TRUE CRIME JAPAN

DEDICATION

This book is dedicated to my wife Maki and our children Nao, Aaron, and Cathal.

PAUL MURPHY

TRUE CRIME JAPAN

THIEVES, RASCALS, KILLERS, AND DOPE HEADS:
TRUE STORIES FROM A JAPANESE COURTROOM

WITHDRAWN
DES PLAINES PUBLIC LIBRARY
1501 ELLINWOOD STREET
DES PLAINES, IL 60016

TUTTLE Publishing
Tokyo | Rutland, Vermont | Singapore

ABOUT TUTTLE
"Books to Span the East and West"

Our core mission at Tuttle Publishing is to create books which bring people together one page at a time. Tuttle was founded in 1832 in the small New England town of Rutland, Vermont (USA). Our fundamental values remain as strong today as they were then—to publish best-in-class books informing the English-speaking world about the countries and peoples of Asia. The world has become a smaller place today and Asia's economic, cultural and political influence has expanded, yet the need for meaningful dialogue and information about this diverse region has never been greater. Since 1948, Tuttle has been a leader in publishing books on the cultures, arts, cuisines, languages and literatures of Asia. Our authors and photographers have won numerous awards and Tuttle has published thousands of books on subjects ranging from martial arts to paper crafts. We welcome you to explore the wealth of information available on Asia at www.tuttlepublishing.com.

Published by Tuttle Publishing, an imprint of Periplus Editions (HK) Ltd.

www.tuttlepublishing.com

Copyright © 2016 by Paul Murphy

All rights reserved. No part of this publication may be reproduced or utilized in any form or by any means, electronic or mechanical, including photocopying, recording, or by any information storage and retrieval system, without prior written permission from the publisher.

Library of Congress Cataloging-inPublication Data in Process

ISBN 978-4-8053-1342-8

First edition
20 19 18 17 16
5 4 3 2 1   1604CM

Printed in China

TUTTLE PUBLISHING® is a registered trademark of Tuttle Publishing, a division of Periplus Editions (HK) Ltd.

Distributed by

North America, Latin America & Europe
Tuttle Publishing
364 Innovation Drive
North Clarendon, VT 05759-9436 U.S.A.
Tel: 1 (802) 773-8930
Fax: 1 (802) 773-6993
info@tuttlepublishing.com
www.tuttlepublishing.com

Japan
Tuttle Publishing
Yaekari Building, 3rd Floor
5-4-12 Osaki, Shinagawa-ku
Tokyo 141 0032
Tel: (81) 3 5437-0171
Fax: (81) 3 5437-0755
sales@tuttle.co.jp
www.tuttle.co.jp

Asia Pacific
Berkeley Books Pte. Ltd.
61 Tai Seng Avenue, #02-12
Singapore 534167
Tel: (65) 6280-1330
Fax: (65) 6280-6290
inquiries@periplus.com.sg
www.periplus.com

CONTENTS

ACKNOWLEDGMENTS

I wish to thank my wife Maki for her love, support and wise insights about Japanese society and who, along with our daughter Nao, made an invaluable contribution to the research for this book. I also want to thank my brother David whose East Asian journalistic experience I have long tapped and who has been a sturdy influence in my life. Thanks as well to veteran Tokyo-based correspondent David McNeill for being a constant source of well-articulated wisdom on things Japanese and a great supporter and friend. Gratitude also to my other brother John for reading and commenting on certain chapters and to Ryann Connell, a generous friend and expert on Japan, for doing likewise.

I am indebted to the ever-professional clerks of Matsumoto City's courts and to all who granted me interviews, especially lawyers Susumu Ozawa, Hirofumi Idei and Jiro Yamane, who greatly aided my understanding of Japan's legal system. I wish to thank also Cian Ferriter and Martin Walsh: our long conversation about elderly crime on a train to Nagoya City persuaded me that there may be a wider audience for a book such as this. Thanks also to Diarmaid Ferriter, Mary Ruane and Micheál Ó Siochrú, who in different ways influenced my initial journey to Japan, and to David Malatesta who insisted I learn the language once I got there. I also want to acknowledge the irrepressible Koji Ueda, who recently departed this life, Colm Ó'Comartún, Chie Matsumoto, Paul Rouse, Gregory Prendergast, Frank Shouldice, Masaru Misawa,

ACKNOWLEDGMENTS

Koichi Terao, Michiko Mutai, David Carlson, Miho and Hideki Shinohara, Shin and Rie Mutai, Angela Chen, Paula Brudell, Cormac Behan, Dónall King, Shane McGonigle, Mick Ryan and Takatsugu Nakayama. Very sincere thanks too to best-selling author and veteran crime journalist Jake Adelstein for sparing time from a hectic schedule to read a final draft and write a very kind endorsement. Finally, I wish to thank the staff of Tuttle Publishing for their encouragement, especially Cathy Layne for her impeccable advice and diligent editing skills and also Terri Jadick who so ably took up when Cathy departed to other pastures.

INTRODUCTION
ORDINARY PEOPLE

Criminal court cases in Japan begin with the fairly predictable—the defendant pleads guilty—and end with the utterly predictable—the defendant is found guilty. What happens in between is the interesting bit. This book is about the "in between." It is about the tales of perverts, arsonists, mobsters, shoplifters, pimps, embezzlers, fraudsters, killers, and others who came before the courts of Matsumoto City in central Japan over a 12-month period.

So it is a book about crime and criminals, but it is also a book about Japan. While members of Japan's mafia, the yakuza, feature in many cases, the great majority of defendants are not career criminals; they are ordinary people. People such as Kesae Shikada, a hard-of-hearing octogenarian shoplifter; accountant Satoru Hara and his wife Hitomi, who planned to kill themselves and their daughter because their house had been repossessed; former retail manager Shinji Horiike, who was obsessed with filming women in toilets; and carpenter Takeshi Tomioka, who beat his 91-year-old mother to death and went to work the following day, leaving her body for his wife to find.

Their stories and others from Matsumoto's courtrooms provide a window to a fascinating society that can be difficult to figure out even for those who, like me, have lived in Japan for many years and understand the language. It's not uncommon, for example, to work alongside someone and know virtually nothing about their personal life, perhaps only knowing their family name and not their first name. One Japanese man I consider a friend, for example, got married and divorced without telling me of either. I learned of his marriage about six months after the event; he has yet to tell me of his divorce.

Part of the problem, especially for a foreigner seeking to understand Japan's people, is that relaxed conversation is regulated, and usually stymied, by custom and the structure of the language. Almost every sentence carries a status marker: a word, the absence of a word, or a verb ending that indicates whether you are senior, junior, or equal in status to the person you are speaking with. It's easy in Japan to ask a question that is considered too personal or too familiar and therefore rude.

This is true in just about every setting, but not in the courtroom—the very place where you might expect more, rather than less, formality. Their language may be polite, but judges, prosecutors, and lawyers ask personal and direct questions of defendants that they wouldn't dream of asking any other stranger. Even for very minor crimes such as the theft of a soda or a book, an hour of court time is usually allotted, and almost without exception the accused is cross-examined at length by their own lawyer, the prosecutor, and often the judge, about their personal circumstances as well as their crime. And because defendants have a worse than 700-to-1 chance of acquittal, their best avenue to a lenient sentence is to show remorse by answering questions as honestly as possible.

This was obvious from my first day in the courts of Matsumoto, an attractive city of 243,000 people about 140 miles west of Tokyo. There are two courtrooms in the city that handle crime by adults: the Summary Court, which deals with minor cases, usually theft; and the District Court, which hears more serious cases, including murder, sexual assault, and robbery, as well as other offenses that are considered serious in Japan, such as smoking marijuana or leaving a restaurant without paying the bill. Cases are usually tried in front of a single judge, and defendants are generally represented by a state-funded lawyer. Defense lawyers sit on the opposite side of the chamber to the prosecutor, who typically swats away any aggressive attempts at defense, safe in the knowledge that the accused will become the convicted. Aside from the court clerk, the only others in the courtroom on most days are a reporter from the local *Shinano Mainichi* newspaper and a friend or family member of the defendant, or sometimes a member of the public.

I became a regular at the courts from the middle of 2013, after moving to the city with my Japanese wife and two sons. Though a journalist by trade, I initially went there out of curiosity rather than on assignment. The first case I attended involved a middle-aged man named Iwao Aiba, who had stolen a bicycle and then broken into an office and taken a DVD player, which he later sold at a resale shop for 200 yen (US$2). The prosecutor read out the details of the theft and burglary charges. Mr. Aiba, replying with a deference and softness of speech that belied his thuggish-looking, head-shaven appearance, pleaded guilty.

His mother was in court as a character witness: an elderly lady in a worn purple coat and a dressy black hat that looked like it had cost a lot of money many years ago. I presumed that she was there to plead on behalf of her only son to the judge, Koji Kitamura. Perhaps she would dodge the fact that Mr. Aiba was a repeat criminal and focus instead on the more appealing aspects of her son's character. But I was wrong. Under cross-examination by the defense lawyer, she painted a dismal portrait of her unemployed son. He had brought "shame" on the family and was "untrustworthy," she said, adding that he was useless around the house and "unable to cook."

"I told him not to thieve ever again," she said in a voice full of heartbreak. "He promised not to do it. Stealing! I am mortified… He used to work, and when he worked he didn't do any of this type of thing…I am so angry."

Her son stared at the floor as he sat flanked by two guards on a long bench, wearing an incongruously bright yellow sweatshirt with the words "Exciting World of Surf" written on it. His face was suffused with embarrassment. Soon it was his turn to be cross-examined. His lawyer got to his feet and berated him further.

"Why did you steal the bicycle?"

"I needed it. I checked lots of them and found one that wasn't locked."

"What about the owner? You didn't care about the trouble you were causing him?"

"I did, I left the bicycle where I thought he might find it later."

"Did you know you were doing something wrong?"

"Yes."

The questioning broadened into a review of the defendant's daily life, his battles with mental illness, his fraught relations with family members, his previous work history. We learned, too, of the tough approach of Japan's welfare system—Mr. Aiba didn't qualify for a regular welfare payment because he lived with his pensioner mother, so when he was penniless he would go to the welfare section in City Hall and ask for an ad-hoc handout. On the day of his crime, City Hall had given him 500 yen (US$5), enough to get a couple of noodle dishes in a convenience store. Mr Aiba was jailed for 18 months. His case was not especially fascinating, but there was enough of interest to suggest that the local courts could be a treasure for anyone wanting to learn more about Japanese society.

During his hearing, Mr. Aiba repeatedly expressed remorse for his crimes. His atonement contrasted thoroughly with what I had seen in my only previous visit to Japan's criminal courts. A few months earlier, working for Irish media, I had covered the trial of two Americans who had committed serious crimes in Tokyo. Memphis musician Richard Hinds had murdered Irish student Nicola Furlong; his friend, a Los Angeles dancer called James Blackston, had sexually assaulted two other non-Japanese women. In both trials the defendants had point-blank denied the charges in the face of overwhelming CCTV footage and other evidence. Both gave meandering versions of events leading up to their crimes that were clearly untruthful, heaping pain on the surviving victims and the family of the murdered woman. In the 119 Matsumoto court cases that I followed over hundreds of hearings from opening statement through to verdict, and dozens of others that I sat in on, I never witnessed anything remotely similar to the remorseless courtroom attitudes of Mr. Hinds and Mr. Blackston.

Of those 119 cases, the ones included in this book have been chosen because they tell us something about intriguing aspects of Japanese society, good or bad. While courtroom dialogue is at the core of the book, I also interviewed others connected to the defendant, such as family members, neighbors, and victims, as well as lawyers and police. My aim has been to write something that will be of interest to people who are interested in Japan. I hope you enjoy it.

HOUSE PROUD

Twenty-one-year-old Michiru Hara didn't have a cell phone around the time her parents were planning to kill her—a sure sign of a loner. In Japan, those without a cell phone are typically the very aged, the super-rich, the extremely poor, and the friendless. Michiru Hara appeared to be the latter. Neighbors told me they never noticed her with pals, and Michiru herself told Matsumoto District Court that she felt very lonely. Nobody sat with her in the court's public gallery during the three-day trial of her parents for attempted arson of their home.

A pleasant, shy girl, Michiru had big ambitions. She wanted to become a doctor, but had failed to get into medical college. So once she graduated from high school, she went to an expensive prep school to prepare for another attempt at the college entrance exams. Every weekday, her mother, Hitomi, or her father, Satoru, dropped her off at the local station so she could catch the train bound for her prep school in Matsumoto City.

In the evening, she took the 7:08 train back to her nearest station, Hakuyacho, nine stops from Matsumoto station. She was always collected by one of her parents. Her house was about three miles from the station; unlike the typical student, she didn't use a bicycle. And she didn't want to walk home. "After 7:30 p.m., it's dark," she said. "There are hardly any street lights, so I'd have to use a flashlight."

At home, the family ate dinner together; she chatted with her father or mother, but not about matters of importance, it seemed.

When her dad changed jobs, for example, he never mentioned it.

"So what did you talk about at home?" a judge asked.

"We talked about everyday things, about my school and what was happening on TV programs, just regular chitchat and gossip," she replied.

Michiru's world revolved around her mother and father. She even slept in the same room as her mother. Until they are around 10 or 12 years old, Japanese children often sleep in the same room as their parents. The entire family typically sleeps on futon mattresses laid on a tatami-mat floor. It isn't unheard of for offspring with an unusual level of attachment to share a bedroom with their parents into adulthood, but it's unusual. Michiru was one of the unusual ones.

Her parents had been married for 29 years and had ceased meaningful talk with one another. But Michiru got along with both of them, and though the word "love" was not mentioned in court, it seemed clear that she loved them and they loved her. By the time Michiru testified at her parents' trial, she had dropped out of her prep school and moved into a small apartment in an area not far from her family home. She had been thrust into a reluctant independence, working three hours a day in a supermarket, earning around 60,000 yen (US$600) per month. She also got some money from her local social welfare office. Between the two incomes, she was left with about $800 per month after she paid for her rent. When she wasn't working at her part-time job, she studied on her own, still aiming to get into medical school.

She took the witness stand in the center of the courtroom, facing the judges. Her hair tied in a bow, she wore practical flat leather shoes and a dark business suit of a type popular among graduating university students who are job-hunting. While she had lost some weight since her parents' detention, she was still chubby, and her face was covered in red blotches due to an ailment called Multiple Chemical Sensitivity (MCS), a condition that she shared with her mother and which, as we will see, was crucial to the tragic story of the Hara family.

Michiru read out the court oath, promising to obey her conscience, to tell the truth, and not to lie or embellish her testimony. She spoke clearly, though in a quiet, high-pitched voice. She was then reminded, as all witnesses are by the presiding judge, not to perjure herself. Her parents were represented by separate lawyers, who sat together across from two prosecutors. Her father's lawyer began the questioning.

"You are living alone now?" he asked.

"Yes. My relatives visit me and help me out sometimes, but I am mostly alone every day. I go to my job from 7 a.m. to 10 a.m., and after that I study for the university entrance exam."

"Did you ever live alone before the incident?"

"No."

"What do you do for food?"

"I eat food from the supermarket. Apart from cooking classes in school, I don't have any experience of cooking."

"You lost weight."

"Yes, I don't know how much because I don't have a scale, but I think I lost about 10 kilos [22 pounds]."

"Your clothes got loose on you?"

"Yes."

"What about your laundry, how do you do it?"

"I hand-wash it."

"What about using a washing machine?"

"I have one, but I don't use it. I'm not confident in operating it, and I don't want to waste money on electricity and water."

Her life seemed lonely and hard, but Michiru was lucky to be alive. Her parents may have been on trial for attempting to burn down the family home, but their grand plan also involved a family suicide. In reality it was more like a murder-suicide, since Michiru knew nothing of the scheme. After setting the house on fire, the parents had planned to drive off a cliff with Michiru sitting in the back seat. It was to be a dramatic finale to a most mundane family story.

"Why did you want to make your daughter die?" the prosecutor asked Satoru Hara, a wiry and extremely deferential 58-year-old man with big hair, a small head, and very narrow shoulders.

"To leave her on her own would be bad."

"You didn't ask her?"

"No."

"But you knew that she wanted to be a doctor?"

"Yes."

"And you still thought that you all should die?"

"Yes."

So what caused Mr. and Mrs. Hara to morph from an apparently dull couple who didn't communicate much into defendants who had planned to wipe out themselves and their only child, and who were now facing up to 10 years in jail for attempted arson? It was all because of a house. In 1998 they had spent 37 million yen (US$370,000) to build a house on land given to them as a present by Mrs. Hara's father. Thirty-seven million yen can build a fine house anywhere in Japan, especially in a region like Nagano Prefecture, where the city of Matsumoto is situated. Nagano's forests provide a ready supply of wood for building, and labor costs in the prefecture are relatively low. But the Haras weren't building a palace; their house was 1,528 square feet, only 10 percent bigger than the average Nagano dwelling. (Japanese homes are widely thought of as being very small, and in Tokyo they are, but the average newly built home nationwide in 2008 was 990 square feet, which is significantly larger than the average size of 818 square feet in Britain). The Hara family house was two stories, black and white, set high above sea level overlooking some pleasant, though not spectacular, countryside. It was built about a hundred yards from the house where Mrs. Hara had grown up. A neighbor told me that her parents had moved from the nearby village of Maki around 70 years earlier, and had been well regarded for the quality of the flower seeds that they harvested and sold.

The main reason the house cost so much was because of Mrs. Hara's and her daughter's MCS. To the greatest possible extent, chemical-free materials had been used to build the home.

"Some smells give me a headache," Michiru told the court. "If I use regular shampoo I get a pain in my head. My mother has similar symptoms."

"When you are at home, do you have those symptoms?" her mother's lawyer asked.

"No, I don't; not when I'm inside the house."

Special chemical-free paper for the traditional-style *shoji* screens was ordered from the southern island of Okinawa, about 1,200 miles from Nagano. The Haras didn't use any plywood, as it contains chemicals. Instead, wood was transported by a supplier about 400 miles away in Aomori Prefecture. They also put charcoal under the floor to help keep the air pure. And they had the walls plastered with a natural stone-powder material called *keisodo*. That meant their walls didn't require wallpaper, which "would need adhesive," explained Mrs. Hara. A local builder informed me that using the natural wall covering of *keisodo* instead of wallpaper would add about a million yen (US$10,000) to the cost of a house of that size.

"Who had the strongest view on how the house should be built?" Mr. Hara was asked by his defense lawyer.

"My wife. I didn't have those symptoms." She had also been obsessive about the design and the details. The couple had met with their architect some 40 times.

Fostering communication within the family was at the core of the plan. "I designed it so that you couldn't go to the porch without first going through the living room and dining area. It was a house where the family would always see each other's faces," Mrs. Hara said.

"What type of house was it?" her lawyer asked.

"For me, it was a treasure."

"Was it a happy place?"

"Yes."

"When was the happiest time?"

That was nine months after they moved into the house, when they held a sixth birthday party for Michiru. "I invited my parents, my father and mother. My father praised me, saying I had done well with the house. He died one year and two months after that. It was the first and last time he praised me."

Like many countries, Japan has become a gentler place for children. Until the late 1940s, the sale of children into servitude by impoverished families was not uncommon. Children are more cherished now, but Japan is still a society where praise for kids, as well as other family members, is much rarer than in the Western world. Standing in the dock, Mrs. Hara struck a plaintive figure, a 59-year-old woman who was so affected by the absence of praise from her father that it evoked rare tears to talk about the single occasion it was given.

A picture emerged from the court testimony of just how much the house meant to Mrs. Hara in particular. She had designed it, had personally chosen the construction materials to create a chemical-free haven, and associated it with a very special moment in her relationship with her father. The house was not a place she would give up lightly.

It didn't become apparent for some time, but the home to which they had become so attached was turning into an unbearable financial burden. Mr. and Mrs. Hara had borrowed 34 million yen (US$340,000)—about 90 percent of the housing cost—over 25 years. Mr. Hara had dealt with the bank; he handled correspondence, and repayments were from his bank account. He had a permanent job in the accounts department at a construction company, and initially could easily afford the loan repayments of 85,000 yen (US$850) per month with two additional payments of around 275,000 yen (US$2,750) each from his semiannual bonuses. Japanese firms typically pay a bonus twice a year of around three or four months' pay in total; this can be more when times are good. Although these payments are called *bonasu* (bonus) in Japanese, and can be more easily raised or lowered compared to a worker's regular salary, they are not fully discretionary. In fact, they are considered sufficiently a part of core pay that banks usually structure customers' mortgage repayments around them. But by 2008, 10 years after taking out the mortgage, Mr. Hara's income began to look uncertain, because his company had started edging him out.

Corporate Japan has an image of providing lifetime employment to its workers, but this is not the case. A mere 20 percent of workers have ever enjoyed lifetime employment. ("Enjoy" may not be the correct verb; in return for job security, companies demand unstinting loyalty with long hours and much unpaid overtime. They also often move their workers around the country every few years, so those with children are forced to choose between uprooting their families or moving away from home by themselves and living alone in a company apartment). About 37 percent of the workforce is in part-time or temporary employment. Even large Japanese companies operate with a multi-tiered labor force. Toyota and Panasonic, for example, provide so-called "jobs for life" for most employees, but also hire armies of seasonal workers on a casual basis and dispense with them when the need abates.

Mr. Hara had expected to be kept on by his company until his retirement, but when times got tough he was pressured to quit and take a job at a hotel owned by an affiliate, where he earned less than half of his previous salary. Though he was clearly pushed out of his job, he repeatedly referred to it in court as a "retirement." His unwillingness to admit to the humiliation of being forced from the company was a huge factor in the crime that was to come. He bottled up his troubles, telling nobody—not even his wife or daughter—about the loss of his job. At age 54, he found himself with a large mortgage, a reduced salary, and a daughter who would soon be of university age.

Paying for a university education is a significant burden on an ordinary family. Michiru Hara was aiming to go to a national university for her medical studies, which she said would cost about 800,000 yen (US$8,000) in fees per year. Families with academic ambitions typically have insurance to pay for these fees. (Japan is insured up to its neck: despite comprising only 1.7 percent of the world's population, Japanese pay 18 percent of the world's insurance premiums, according to insurer Manulife.) But the Haras didn't have education insurance. So with an ambitious daughter, Mr. Hara was facing an uphill financial struggle.

"Didn't you think about asking your wife to work?" the prosecutor asked.

"No, I didn't think of it. She was minding the house and look-ing after our daughter. I always made the money, and we didn't plan for her to work."

"Didn't your wife ever offer to get a job?"

"I think she wanted to work, but she didn't," he replied.

Another reason for not asking his wife to get a job was that he would then have had to explain just how desperate their financial situation had become. His wife had no idea of the financial peril the family was in, or that they were on the verge of losing her beloved house. It was only during police questioning that she first learned her husband had lost his job and now worked at a hotel.

"Was there no conversation in the house?" her lawyer asked her.

"Almost none. When he left the house to go to work, I'd tell him to do his work well, and he'd say that he would. If he wasn't coming home from work he would call to say so, but we never talked on the phone otherwise."

If the body language in court was any indicator, communica-tion in the Hara family hadn't improved post-arrest. Not only did they not speak to each other, but they didn't even make eye contact during the trial. And when their daughter went to visit her parents in detention, none of the three of them, it seemed, was prepared to talk about the elephant-in-the-room issue of why they had been planning to kill her.

"How many times did you visit your parents in detention?" a defense lawyer asked Michiru.

"I didn't count, but about once a week."

"Did you see them together?"

"No, I could only see one of them one week and one the next."

"You said you didn't talk about the incident. Didn't you have something to ask them?" a judge asked.

"I didn't want to talk to them about it," Michiru replied.

"So they didn't mention it?"

"Not really. They just said they were sorry for what they had done."

"What did you talk about?"

"I talked with my mother about cooking. My dad and I talked

about everyday things, like the increase in consumption tax."
(Japan's sales tax, which had risen from 5 percent to 8 percent in
April 2014, was a big topic of public discussion).

"Did you talk about the incident?"

"No, not really."

Mr. Hara told the court, "We didn't have a concrete conversation about the arson. But what has happened has happened. I
wrote her a letter and told her that, in the end, it had come to this."

"Did you talk about the family suicide?" his lawyer asked.

"I said we should go forward together."

Mrs. Hara was also asked about her daughter's visits to the
prison where she and her husband were on remand. "Your daughter said you didn't talk much when she visited you," her defense
lawyer said.

"It took her about two hours to get to the prison, and we had
only 30 minutes to talk. During that time I thought there was no
need to darken the mood with talk of the incident. I wanted to be
cheerful and encouraging," Mrs. Hara said. "I felt pathetic, guilty;
her parents are criminals and she is now living alone. She was trying really hard…she kept crying," she added.

"What do you want to do now?" the lawyer asked.

"My daughter wants to go to college and I am ready to do whatever I can to help. As a family, all three of us, I want to repair
things, while living and laughing together."

The lawyer questioned Mrs. Hara about events leading up to
the attempted arson. Mrs. Hara spoke of her shock on the day she
answered the door to see the president of a local real-estate firm
on her doorstep. He told her that he had just bought her house at
an auction of foreclosed properties and she had to move out. She
hadn't even known it was for sale.

"When you were told to leave the house, what did you feel?"
her lawyer asked.

"Is it a dream, is it a nightmare? I couldn't sleep. Almost every
day, I couldn't sleep. I hid it from my daughter. I didn't talk to my
husband, I kept everything to myself."

Japan has a fairly simple system for selling foreclosed homes.

It advertises them—sometimes with pictures of the interior, but often not—and puts them up for auction. Hopeful purchasers put in sealed bids to the local court, and on the day of the auction the bids are opened; the highest one gets the property. The benefit for the purchaser is that they can get properties cheaply. Securing a property for around two-thirds its market value is common in auctions in bigger cities like Tokyo, while properties commonly go for around half the market value in the countryside. The Hara house and site sold for 11 million yen (US$110,000) at auction— less than one-third of the building cost alone. The disadvantage to buying foreclosed properties, however, is the same as anywhere around the world: you could be buying a house whose previous owners are unhappy about the sale. People, that is, like the Haras.

Initially, after Mrs. Hara received the shocking eviction news, her husband negotiated with the new owner, who agreed to sell the house back to him at a price of 15 million yen (US$150,000). But given their dreadful credit history, the Haras' loan requests were turned down by banks and credit unions. Mr. Hara approached his older brother, but he could not help them either. It was now November 2013; almost six years had elapsed from the time Mr. Hara had stopped paying the mortgage in February 2008.

In desperation, they even approached a man called Fukuzawa. "I didn't know him," Mr. Hara admitted in court. "My wife's parents knew him; he used to have a business around here." The connection with the friend of his parents-in-law was tenuous. "In 2005, my wife's mother died, and he told us at the funeral that if there was ever anything he could do for us, we should let him know." Mr. Fukuzawa had presumably forgotten those words uttered at the funeral eight years earlier, but the Haras hadn't, and he was their final hope. Mr. Hara drove about an hour to Mr. Fukuzawa's home in southern Nagano Prefecture to ask him for a loan. It must have been a difficult conversation; Mr. Hara is an extremely mouse-like man, lacking in presence and very deferential in manner even by Japanese standards. It is hard to imagine him making a persuasive or forceful case to borrow $150,000 from a man whom he had met only once. Mr. Fukuzawa said he would need time to consider the proposal, so Mr. Hara returned a few days later, on November 9.

"What was the response?" the prosecutor asked.

"He said it was *muzukashii*." Though it means "difficult," *muzukashii* is—often confusingly for foreigners—used as an indirect and therefore more polite way of saying "impossible," which can be considered too direct.

Once Mr. Fukuzawa had refused, Mr. and Mrs. Hara had run out of options. "We thought there was nothing we could do, but my wife and I felt strongly that we didn't want to hand over the house."

The desperate husband and wife met at a convenience store parking lot to discuss their position—they didn't talk about their financial problems when their daughter was at home. It was in the parking lot that they agreed on the plan to torch the house they had built from scratch and then kill themselves and their daughter.

"Who suggested the plan to burn down the house and commit family suicide?" his lawyer asked.

"The words came from me," Mr. Hara said.

"And what did your wife say?"

"She agreed."

"How did your wife appear?"

"Not normal, well, neither of us was normal. We thought it was the only way—for the three of us to die."

Actually, they had lots of options, the most obvious one being to give up their house and move across the field to the house where Mrs. Hara had been raised. It had been left to her and her older brother, who had his own house, and remained unoccupied.

"Why didn't you move into your family home?" Mrs. Hara's lawyer asked her.

"It would have been hard to watch someone else living in our house," his wife said. In response to a similar question, Mr. Hara said, "If we had done that, the people in the area would have known that something had gone wrong regarding our house."

Considering that Mrs. Hara was born and bred in the area and she and her husband had lived there for 15 years, the neighbors knew surprisingly little about them. Of people in six neighboring households that I spoke with, only one person said she would recognize Mrs. Hara's face, though she added that she didn't know her family name. None of the others said they would recognize her. An elderly man who lived all his life about 500 feet away from the house where Mrs. Hara grew up, and closer still to the house she had tried to burn down, said, "I have been living here for 47 years, and if I saw her walking on the road I wouldn't know her face. She was in the house all the time. The husband was active in the residents' association, always happy to do his bit, but he didn't say much." Other neighbors said that they never saw any visitors to the house.

Another obvious solution to the Hara's financial problem would have been to ask their daughter to give up studying at her prep school. She could have studied at home to prepare for the college entrance exam, as she was later forced to do. Her prep school fees were about 1.2 million yen (US$12,000) per year, Mr. Hara said—equal to 75 percent of the mortgage payment.

"Did you think about asking your daughter to give up on the idea of going to the school and study at home instead?" Mr. Hara was asked by his defense lawyer.

"No."

"Why didn't you tell your daughter you were short of money and ask her to give up school?"

"I didn't want to worry her before her exams," Mr. Hara replied. "On November 9, we decided to burn down the house and commit family suicide, but we hadn't yet worked out how to go about starting the fire. When we went to Watahan [a home-improvement chain store which sells everything from car tires to curtains] we thought about it," Mr. Hara said.

As they walked up and down the aisles of Watahan, they checked out which goods would suit their still half-baked plan. They decided on some cushions and light wooden pallets used to lay futon mattresses on. The Haras also bought some kerosene at Watahan, but instead of simply dousing the house with the fuel and setting it alight, they had a slow-burning plan. They decided to light three kerosene heaters and put wood, towels, and clothes on or near them, expecting they would catch fire gradually. They also planned to put lit cigarettes onto cushions, hoping that they would smolder and eventually catch fire.

So why were they so concerned about a creating a slow-burning fire? "It was daytime and there were people working nearby," Mr. Hara explained. "If the fire started suddenly, it would be noticed, and there would be a commotion." Creating a fire that would take time to burn would give them ample time to escape from the scene, pick up their daughter from the train station and drive to their suicide. The Haras already had a kerosene heater in the house, and Mr. Hara brought in two extra heaters from their shed. Mrs. Hara laid paper on the floor as the heaters were carried in. "So the floor wouldn't get damaged," she explained.

"But if you were planning to burn down the house, why worry about the floor?" a judge asked.

"Out of habit, I suppose," she replied.

In what a police scientist characterized as the most dangerous part of their arson plan, the Haras lit one heater and hung towels close to it.

"What did you think would happen?" Mr. Hara was asked.

"I was thinking it would catch fire. If the towels caught fire they would fall to the ground and the things on the ground would then burn."

He explained that in neighboring Niigata Prefecture, where he had grown up, "people often dried clothes near a heater and they sometimes caught fire."

"So you put the towels near so they wouldn't light immediately."

"Yes."

"Who thought of that?"

"It was me, I think."

His wife left the house for a little while during the arson preparations. She walked the short distance to the family home, which had stood empty since the death of her mother. "I went to leave our second car there and to apologize to my parents," Mrs. Hara said. She went to pray at the family *butsudan*, a Buddhist shrine in people's homes where offerings, often of rice or fruit, are made to deceased ancestors. Although Japan is not a religious country in a

Western sense—religious observance is usually limited to a visit to a temple or shrine once or twice a year, and polls show most Japanese do not believe in God—there is a widespread belief that something exists beyond this world, and that there is a connection between the dead and the living.

"What type of apology were you making to them?" the prosecutor asked.

"I was apologizing that we were going to disappear," she replied. For only the second time in her testimony, Mrs. Hara's voice broke and she shed a tear.

Meanwhile, Mr. Hara had inspected the arson preparations and made some alterations. Things weren't quite ready. For example, his wife had a pot on one kerosene heater with just dried tofu in it, in the hopes that the pot would heat up and the tofu would catch fire. It may have been the first-ever case of dried tofu being used as an arson accelerant. Mr. Hara wasn't convinced, however. He added kitchen paper to the pot. "I thought it wouldn't burn if it was just the tofu," he said. He also moved the towels closer to another of the kerosene heaters.

"How close?" the prosecutor asked.

"Around an inch away."

"Apart from that, did you notice anything that needed to be changed?" the prosecutor asked.

He had. He could see that the lit cigarettes placed on cushions weren't catching fire. "My wife told me to put extra cigarettes on the cushions."

"Your wife said to put them on?"

"Yes, she thought it would burn with extra ones."

The arson attempt was so pitiful that both Mr. and Mrs. Hara had to emphasize in court that they were serious.

"Did you really want to burn down the house?" a judge asked Mrs. Hara.

"Yes, I didn't want to give it to someone else, I wanted to destroy it."

"When you left the house were there actual flames?"

"No."

"Was there smoke?"

"In my daughter's room upstairs, the fire was starting to burn," she said.

So with the tofu and paper in one pot on one kerosene heater, thin wooden pallets on another, and towels hanging in proximity to the third heater, Mr. and Mrs. Hara left the house and embarked on part two of their plan: pick up their daughter, get some food, and find a place to die. The only mementos Mrs. Hara took with her were some pictures of her daughter. She said she "wanted to be holding them" when the family died. They drove to the train station.

"I had to go and pick up my daughter," said Mrs. Hara.

"You wanted to bring her to the place for family suicide?" the prosecutor asked.

"Yes," she replied.

The Haras' crime was considered sufficiently serious for them to be tried before lay judges (see chapter 9 for a detailed explanation of Japan's lay judge system), which meant they were being judged by six regular members of society as well as three professional judges. In a lay judge trial there are a lot of breaks, usually at least five a day. During each of the breaks, which apart from lunchtime last about 15 or 20 minutes, Mr. and Mrs. Hara were handcuffed and led out separately. Once the break had finished, the presiding judge would return to the court and the lawyers and people in the public gallery would rise and bow. The court clerk would then phone the guards to bring the two defendants back in. Mrs. Hara always came in first, turning and facing the corner near the door before the guards took off her handcuffs. She then walked toward her seat with her head bowed, not looking at her daughter, who sat about 10 feet away. Then her husband would be brought into the courtroom; his handcuffs, like his wife's, were removed just inside the door. Apart from an occasional curious glance at me, the only foreigner in the courtroom, he remained with his head bowed for virtually the entirety of the court proceedings. He looked at neither his wife nor his daughter. Once the defendants were in place, the remainder of the judges would enter, always in the same order—the first lay judge followed by the other five in order of their seating position at the bench; the two back-up lay judges; and finally the two junior professional judges. The judges would remain standing momentarily. The court clerk would bark a sergeant-major-like "*Kiritsu!*" (stand up) to everyone else in the courtroom, then order, "*Rei*" (bow) and "*Chakuseki*" (be seated). Then the proceedings would resume.

As Mrs. Hara's cross-examination drew to a close, one of the lay judges asked her, "You told us that the house was a treasure for you, but why didn't you consider burning the house with all of you in it?"

"Of all the ways to die, I had heard that a house fire is the worst," Mrs. Hara replied.

"So you didn't want to die in a house fire?"

"Absolutely not."

Although driving off a cliff was the Haras' preferred method of suicide, they had been so busy with their arson preparations that they hadn't picked a spot from which to plunge to their deaths. Mountainous Nagano Prefecture provides many possibilities of a steep drop, though there is often a crash barrier in dangerous locations. And if the mountains didn't yield a likely spot, they planned to head to Niigata Prefecture's coast, a couple of hours' drive from home, and find a cliff there. They collected their daughter at the train station and, telling her that a relation was on the verge of death, began to drive north toward Niigata. On the way they pretended they got a message to say the relation had suddenly recovered. They then told the daughter that they would turn the trip into a short holiday and stay overnight in their car (it apparently wasn't the first time for the family to sleep in their car rather than a hotel while on a trip).

"Did your parents tell you about the suicide plan?" Michiru was asked by a defense lawyer.

"No, it was like a happy family trip, it was something we hadn't done in a long time." But in typical fashion for a country obsessed with food (Japan has more three-star Michelin restaurants than any other country, even France), Mrs. Hara wanted the family to have one last delicious meal before they died. They went to a seafood restaurant. "My daughter likes sea urchin," Mrs. Hara said, "I thought we would eat it as a final meal."

"How were you going to carry out the family suicide?" the prosecutor asked Mr. Hara.

"We were going to do it as a car accident," he answered calmly.

"But you didn't. Why?"

"My daughter usually sleeps when we are on a long drive, but she didn't on that night."

"Your daughter didn't sleep, so that's why you didn't do it?"

"Yes. It would have been just too difficult to do it if she were awake."

Though Mrs. Hara got emotional at other parts of her testimony, she appeared as unruffled as her husband when explaining their plan. "We were going to die," she stated. "We would go together and the house would also go."

"Did you have any resistance to dying by driving off a cliff?" her lawyer asked.

"No resistance, I thought it was the way."

"Why couldn't you do it?"

"If Michiru had slept we would have done it, but she wouldn't sleep for us." In the end, with Michiru awake in the back of the car, Mr. Hara pulled over and they all fell asleep in the car for the night. The family suicide would have to wait until the following day. However, early the next morning, the new owner of their house arrived, expecting to get the keys from the Haras, but found it locked and empty. He called a locksmith, and when they finally got into the house it was "like a sauna" from the kerosene heaters. There was no significant harm done to the house, however. The arson attempt had been a damp squib, causing some minor smoke damage, nothing else.

The police put out an alert for the family, and they were picked up after their car was spotted by officers outside a convenience store.

"If you hadn't been captured, what would have happened?" a judge asked Mr. Hara.

"We would have found a place to have an accident," he replied.

"Is your daughter important to you?" a judge asked Mrs. Hara. "Yes."

"But in the end you were going—this is perhaps a severe way of expressing it—but you were going to make her die." This delicately prefaced statement was the closest anyone came to blaming the Haras for their plan to kill their daughter.

The parents were not charged with conspiring to kill Michiru, only with arson, so the suicide element was not dealt with at any length in questioning by either the prosecution or the defense. Some local media reports on the trial also failed to mention this angle. The well-regarded Nagano daily newspaper, the *Shinano Mainichi Shimbun*, didn't mention the family suicide plan in any of its four reports on the case, sticking purely to the arson aspect.

At no stage did anyone in court use the Japanese verbs "to kill" or "to murder" when referring to the plan to drive the unwitting daughter to her death. The closest was the phrase *shinaseru*, used by a couple of judges, meaning to "make (somebody) die."

While individual suicides are generally viewed as heartbreaking and/or selfish in Japan, there is also some degree of cultural empathy, with the idea that suicide is an honorable way out of shame or disgrace. Japan's suicide rate is one of the highest in the world, and twice that of the United States. And, of course, Japan was the first-ever state to use suicide bombers as a strategy of war when it sent kamikaze pilots to their deaths in World War II. Even so, I was surprised at the lack of blame toward the defendants for their family suicide plan. The judges were more critical in their questioning than the prosecutors or defense lawyers, but even their views were mildly stated. There was no aggressive blaming.

I asked some ordinary Japanese living in Matsumoto City why they thought this was so. The answers were broadly similar, most cogently expressed by an acquaintance who works as a security guard. "In Japan," he said, "the child belongs with the parents. This is what we believe: the parents and the children are one. The parents presumably thought that to leave the child on her own would be a terrible thing to do. In their own minds, they weren't murdering her, they were bringing her with them."

This type of thinking is echoed in the first line of a police sign at the bottom of Japan's emblematic Mount Fuji. The sign is close to an entrance to Aokigahara Forest, also known as Suicide Forest, where in the first decade of this century one or two people killed themselves every week. "Your life is a valuable gift from your parents," the sign reads. "Think once more, quietly, about your parents, your siblings, and your children. Don't worry alone, talk to someone."

In a twisted way, it seemed that Mr. and Mrs. Hara believed they were thinking of their daughter when they planned to kill her. They weren't going to leave her alone; it was in her best interests that she come with them, they thought. As Mrs. Hara put it, "We were going to a different world, and we would be together."

"But your daughter was going to university. Did you know her ambition, her dream? You were going to cause the death of your daughter who wanted to be a doctor," a judge countered.

"There was no other way, I thought. I wanted us to be together always. And I didn't want to hand over the house."

"It seems to me that you weighed up the importance of the house and weighed up the importance of your daughter and her future and you chose the house," another judge said.

"I thought she would want to be with us."

"That was how you thought, but what about your daughter's feelings?"

"At that time I didn't think about my daughter's feelings."

Fortunately for her parents, Michiru was the forgiving type.

"When you heard about your parents' plan to carry out a family suicide, what did you think?" a prosecutor asked her.

"I was surprised," was her brief response.

"What do you think of your parents' decision?" the prosecutor pressed.

"I think there must have been a different way."

If the daughter had any hatred, disgust, or even confusion it didn't show.

Her father told the court, "I was thinking of taking her life. I feel sorry for that."

"At some stage you will be rehabilitated and return to society," his lawyer said to him.

"As a family we will live together, and I will find work in Matsumoto."

"Where will you live?"

"First, we will look for a place where we can all live."

"Can you promise not to commit a crime again?"

"Naturally, I promise."

"Are you thinking of suicide?"

"No. Not now."

His wife also assured the court that she, too, was looking to the future. "I did a really stupid thing," she said, "we should just have moved quietly from the house in the first place."

"What will happen with your relationship with your husband?" her lawyer asked.

"I want to repair it."

"Do you intend to live together?"

"Yes."

"Will you get a job?"

"Yes, I will work."

The trial had begun on a Tuesday and ended on a Thursday. On the following Tuesday, the nine judges and two defendants filed back into court in the same order as they had done during the trial. The presiding judge, Toshihiro Honma, read out the verdict—guilty of attempted arson—followed by the sentence: three years in jail, suspended for four years. He explained to the Haras that if they committed no crime over the following four years, they wouldn't have to go to jail. It was a "selfish" crime with a "self-indulgent" motive, he said. But the facts that their arson efforts were so amateurish, they had no criminal records, had paid compensation for the smoke damage to the real-estate company that had bought their foreclosed home, and that the president of the company had written a letter seeking clemency all went in their favor.

Judge Honma ordered Mr. and Mrs. Hara not to go near the house or its new residents in the future. He told them that their daughter gave them a reason to live and that they should rebuild their lives. Mrs. Hara cried at the verdict, and Michiru was obviously happy. She had earlier told the court that she would live with her parents once they were freed from detention, and that their release would "lift my spirits psychologically."

"What do you want your parents to do once they are out?" she was asked during her testimony six days earlier. "The first thing I want them to do," she said, "is drop me off at the train station."

POSTSCRIPT

Three months after the verdict, I visited the new occupants of the house that the Haras had tried to destroy. The current owners paid 18 million yen (US$180,000) for it, yielding a profit of around 60 percent for the realtor who had bought it at the foreclosure auction. "It's a really well-built house," the new owner said, though she added that if she had known more about its history she might not have bought it. The quality of the house's walls and wooden floors was striking. The bottom half of the walls were paneled in wood, the top half with the pricey *keisodo* natural plaster.

I then visited the empty house nearby where Mrs. Hara was brought up. I hoped that I might meet Mrs. Hara's brother, who, I was told, dropped by once a week to check on it. Her brother wasn't there, but, coincidentally, Mr. Hara was. He looked much healthier and less stressed than the last time I had seen him in a courtroom. He was still a thin man, but he had put on a few pounds and he had gotten a hair cut.

I introduced myself as someone writing a book about district court criminal cases and he said he remembered me from his trial. He said that he was currently living with his wife and daughter in a rented accommodation, and that his daughter was still studying hard. He was still looking for a job, though he added that his psychological and physical recovery was a slow process. I asked if he wanted to do a proper sit-down interview about the "incident."

"No," he said, "I want to forget all about it."

LATE IN LIFE

WEEDKILLER

Yoshimatsu Matsumoto was a latecomer to crime. At 74, he was facing prison for the second time in his life. Charged with theft, he was led by two prison guards into Matsumoto City's Summary Court, handcuffed and on a leash. One prison guard walked in front and another behind, holding the blue rope that wrapped around the old man's waist and connected to his handcuffs.

Moments before the judge arrived in the courtroom, Mr. Matsumoto was released from his handcuffs. He had been in detention since he was arrested for stealing from a megastore called Cainz three months earlier. The retired factory worker had first been caught thieving when he was 69. That crime was dealt with out of court. Then he was caught again and given a suspended jail sentence, meaning he didn't have to serve time if he behaved well. But he didn't behave well. Soon after, he was caught stealing a digital camera. That landed him a prison sentence. This was his fourth offense, and another spell in jail was a near certainty.

In a country where people generally age well, Mr. Matsumoto's slouched shoulders, bushy gray eyebrows, balding head, and dowdy tracksuit made him look older than he was. While defendants in Japanese courts typically appear anxious or keep their heads bowed and eyes closed in shame or contemplation, Mr. Matsumoto stared ahead, expressionless. He was before the court because he had stolen weed killer, as well as something that few under-60s would have any use for—blank cassette tapes. He took the witness stand, shadowed again by his guards, who appeared ready to pounce should the shuffling septuagenarian make a break for it.

So why cassette tapes? Mr. Matsumoto explained to the judge that he liked to listen to *enka*, a traditional style of ballad singing popular with older generations in Japan. He had four cassette players in different rooms in his house, and wanted the tapes to copy music by famous *enka* singer Yoshio Tabata, a former steelworker who had first made a name for himself singing sugar-coated patriotic anthems such as the 1941 hit *Ume to Heitai* (The plum and the soldier). Perhaps Mr. Matsumoto was feeling nostalgic when he stole the tapes: Mr. Tabata had died of pneumonia aged 94, a month before the crime.

Mr. Matsumoto took the tapes and containers of weed killer concentrate from Cainz, a chain that sells everything from bicycles to beer from rice cookers to *kabutomushi* (large beetles that Japanese children keep as pets). When a store worker apprehended him in the car park, Mr. Matsumoto had seven containers of weed killer in his rucksack. He admitted to police that he had also stolen the same brand of herbicide on a previous occasion, all for the patch of land in front of his wooden house measuring only about 15 square yards. Half a container would have been more than ample.

"Why did you steal so much weed killer?" his defense lawyer asked. "Were you sowing rice?"

"No."

"Did you not know that you are supposed to dilute it with water?"

"I only heard that later."

"Were there no instructions (on the label)?"

"The writing was very small, I couldn't see it." That was an unlikely excuse. Perhaps Mr. Matsumoto didn't want to admit that he was stealing something that he didn't have any use for.

He was all alone in court; over the four hearings it took for his case to be completed, not a single relative or friend came to show him they cared. He was once married and has two adult children, but they were nowhere to be seen.

"Why did you get divorced?" his lawyer asked.

"She wanted to get divorced."

"Did she give a reason?"

"Nothing special."

He couldn't remember the last time he had seen his children, but said he had probably met his youngest son about ten years before. Asked why they didn't meet, Mr. Matsumoto told the judge that the son was married. "He's busy," he said. He didn't seem to be deliberately trying to paint a picture of a pathetic life.

He told the judge that he had friends who sang karaoke with him. But during his months of pre-trial detention, nobody made the 15-mile trip from the hamlet of Ono, where Mr. Matsumoto is from, to the detention center in Matsumoto City where he was being held until his trial concluded. It wasn't as if his friends or neighbors were ignorant of his troubles. They all seemed to know about his recently acquired penchant for shoplifting and his arrest. One of them told me that it had been rumored in the area that he had been going to the Cainz store on shoplifting trips even before he was caught in the act. Nonetheless, if a handful of conversations with neighbors are any barometer, Mr. Matsumoto was apparently still liked, albeit pitied, in the area.

The absence of relatives willing to attend the trial as a show of support or, even better, to testify as character witnesses, was a bad sign. Judges like to see a parent, a sibling, even a child testifying for the defense. Failing that, an employer or a family friend will do as a poor second-best.

Character witnesses, especially if they are family, are usually not there to paint a pleasing portrait of the defendant. In fact, family witnesses often take the opportunity to criticize him (defendants are usually male), telling the judge of the shame that has been brought on the family, and, in the case of recidivists, how they have been a constant burden. Sometimes the testimony is tearful, sometimes stonily bitter. Rarely does a family member on the witness stand draw attention to an attractive feature of the defendant's character. They invariably apologize to the court for the trouble their relative has caused, typically bowing deeply to the judge before and after their testimony, and often bowing to the prosecutor as well. Not infrequently, the relative will also give another deep bow to whoever happens to be in the public gallery, apologizing for the bother that their family member has caused. Those bows are usually about 70 to 90 degrees, to show profound humility and apology—significantly more than the 15- to 30-degree bow that is used in formal greetings and farewells.

The bows are typically most plentiful and held for the longest time if the witness is a mother. Japanese parents, especially the older generation, are generally undemonstrative towards their children, rarely praising them or embracing them. In what might be considered a universal truth, however, mothers typically have a stronger bond with their children than fathers do. Consequently, when their child breaks the law, they feel the greatest shame. Perhaps this is why testimony from a mother, particularly if their son is a repeat offender, can verge on vitriolic.

It is one of the curiosities of the Japanese courtroom that everyone gets to pick on the defendant. It's not just the family member, who, after all, may have more reason to feel aggrieved than even the victim. The most belligerent questioning often comes not from the prosecutor or the judge, but from the defense lawyer, whose tone of questioning is sometimes condescending, often accusatory, and, on occasion, even downright angry.

In the following cross-examination, a defense lawyer in Matsumoto District Court lambasted his client, a thief and embezzler, for not showing sufficient remorse. "I'm at a loss for words when I look at all you did…When I listen to you I feel uneasy…You need to think long and hard about what you've done instead of just standing there speaking as if you've done nothing wrong. Can't you show some remorse? What you have done is terrible."

Indeed, it is far more unusual to see a prosecutor aggressively questioning a defendant than it is to see a defense lawyer getting snappy with their client on the witness stand. When the defendant pleads guilty—as around 91 percent have done in recent years, according to official statistics—the defense lawyer, whose questioning generally comes first, cross-examines the witness to establish the facts of the crime and the motive, and to elicit from the defendant statements of remorse and pledges that he will not do it again. There is usually not very much for the prosecutor to do once the defense lawyer has finished cross-examining.

The expressionless demeanor of Yoshimatsu Matsumoto, the cassette-tape and weed-killer thief, didn't convey much of a sense of guilt, but he did say in words how sorry he was.

"Do you know it's bad to steal?" his lawyer asked.

"Yes."

"Is it bad enough to go to jail?"

Mr. Matsumoto nodded.

"Is it worse to punch someone or to shoplift?"

"Shoplift."

"Is it worse to stab someone or to shoplift?"

"Shoplift."

"What about murder?"

"Murder is worse."

Anything that indicates a lack of remorse, such as a not-guilty plea, is frowned upon by judges. That is true of any country, but even more so in Japan. Very rarely does a defense lawyer put up any kind of a robust defense.

The University of Hawaii's David Johnson, a veteran observer of Japanese court processes, wrote in his book *The Japanese Way of Justice* that in some cases the defense arguments are so "perfunctory" and "incomplete" that "if judged by American standards they could constitute malpractice." Johnson also pointed out, however, that by the time a defendant is put on trial, the police and prosecutors have done their job. Cases with uncertain evidence are rarely prosecuted. Often, Johnson wrote, "there is little even the most zealous, skilled attorneys can do except try to mitigate the severity of the sentence."

Official statistics back up the conclusion that only the most rock-solid cases typically make it to court. In 2011, only 10 of 8,626 defendants appearing before Japan's summary courts—which, as mentioned previously, handle mainly minor theft cases—were judged not guilty: in other words, just one in 862 defendants. At that rate, the judge at Matsumoto Summary Court who delivered judgment on 69 cases in 2013 (all guilty) will deliver a not-guilty verdict every 12 years.

For those defendants who appear before a district court, the chance of a not-guilty verdict is slightly higher, but still remote. In 2011, just one defendant in 723 throughout Japan was fortunate enough to be found not guilty. In 2013, Matsumoto District Court judges found one person not guilty (in a theft case) out of 163 judgments delivered. Accordingly, by the law of averages, a not-guilty verdict at Matsumoto District Court occurs roughly every four or five years.

Mr. Matsumoto's lawyer, however, was different: he had a plan. Although the elderly man admitted to shoplifting, his lawyer entered a not-guilty plea on the basis that his client was not criminally responsible because he was senile. If the judge accepted that he was senile, then Mr. Matsumoto would walk free.

"Do you forget a lot?" the lawyer asked.

"Yes."

"How much savings do you have?"

"I can't remember."

"Did you ever go to jail before?"

"Yes."

"Which jail? Do you remember?"

"No."

"I am going to ask about vegetables. Say the names of 10 vegetables."

"Tomato, beans, eggplant," replied Mr. Matsumoto, adding one other that was inaudible.

"Where are you?"

"In court."

"Whose court?"

"My court."

"Take seven from 100."

"93."

"Take another seven off."

"86."

Answered quickly and correctly, things weren't going so well.

"Say 286 in reverse."

"682."

So far, so bad. Mr. Matsumoto's mental faculties were holding up reasonably well apart from his failure to name 10 vegetables and recall which prison he was in previously. The defense of senility was looking weak.

"Say 9253 in reverse."

"9368." Finally, Mr. Matsumoto had really fluffed it. But it was too late. He came across as somewhat doddery, but not at all mentally incapable. Later, the prosecutor read from letters by psychiatrists who had assessed Mr. Matsumoto's mental health and judged that he was capable of deciding right from wrong and wasn't senile.

The judge asked Mr. Matsumoto about his life.

"Who makes your food?"

"I make it."

"For example?"

"Curry with rice."

"Do you buy the vegetables?"

"Yes."

"And you cut them?"

"Yes."

"What do you do about taking a bath?" the judge asked. (The question is not as odd as it sounds: government figures from 2008 show that 4.5 percent of Japanese dwellings had no bathroom, one of the reasons for the ongoing, though declining, popularity of public bathhouses known as *sento*. A greater number of homes have no indoor toilets. OECD figures released in 2014 show that 6.4 percent of homes have no indoor flush toilet, compared to 0.1 percent in the United States and 0.3 percent in the United Kingdom).

"I have a bath at home."

"Do you use it?"

"Yes."

"Do you have any difficulty looking after yourself?"

"No."

"Do you have home help?"

"No."

"You do everything?"

"Yes."

"When you return to society, where will you live?"

"At home."

Here again, the answers given by Mr. Matsumoto showed a man who was capable of performing everyday tasks. He was never going to be one of the lucky few to win a not-guilty verdict. Once his senility defense faltered, his fate was sealed. Though the value of goods stolen may have been small, amounting to just 5,698 yen (US$57), he is part of a worrying trend emerging in Japanese society. There are thousands of elderly men and women like Mr. Matsumoto who have led hardworking, respectable lives unblemished by criminal wrongdoing, but who become repeat criminal offenders after they retire.

PENSIONER CRIME WAVE

A Ministry of Justice White paper on crime in 2012 said that overall crime by those over age 65 was 6.3 times higher in 2011 than it had been in 1992; the number of elderly citizens had only doubled. Assaults by the elderly rose even more spectacularly in the same period, leaping around 50-fold, albeit from a low base. Murder by the aged also rose at a time when the nation's overall murder rate fell.

In 1992, about seven times as many people in their 20s were found guilty of crime compared to over-65s. But by 2011, offenses by over-65s actually exceeded those committed by 20-somethings. Much of the media focus on elderly crime has been on sensational incidents, such as the 80-year-old chief of a fish processing company arrested in 2012 for killing his wife and hiding her body in a freezer for a decade, the 97-year-old man arrested for the attempted murder of an 84-year-old woman with a sword, and the 79-year-old woman who, allegedly harboring resentment against her husband for extramarital affairs he had had four decades earlier, beat him to death at their home near Tokyo.

But the vast bulk of elderly crime, and the vast bulk of the increase in elderly crime, has been plain old theft. Police figures show that different forms of theft accounted for 86 percent of all non-traffic-related crime by the elderly in 2011.

So what lies behind the phenomenon of pensioner crime in this predominantly law-abiding country? Figures from the United Nations Office on Drugs and Crime (UNODC) show that, proportionate to population, you were six times less likely to be assaulted in Japan than the United States in 2011, 39 times less likely to be robbed, and 16 times less likely to be a victim of murder and non-negligent homicide—even as US homicide rates dropped to levels not seen since the 1960s. Figures for 2010 show that people in Japan were 1,328 times less likely to be killed with a gun than those in the United States. In that year, there were only three gun murders in Japan, where about 1 percent of homicides are committed with a firearm, compared to about 65 percent in the United States. Even compared to its East Asian neighbors also known for low crime rates, Japan is socially very calm. You are 15 times more likely to be assaulted in South Korea, and three times more likely to be robbed there, UNODC figures suggest. But while Japan's National Police Agency figures show the overall number of crimes in Japan plummeted by half, from 2.85 million in 2002 to 1.48 million in 2011—partly thanks to better anti-theft technology in cars, homes, and shops; widespread use of CCTV; and improvements in DNA technology used to detect criminals—the portion of crime committed by the elderly spiraled.

One of the most common questions put to elderly defendants in the courtroom by the prosecution, the judge, and the defense lawyer is "Why?" It's also a big question for all of Japanese society. Why are so many elderly in one of the wealthiest and most socially obedient countries in the world turning to crime? There is hardly ever a satisfactory answer. Most elderly criminals are convicted for thieving, which would suggest poverty as a cause. Fully 46 percent of the 32,180 elderly men found guilty of crime in 2011 were convicted for shoplifting. For elderly women, the percentage was even higher: 81 percent of the 16,457 female offenders were shoplifters.

In 2012, the number of over-65s arrested in Tokyo for shoplifting exceeded teenagers for the first time ever. Whereas teenagers are more likely to steal game software or other items that can be easily resold, the most common item stolen by the elderly is food, which would appear to back up the theory that people are being forced to steal through financial desperation. But while poverty is presumably the driving force for some elderly crime, it does not persuasively explain the dramatic rise in criminality among Japan's grandparents. Firstly, over-70s are the wealthiest group in Japan. Government figures from 2008 show that the average household of two or more headed by a person over 70 had net financial assets of 23 million yen (US$230,000)—10 times the assets of households headed by a person in their 20s. If poverty is driving the surge in elderly crime, why has "silver shoplifting" become so prevalent at a time when the over-70s are doing much better financially than their parents' generation?

The current generation of over-70s have benefitted more than others from stable employment and a traditional seniority-based pay structure: in the past, in many companies, all that was necessary to get paid more was to grow older. While cost-of-living pay raises became uncommon due to deflation—which caused consumer prices to stagnate for the best part of two decades—many larger companies continued to increase salaries based on seniority.

Once workers retire, their income obviously drops, but it can remain substantial. According to government statistics, yearly income in Japan in 2012 for households of two people that were headed by a person in their 70s was 6.2 million yen (US$62,000). This is a significant sum, given that social services such as health are available at low cost thanks to public subsidies similar to those in Europe, while income-tax levels for low-to-mid-income earners are more akin to those in the United States. The over-70s household income is well ahead of the 4.4 million yen (US$44,000) earned by households headed by a person in their 20s. And over-70s are—as would be expected, given banks' reluctance to lend to the elderly—by far the least indebted with debts of 1.7 million yen (US$17,000) compared to 10 million yen (US$100,000) for households headed by people in their 40s, the most indebted group.

There are, of course, many elderly people who have no nest egg and no occupational pension, but there is a social welfare system in Japan. It is slightly bureaucratic to access, but it exists and provides a subsistence income. There is very little of the abject poverty in Japan that is visible on the streets of other rich countries. But if it's not poverty that lies behind the rapid increase in elderly crime, then what is it?

Keita Ochi, a criminologist from Hosei University, told the *Yomiuri* newspaper that some elderly feel they have contributed so much to the nation's economic growth that they will be forgiven for minor transgressions. In other words, shoplifting is a form of payback. Tomomi Fujiwara, who in 2007 wrote a book titled *Bosou Rojin* (Out-of-control old people), believes that in modern Japan, because family and community bonds have weakened, older people have become more isolated, and are therefore more likely to steal, stalk, and even assault: one in 13 offenses is a crime of violence, a higher proportion than for any other age group. In the debate over Japan's "silver crime," this is the most common explanation: old people commit crime because they are lonely and isolated.

Certainly Mr. Matsumoto's neighbors in Ono, where he was raised, reckon they knew why he did it. "He was lonely. I feel sorry for him," said a neighbor who remembered the 74-year-old as someone who readily cleared the snow from the footpath in front of his house, an appreciated gesture in the harsh winters of Nagano Prefecture, where snow is quick to freeze into packed ice. (She also remembered, less fondly, hearing *enka* music blaring through Mr. Matsumoto's open windows in the summer.) Mr. Matsumoto's life revolved around Ono, she said, recalling that his friends were mostly people that he had started elementary school with almost 70 years earlier. "Some of them have died in the last few years," the neighbor told me. "One of them died recently of a brain hemorrhage. He misses them."

Another neighbor concurred with the loneliness-leading-to-shoplifting theory. Although Mr. Matsumoto was friendly to people, and decent, he lived alone and must have been lonely, he said. Neighbors appeared to know little about his family life. They were aware that he divorced a long time ago, that his ex-wife and children had moved to a place about 10 miles away and seemed to have little contact, though a neighbor did say Mr. Matsumoto used to send money to his estranged family.

FRIED CHICKEN

But if loneliness, or poverty, is the root of elderly crime, what can explain the actions of someone like 82-year-old Takeko Ushikoshi? This tiny old lady tottered into Matsumoto Summary Court charged with putting nine cutlets of *sanzokuyaki* fried chicken—a salty specialty of Nagano Prefecture—into her shopping bag and leaving the supermarket without paying. It was the fourth time she had been caught shoplifting, but only her first court hearing. She had previously escaped court by paying a fine. Mrs. Ushikoshi started stealing when she was 79, to the obvious mortification of her family, two of whom were in the public gallery witnessing her—and their own family's—humiliation. She lived with her husband and their son and daughter-in-law, and their two elementary-school children.

The daughter-in-law testified for the defense. In a country where mothers-in-law are known for lording it over whichever unfortunate bride marries into the family home, it must have been the ultimate indignity for Mrs. Ushikoshi to watch her daughter-in-law take the stand on her behalf. The daughter-in-law, though, gave kindly evidence. Unusually for a witness called by the defense, she didn't blame the defendant. The old lady was a valued part of the household, she said.

"She makes the food in the house, she comes with us on holidays, she is very much involved with the rest of the family." Not much evidence, then, that Mrs. Ushikoshi committed her crimes out of loneliness.

"Did you see what she stole?" the defense lawyer asked the daughter-in-law.

"I thought it might have been things she liked, but when I looked into the bag at the police station, I saw it was the type of fried chicken that the children are fond of."

"Why do you think your mother-in-law stole?"

"I have given it much thought," she replied, "and I don't know, but the only thing I can think of is that because there was a time when life was tough for her, she was afraid to spend her money."

She also said that her mother-in-law contributed financially to the household purse, handing over one-third of her and her husband's pension—50,000 yen (US$500)—every month. Mrs. Ushikoshi and her husband were left with 100,000 yen (US$1,000) for incidentals—not enough to fund luxury living, but certainly enough to pay for a comfortable lifestyle. Mrs. Ushikoshi's husband was ill at the time of the offense, but in Japan, sickness doesn't bankrupt. People pay monthly insurance premiums, but these are related to income, and are a manageable expense for most people. When Mrs. Ushikoshi was arrested, she had 4,000 yen (US$40) in her purse, enough to pay for chicken she had pilfered twice over.

Her lawyer reminded his client that she had been caught shoplifting on a previous occasion and her son had to suffer the humiliation of collecting her from the police station.

"You still did it again—why?" the lawyer asked.

"I knew it was bad, but it seemed I forgot what happened before."

"You couldn't control yourself?"

"No. I go into my own world when I am shopping."

"But if you put something in your bag, it's stealing, and you know that you shouldn't steal."

"Yes."

"Why do you get the urge?"

"I don't know."

"Can you promise not to do it again?"

"Yes."

Mrs. Ushikoshi didn't clearly explain the motive for her theft in court, but in a statement to police after she was first apprehended she said that paying for chicken would have been "a waste of money." She had money at the time of her crime, but she didn't want to use it to buy goods that could instead be furtively stuffed into her bag.

The same was true for the weed-killer and blank-cassette man, Yoshimatsu Matsumoto, who seemed to have no financial problems. Mr. Matsumoto shoplifted in style. We may never know what drove him to crime, but we do know what drove him to the scene of the crime: a taxi. To steal $57 worth of merchandise, he took a $30 cab ride to the Cainz home-center store. The taxi driver waited outside with his meter running, an unwitting would-be getaway driver, while his customer was inside the shop filling his small backpack with pilfered merchandise. Apprehended by a store worker just as he was getting back into the taxi, Mr. Matsumoto made sure to pay the taxi fare.

It turned out that Mr. Matsumoto had enough savings to pay for thousands of similar taxi fares. The prosecutor located 8.5 million yen (US$85,000) sitting in his bank account, and Mr. Matsumoto told prosecutors that his total savings amounted to around 20 million yen (US$200,000). In a sign of contrition, he paid the shop 200,000 yen (US$2,000) in compensation prior to his court appearance.

"So why did you steal?" his defense lawyer asked.

"I wasn't thinking properly."

"Why did you pay for the taxi and not the goods? What's the difference?"

Mr. Matsumoto didn't reply.

"You have no answer?" his lawyer pressed.

Again, no reply.

"Did you know you might be caught?"

"Yes."

The judge also had questions for Mr. Matsumoto.

"When you put the goods in your rucksack, did you intend to pay?"

"I was of two minds."

"Did you decide halfway through not to bother paying?"

No response.

Like Takeko Ushikoshi, the 82-year-old fried-chicken shop-lifter, Mr. Matsumoto told police that he had money but didn't want to spend it. He even used the same phrase: "It's a waste of money" (*okane wa mottainai*).

"You said it was a waste of money to pay," the judge stated. "You said you didn't want to spend your money, so you shoplifted in Cainz. What did you mean by that?"

Again, Mr. Matsumoto gave no response.

FRIED PORK

On the day that Takeko Ushikoshi appeared at Matsumoto Summary Court for sentencing, a dapper-looking old man, well groomed and well dressed, sat in the public gallery watching the proceedings. Like Mrs. Ushikoshi, he was tiny; about 150 centimeters (5 feet) tall. He could have been her brother. But he wasn't: his name was Kesae Shikada, and he was the next defendant. It turned out that he shared many things in common with Mrs. Ushikoshi. Like her, he lived with a son and daughter-in-law and their two children—though unlike Mrs. Ushikoshi, his spouse had died. Like Mrs. Ushikoshi, he did the lion's share of the housework; however, he complained bitterly about it. "I do everything—the cooking, cleaning, laundry," he moaned more than once to the court. Like Mrs. Ushikoshi, Mr. Shikada was a latecomer to shoplifting. He even stole from the same supermarket chain, Nishigen, though a different branch. And like Mrs. Ushikoshi, fried food was his downfall—though in Mr. Shikada's case, it wasn't chicken: he was caught with his pockets stuffed with deep-fried *tonkatsu* pork as well as rice balls.

Like Mrs. Ushikoshi, Mr. Shikada had stolen small items on a few occasions before, but had never spent time in jail. He also had savings, about 2 million yen (US$20,000), and received 150,000 yen (US$1,500) in pension payments each month—the same as Mrs. Ushikoshi and her husband combined. And like Mrs. Ushikoshi, he was also a retired factory worker. He was one year older, 83, and was also in apparent fine physical health, apart from his hearing disability.

The court clerk asked, "Did you bring your hearing aid?"

"What?"

"Did you bring your hearing aid?"

"What?"

The clerk fetched an earpiece used for simultaneous translation on the rare occasion when the defendant is a foreigner. "Here, please use this."

After a brief opening statement by the prosecutor, the defense lawyer entered a not-guilty plea. The facts weren't in dispute, he said; his client had stolen the food, but he was of feeble mind when he did so and shouldn't be held criminally responsible. The prosecutor then described the contents of the book of evidence, including a brief description of the defendant's educational background, witness statements, victim statements, CCTV still images, and other items. The judge explained to the defendant that he would first be questioned by his lawyer.

But before his lawyer could open his mouth, Mr. Shikada loudly interjected to tell the judge about his remorse: "I can't sleep," he said, "I did something terrible. I can't sleep." As the lawyer began his questioning, it soon became clear that he and his client were at cross-purposes. Mr. Shikada had come to court to admit his crime and show his repentance as melodramatically as possible. But his lawyer had a list of questions he wanted to get through, apparently in the hope that his client's responses would indicate he was senile.

"When did you finish school?"

"I don't know. It was a long time ago."

"When did you start work?"

"It was a long time ago."

"When you left school, where did you work?"

"Nagano Denwa, it was a phone company."

"How long did you work there?"

"One year."

"After that where did you work?"

"I can't remember. Oh! It was on that road..." He paused to think about which road it was on but the lawyer moved onto the next question.

"How many companies have you worked for?"

"Around three."

"Which was the one you worked for longest?"

Mr. Shikada named a manufacturer, adding, "You are asking questions about things from a very long time ago. But I am more concerned with the terrible offense I have committed."

The lawyer ignored him. "Do you know where you are?" he asked.

Mr. Shikada ignored the question. "I don't know why I did it. Nishigen [the supermarket] is near my home, I see it every day. I can't live with myself. Why did I do such a bad thing? I did such a terrible thing, I can't think about anything else. Every day, it's all I think of."

"That's enough," said the lawyer. "My question is: Do you know where you are?"

Mr. Shikada stated his address.

"Not *your* address, do you know where you are now?"

"In court."

"Why?"

"I did a bad thing, I think of it every day."

His lawyer tried again: "Why did you shoplift?"

"No matter how much I think about that, I still don't know."

"Was it done without thought?"

"Yes."

"Why didn't you use money from your savings?"

"I don't know."

"Was it because you didn't want to eat into your savings?"

"I wasn't thinking in that way at all."

The defendant explained again that he lived with his son, his son's wife, and two grandchildren, and repeated his complaint about his unfair share of the housework burden. "We all live together but I do everything: the cooking, cleaning—I do it all," he said animatedly. He told the court that he had borrowed 12 million yen (US$120,000) from a bank to refurbish the house when his son's family moved in with him about a decade before. About 80 percent of his income was spent on mortgage repayments, he said. "It's my house and my loan, I am paying everything."

He insisted that he could live on what was left of his income once the loan repayments were made, though he said he sometimes dipped into his savings. He was emphatic that his shoplifting was not caused by a lack of money.

And so it went on. The questioning from his lawyer lasted for about 30 minutes: He asked about Mr. Shikada's deceased wife, which *kanji* characters were used to write her name; about his grandchildren, and the *kanji* characters used to write their names; his previous offenses; his smoking (five cigarettes a day); his drinking (just a cup of sake every day); his pension; his son and what type of work he did (the son had a part-time job); and his own living situation.

"What is your daughter-in-law's first name?" the lawyer asked.

"I don't know. I don't talk to her."

"So you don't remember. That's your answer?"

It was. In Japan, as already mentioned, it isn't unusual not to know the first name of even someone you know reasonably well, because colleagues almost always address each other by family name only, and friends usually do as well. But to not know the first name of a daughter-in-law indicates either an extraordinary lack of interest in her, or—as Mr. Shikada's lawyer was attempting to persuade the court—senility. The problem was that Mr. Shikada's crime appeared deliberate and calculated, not really something that a senile man would be likely to perpetrate. He had stuffed some goods in his pocket, but had placed others, such as kimchi vegetables and udon noodles, in the shopping cart, and had paid for them at the cash register.

The prosecution called as a witness a worker of the category known colloquially as "*manbiki* G-Men": store detectives hired by supermarkets to catch shoplifters. (*Manbiki* means shoplifting; "G-Men"—also a US slang term for FBI agents—derives from a popular Japanese detective drama called *G-Men 75*, which aired in the 1970s and early 1980s.) Despite their moniker, *manbiki* G-Men are usually women who pose as ordinary shoppers.

On the day in question, Mr. Shikada aroused the suspicion of the store detective because he looked to his left and right after picking up some deep-fried pork. "He had a basket in his right hand and he was carrying the fried food in his left hand. That looked suspicious to me," she said. He didn't put the goods straight into the basket as shoppers usually do; instead, he whipped the food into his pocket. The store detective watched Mr. Shikada, pocket bulging, pay for the food that was in his basket and followed him out to the car park. "I went after him, and called to him, 'Excuse me. Don't you have food that you didn't pay for?'"

"He said, 'No,' and had a very rebellious attitude. I then pointed to the fried pork and rice balls in his pocket, and he just said he would pay."

But the matter wasn't simply resolved by Mr. Shikada paying for the goods he had tried to steal. The supermarket called the police anyway.

"How long have you been doing this job?" the prosecutor asked the store detective.

"Since 2003."

"How many people do you usually catch per month?"

"About seven or eight."

"In your 10 years' experience, how many people did you catch who turned out to have a sickness?"

"Two. The last time was about three or four years ago."

"What happened?"

"When I asked whether they had food, they didn't reply. That person had dementia."

"What about the defendant?"

"He replied without hesitation, and he followed me into the office when I asked him to."

Once the store detective had finished giving evidence, that day's hearing ended. Mr. Shikada walked into the corridor with his lawyer.

"Who was that woman?" he asked.

"She works in the supermarket as shoplifting security," his lawyer replied.

"Oh, really?" It was the closest that the defendant had come to sounding senile, and it happened out of earshot of the judge.

Mr. Shikada's trial for fried-pork theft was far from finished, but by now the crime had taken up about three hours of court time over three hearings. The elderly man had given no answers about motive—not in court, anyway. According to a statement he gave police soon after he was caught, however, he said he stole because "it was a waste of money" to pay for the goods. Just like Mrs. Ushikoshi, who stole fried chicken, and Mr. Matsumoto, who stole cassette tapes and weed killer, Mr. Shikada had money but didn't want to use it, like a squirrel afraid to eat into his stores.

Among the explanations for the surge in elderly shoplifting, this, I believe, is the most likely. Elderly people like the three featured in this chapter shoplift not because they are poor now, but because they are afraid they may become poor. There is a wide sense of foreboding in Japan about the nation's future, a sense that Japan's best years are in the past. People like Mr. Matsumoto lived most of their life in a country that could seemingly do no wrong economically. For 52 years, from 1946 to 1998, Japan's economy grew every year, apart from a 1.2 percent drop in the "oil shock" year of 1974. For the nation it seemed there were no boom-and-bust cycles any more, just cycles of lower growth and higher growth.

In 1964, Japan overtook West Germany as the second-largest economy in the world. The economic disaster of the 1930s and 1940s, brought on by the nation's warmongers, became a distant memory as Japan recorded growth rates similar to those of modern-day China. For seven years of the 1960s, GDP growth exceeded 10 percent. By the 1980s, a combination of pronounced state influence in the economy, protectionism, and a hard-working and well-educated populace—combined with low crime and high employment—made Japan appear economically invincible. The possibility of Japan even overtaking the United States as the world's most powerful economy began to seem realistic, and books titled with variants of "Japan as Number One" became bestsellers. The country never did become number one, however, and now it is no longer even number two. In 2010, China became the largest Asian economy.

Even when it comes to electronics Japan is no longer a world-beater. In and after 2012, the electronics giants that once made Japanese proud—Sharp, Panasonic, and Sony—were downgraded to so-called junk status by ratings agencies. If those companies are to win back market share they will have to once again start making gadgets that people can't do without. As it stands, Japanese companies have an insignificant share of the personal computer and smartphone market, losing out to companies from South Korea, Taiwan, the United States, and China.

Steven Vogel of UC Berkeley cites a Japanese government report that the country's electronics makers produced 70 percent of the components of an iPod in 2005, but only 20 percent of the parts of an iPad in 2010. In an *Asia-Pacific Journal* article titled "What Ever Happened to Japanese Electronics?: A World Economy Perspective," Vogel points to figures that show Japanese manufacturers' share of DRAM chip production worldwide slumped from 76 percent to 3 percent between 1987 and 2004, and their share of liquid-crystal displays in phones and TVs went from 100 percent in 1995 to 5 percent a decade later.

Japan has been stuck in something of an economic rut for 20 years. While it has not been doing as badly as many say—Japanese and foreign commentators often refer to the 10 years from 1992 as Japan's economic "lost decade" even though unemployment never even reached 6 percent, and GDP only declined in two of those 10 years—there is a sense of malaise.

Japan has a pension system that has delivered to date, but there is a widespread belief that, as the nation ages, there won't be enough funds to give people a living income. The average life expectancy from birth in Japan is 83.5 years, but, as the OECD notes in its "Pensions at a Glance 2013," those who reach 65 can be expected to live another 21.7 years—in other words, until they are almost 87. In 1980, 9 percent of Japan's population was over the age of 65. By 2040, that share is expected to reach 34.4 percent, compared to 20.4 percent in the United States. Japan's elderly are projected by the Ministry of Internal Affairs and Communications to make up 38.8 percent of the population by 2050.

Part of the worry for older Japanese is that, even though the average Japanese senior has significant assets, they are heavily reliant on pension income, since their assets provide so little revenue. About three-quarters of such assets are in ultra-low-interest bank deposits or real estate that yields little or nothing. Money in the bank gives a pitiful yield. As of early 2015, fixed-term deposits at Postbank, the post office bank that is the largest savings institution in the world, offered yields as low as 0.035 percent. Put 200,000 yen (US$2,000) on long-term deposit and you will have enough to buy a postage stamp after a year; lodge the equivalent of $10,000 and you'll make enough to buy a coffee; leave $30,000 on deposit, and you'll have enough after a year to buy a pint of Guinness (at the local price of about $10).

Property has also proven to be a poor investment in most of Japan. After peaking in 1991, land prices in urban areas have fallen every year since. As of 2012, land prices in urban areas outside of the six biggest cities were down 49 percent, and commercial prices down 76 percent. While Tokyo's real estate market shows signs of recovery, in other regions the property market has remained generally lifeless. This is especially so in smaller cities like Matsumoto, where you can pick up a dated but decent family apartment for as little as $30,000. "There is no investor market in Matsumoto," says Yoshinori Ichikawa, a local real estate agent. "There are too many vacant apartments, so people don't want to take a risk."

While all of East Asia is racing toward an aging society, Japan is galloping faster than its neighbors. The UN estimates that South Korea's population will fall 8 percent, to 44 million people, by 2060; China's will drop 10 percent to 1,211 million. But Japan's will plunge 32 percent, to just under 87 million. A declining population is obviously never good for a property market.

And there are other worries for asset-rich old people. Seeking to replace deflation with 2 percent inflation, Japan, under Prime

Minister Shinzo Abe, implemented fiscal and monetary policies known as "Abenomics," which center around the printing of trillions of yen. The hope was flooding the market with cheap money would cause prices to rise. Inflation, however, tends to hurt those on fixed income, such as pensioners, more than any other group. Of course, it also erodes debt, but because Japan's elderly have less debt than other age groups, it would benefit them least in this regard.

And if Mr. Abe's policy fails, as previous government stimuli have done, then Japan may be left with more debt and little to show for it. Japan's public gross debt-to-GDP ratio was 226 percent in 2014—the highest in the developed world, and over twice the percentage of the United States. This, according to the OECD, "puts the economy at risk." The risk for the elderly is huge. If Mr. Abe's policies succeed and inflation returns, people on fixed incomes may be hurt. If they fail, and national debt spirals out of control, pensioners could really suffer financially.

Opinion polls suggest that the average Japanese believes that Abenomics will not lead Japan back to the economic glory days, and they are worried about their future. Kyodo News reported on a government survey in May 2014 showing that just over two-thirds of Japanese feel they will not have enough money when they retire. Three-quarters of that group said their provisions for retirement are "quite inadequate." Fewer than one in 50 said they would have enough money to live on, and the remainder believed they would have just a bare minimum. Polling by international research company Pew found that even when the stock market was booming in 2013, the first year of Abenomics, only one in five Japanese respondents described the economy as "good"—the best reading for five years, but dismal compared to recent Pew surveys in China in which between 80 and 90 percent of respondents say they are cheerful about the economy.

We don't know how much attention the elderly shoplifters highlighted in this chapter pay to Japan's fading world role, but their own explanation for their wrongdoing to police suggests that a sense of financial uncertainty, warranted or otherwise, has turned these old people who had worked all their lives into "silver shoplifters."

One of the causes of elderly crime may be uncertainty, but the response of the courts to the surge has been entirely predictable. The Japanese judicial system is not as ageist as some other countries. For a defense lawyer to argue that a defendant who is otherwise healthy should be treated with special lenience due to advanced age would be fruitless. Repeat offenders go to jail regardless of their age.

While fewer than 4 percent of English and Welsh prisoners were over age 60 in 2013, according to UK Justice Ministry statistics, in Japan the figure was 18 percent. Even allowing for the proportionally greater numbers of elderly in Japan, the rate of elderly incarceration is 3.3 times higher than in England and Wales. The trend, moreover, is on a worrying upward trajectory. From 1924, when such records began, until 1991, Japan only once jailed more than 100 males over the age of 70 in a single year—that was in 1953. But in 2012, Ministry of Justice figures show Japanese courts jailed 903 males over 70.

Japanese prisons are no place for those in the twilight of their lives. In 2010, the Nippon TV channel received rare permission to film and interview inmates for a special report on elderly prisoners. Filming inside Kurobane prison in Tochigi Prefecture, the channel showed a prison system woefully unprepared to deal with the increasing numbers of prisoners who are more suited to a nursing home than a prison. The broadcast showed prisoners with Alzheimer's disease who have to be taught and retaught every day how to do simple tasks. The program also showed younger prisoners wearing white coats acting as caregivers for the older prisoners, helping them to bathe and walk. At night, with prisoners in their cells, the prison guards took on the caregiving role for inmates who are senile, incontinent, and disabled. More than 10 percent of the inmates of Kurobane prison are over the age of 65, and many of them clearly shouldn't be in a prison at all. Japan's prison system is ill-equipped to handle elderly convicts suffering from senility.

The Nippon TV crew also showed footage from Hiroshima Prefecture's Onomichi prison, one of the few with a wing specially adapted for the elderly. In Onomichi there are more individual cells for older inmates, who tend to be crankier and less inclined to share cells. Each cell has a rubber mat and padded walls. Prison stairs are fitted with handrails. In 2007, *New York Times* journalist Norimitsu Onishi, who also visited the prison, reported for his newspaper that "In the workroom, adjustable chairs were brought in two years ago. In the locker room, names were added below inmates' identification numbers, which they tended to forget...'Hard of hearing,' read a sign on one door. On another, leading to the cell of an inmate with dementia, a sign instructed prison workers to give him medication before every meal 'even if he did not request it.'"

Older people have it somewhat easier compared to other inmates. They have to work less—six hours compared to the standard eight hours expected of most prisoners. In some jails, the elderly are excused from marching in military formation when moving around the prison. Many elderly prisoners are simply no longer able to march military-style, while others are unable to walk at all without aid.

Mr. Matsumoto, the 74-year-old who took a taxi to go shoplifting, may have been unable to recall the name of the prison he was in previously, but he remembered enough about it to tell the judge he really didn't want to go back.

The judge for Matsumoto Summary Court is Koji Kitamura. He is fairly avuncular, and often gives personal advice to defendants on how to improve their relationships with family, for example, or how to manage their debt. He often smiles at those before him as an uncle might at an errant nephew. There is forgiveness in his smile, but not in his sentencing. He is neither hard nor soft by Japanese judicial standards—he follows the established judicial practice of jailing repeat offenders regardless of the crime, though he jails them with resignation, not enthusiasm. In 2013 he jailed one in three of those who came before him.

Once he had established to his own satisfaction that Yoshimatsu Matsumoto was not senile, the judge made it clear that Mr. Matsumoto would be going to jail. It is, of course, fairly pointless to jail an old man for stealing $57 worth of goods. Mr. Matsumoto was not a physical threat to anyone, and jailing him was arguably a waste of public money and clearly not much of a deterrent to him. But jail is currently Japan's only option for punishing its elderly repeat criminals, petty and otherwise; options such as community service are not employed. Judge Kitamura sentenced Mr. Matsumoto to 14 months in jail with 40 days off in lieu of the time already spent in custody. The old man didn't react; he just continued to look vacant. The two guards flanking him put the handcuffs back on, and he was led out of the courtroom on a rope. The sense of loneliness from this sad man was palpable. But Japanese courts are not sentimental places. Mr. Matsumoto's lawyer argued strongly that he was senile and therefore not criminally liable, but he didn't bother to argue that the defendant should be treated gently because of his age.

Mr. Matsumoto will receive classes in jail to help him change. The Ministry of Justice says that "Guidance for reform is provided through lectures, gymnastics, events, interviews, consultations, and advice, along with other methods." The guidance is meant to encourage prisoners to "understand their victims' feelings and realize a sense of remorse" as well as to "lead a regular life with a sound way of thinking, thereby promoting their own mental and physical health." It is also aimed at helping convicts in "acquiring the necessary skills to adapt to a societal life."

This type of guidance may be appropriate for younger offenders, but is probably not for the elderly like Mr. Matsumoto. His victim, Cainz, is a massive retail chain with sales in 2012 of 341 billion yen (US$3.41 billion). Mr. Matsumoto said in court and in a written apology that he was sorry for his crime, but it's unlikely he'll spend much time trying to "understand the victim's feelings." It is also a fact that the rate of recidivism for the elderly is higher than average. Whatever drove Mr. Matsumoto to thieve will likely still exist after his release from jail.

Likewise for Kesae Shikada, the volubly remorseful 83-year-old who stole the fried pork and rice balls. Mr. Shikada was back in court on a sweltering day in August for his seventh court appearance since his first hearing in freezing-cold January. Mr. Shikada's lawyer was still fighting an unusually valiant battle for his client, arguing a not-guilty plea on the basis of senility. The day's evidence was given by a Dr. Ogiwara, a psychiatrist from Shinshu University Hospital who appeared at the request of the defense. In her opinion, based on brain scans and tests, Mr. Shikada was suffering serious brain degeneration and was showing symptoms of Alzheimer's disease. According to Dr. Ogiwara, Mr. Shikada would have known the difference between right and wrong when he shoplifted, but he would have had difficulty controlling his emotions. She was unable to give a firm opinion as to whether he was sufficiently sound in mind to be criminally responsible.

But Mr. Shikada appeared to hear very little of the evidence. He had brought his own hearing aid to this session, but it didn't work properly. Seven months after his first court appearance, he was still apologetic but no longer punctuated the hearings with outbursts of fervent remorse. At this hearing, he had other concerns on his mind. During a break in court session he went to look out the nearest window. "Just checking if it's raining," he said, "I came here without taking in my washing."

The evidence from Dr. Ogiwara gave him a fighting chance of getting off. But he clearly just wanted the marathon trial to finish. He looked crestfallen when he was told that there would be at least two more hearings before he had finished.

I asked his lawyer, Susumu Ozawa, why he was putting so much work into a relatively minor case for which, as a state-appointed lawyer, his payment would be about half what he would get if he was privately hired. "It would be easy," he said, "to take this case and win a suspended sentence. But shoplifting is often a repeat offense, so what happens if he does it again? If we don't fight this case and have him properly assessed, jail would be a certainty next time round."

In the end Mr. Ozawa got a partial victory. His client, Mr. Shikada, was found guilty, but he didn't get a suspended sentence: He was fined 200,000 yen (US$2,000). That means that if he is caught shoplifting again he will likely be given a suspended jail sentence rather than an actual jail sentence.

Unlike Mr. Matsumoto and Mr. Shikada, 82-year-old Mrs.

Ushikoshi, the fried-chicken shoplifter, was making her first appearance as a defendant because, as mentioned earlier, her previous transgressions had all been dealt with outside of court. The judge sentenced her to 10 months in jail, suspended for three years. Forgiveness should Mrs. Ushikoshi steal again is unlikely. As with their male counterparts, elderly women are being sent to jail in record numbers. In the 69 years from 1924 to 1992, Japan jailed 179 women over 70. The highest numbers were in the years 1934 and 1992, in each of which eight females over 70 were sent to prison. But—and here is a startling statistic—in 2012 alone, Japan jailed 179 women over 70, the same as the total from 1924 to 1992. Older women used to be an invisible part of the prison population, but in 2012, one in 12 newly imprisoned women was over 70.

Mrs. Ushikoshi showed no emotion upon hearing her penalty. The judge warned her not to come before him again: "You don't want to start a life of going in and out of prison." She bowed and thanked him, put her hat back on, and tottered out of court.

GANGSTERS

BETRAYED

Her voice was timid, almost sweet; her answers were hesitant and inarticulate, usually monosyllabic. But Kumiko Harada's replies to each of the prosecutor's questions made the thuggish-looking man sitting in the defendant's seat bristle.

Kenji Kakiuchi, 38, was a local gang boss in the city of Suwa, a small industrial city whose main boast is that it's the home of the Epson printer company. Thin and balding, Kakiuchi exuded confidence, looking like a man who is used to being in charge. He had once been the *honbucho* (general manager) for one of the leading yakuza gangs in Nagano Prefecture before leaving and creating his own scaled-down crime operation.

Whereas virtually all defendants in Japanese courtrooms speak only when spoken to, he laughed and joked, consulted loudly with his lawyer during the hearing, smiled and waved at his ex-wife in the public gallery, and showed outrage about some of the claims that Ms. Harada was making in front of those he initially referred to as "venerable judges." But Mr. Kakiuchi also carried an unmistakable menace. He couldn't see Ms. Harada's face, as she was giving evidence via video link. She could have been in the same building, or she could have been a thousand miles away. What was important to her was that she wasn't in the same room as Mr. Kakiuchi.

"We are doing a video link at your request. Why?" asked the prosecutor.

"I am scared."

"What is scary?"

"Kenji-san is scary."

Kenji Kakiuchi was in court for a typical gang crime. He's a pimp—or, more precisely, he is an *enderi* pimp. *Enderi* is a linguistic blend of Japanese and Japanese-English that only a language as flexible as that of Japan could adopt. The "*en*" comes from *enjo kosai*, a phrase meaning "compensated dating," which originally described the phenomenon of older men paying to go on a date with a schoolgirl but now usually means teen prostitution. The *deri* comes from the English word "delivery," and is a contraction of *deriheru* (delivery health), meaning a call-girl service. *Enderi* therefore means a call-girl service where the prostitutes are either children—which in Japan is anyone under 18 years of age—or else they look young enough to pass for one.

The careful *enderi* pimp would recruit women who are over 18, but Mr. Kakiuchi wasn't careful. The oldest prostitute who worked for him was 30, but most of them were under 18; the youngest was just 14. That meant that he was being prosecuted under child welfare as well as anti-prostitution laws. He was also being charged under child-porn legislation for making videos of teenage girls giving oral sex to men, and he faced yet another charge for being in possession of methamphetamine drugs when he was arrested.

The attraction for pimps of running a call-girl service in Japan is the same as anywhere. There is no need for fixed premises, so there are fewer overhead costs. All Mr. Kakiuchi needed was a mobile phone, an Internet connection, and a driver to ferry his prostitutes to the clients. He used to run the prostitute operations of the main local yakuza gang. But he doesn't look like the kind of man that would be good at persuading young females to work for him. This is partly because he is a generation older than most of his sex workers, but more so because, as Ms. Harada pointed out, he is scary. His friends vouched for him in court as a perfect gentleman, but Mr. Kakiuchi looked like a hooligan: his face remained slightly scarred by the acne of his youth, and his right hand was missing most of its pinkie, a legacy of his yakuza days. He was also quick to anger.

So he needed to hire a younger person to help sweet-talk young flesh into working for him. Kumiko Harada, one his youthful recruiting agents, had just moved into adulthood at 20 years of age. Those aged 18 and 19 are in legal grey areas in Japan, as they are considered neither adults nor children, but minors. Although they are legally too young to buy a packet of cigarettes or a beer, they may be tried as adults in court cases and may also be executed for especially heinous crimes; capital punishment is not allowed for those 17 or under.

Ms. Harada was paid a basic wage of 10,000 yen (US$100) per day, about the standard wage for honest manual work in the region. She also topped up her earnings with a small cut of what the prostitutes earned. She said her monthly earnings were up to 300,000 yen (US$3,000) per month, which was good money for a young unskilled worker outside of Tokyo—and was, of course, tax-free. As Mr. Kakiuchi growled during her testimony, "Where else would she get money like that?"

Mr. Kakiuchi's crew trawled dating sites to find men who were looking for love—or at least sex. Ms. Harada recruited women online, contacting them via bulletin boards and blogs.

"Who told you to do this?" the prosecutor asked her.

"Kenji-san, he wanted to increase the number of women working for him."

But Kenji Kakiuchi had high standards; he liked slim and pretty as well as young. According to a statement Ms. Harada gave to police, he wasn't always happy with her work. He described one woman that Ms. Harada had brought to him as a potential prostitute—a 23-year-old supermarket worker who was looking to earn some extra cash—as a "fat old aunt whose hair was too short," and another, an unemployed 18-year-old, as a "fat, dirty *yamanba*." (The word *yamanba* literally means "mountain hag," but is used to describe an unfashionably dressed woman with too much makeup.)

Ms. Harada and two other foot soldiers organized the logistics between the clients and the prostitutes, and drove the latter to the hotels where the encounters took place. All of Mr. Kakiuchi's crew were signed up to a texting group through a smartphone app so they could communicate as a collective, coordinating the movements of the women. Group texting also meant that, as Mr. Kakiuchi said, "If there was a bad client or one who wouldn't pay, the other guys and I would all speed there immediately." Ms. Harada was also the bagwoman for Mr. Kakiuchi, collecting his illicit takings.

Her boss preferred to arrange the encounters not in regular hotels, but in so-called love hotels, with the client footing the room charges. The attraction of love hotels, often garishly painted with pseudo-neoclassical touches like balconies and balustrades, is that they are highly anonymous—you can often pay for the room via an automated vending machine or by sliding the money to the receptionist through a slot, so you don't actually meet any of the hotel staff. Another attraction of love hotels is that rooms can be rented for as brief a period as one hour, and the rental time can be extended in 30-minute blocks.

For prosecutors, knowing the details of Mr. Kakiuchi's pimping was one thing; proving them was another. They needed an insider to nail him. In the end, they got two of his closest lieutenants to testify against him in court—Ms. Harada and her boyfriend, Yuya Yamada.

"Who told you to recruit the females?" the prosecutor asked Ms. Harada.

"Kenji-san," she replied.

"Did the defendant use the word 'employee' to describe them?"

"Yes." This was an important answer, because under the Employment Security Law, Mr. Kakiuchi faced up to 10 years in jail for recruiting labor with "an intention of having workers do work harmful to public health or morals."

"What do you think 'employee' means?" the prosecutor continued.

Ms. Harada gave no reply.

"Were they working for the defendant?"

"Yes."

"Did he explain how much money he would take and how much they would get?"

"Yes."

And so it went on, with the witness either unwilling or unable to speak in full descriptive sentences. Her monosyllabic answers were clear, however, and each one of them strengthened the case against her former boss.

Mr. Kakiuchi was not just a powerful local gangster. He was also part of a growing phenomenon in Japan's gangland—the yakuza who is no longer part of the yakuza. Japan has traditionally had two categories of criminals: those involved in organized crime and those who freelance—individuals who commit mainly opportunistic crimes such as theft and burglary. The organized criminals are the yakuza; they are legal entities with their own offices and companies. They are involved in businesses that are legal, such as moneylending, and those that are illegal, such as drug dealing.

GETTING TOUGH

In recent years, however, Japan's traditional quasi-tolerance toward the yakuza has been declining. New laws have persuaded many that being in a yakuza gang is no longer worth it. Being a registered yakuza, in other words, is starting to confer obvious disadvantages.

In 1992, Japan's first anti-yakuza law was passed. Under this law, most yakuza groups are "designated," which means they are requested—though not legally obliged—to register their members with the police. Members of designated groups are expected to provide basic information such as name, address, date of birth, and gender; according to the National Police Agency, that data is accessible by police nationwide. Whether a group is designated or not depends on its size and the percentage of members with criminal records. Once a group is designated, the police can issue cease-and-desist orders to yakuza members engaged in specific instances of criminal behavior, such as demanding protection money, or intimidating tenants to vacate properties to facilitate development (a profitable yakuza sideline known as *jiage*). The benefit to the yakuza member is that the cease-and-desist order acts as a sort of warning and is preferable to being arrested, so they generally comply with it.

In the first decade of this century, new or amended laws started to make life far more difficult for the mobsters. Around Japan, prefectures and cities began to pass anti-yakuza ordinances aiming to make gangsters as much social outcasts as well as criminal ones. Such ordinances make it unlawful to deal commercially with the mob. Their scope is extraordinarily wide, essentially banning all business dealings with the yakuza. It has become illegal, for example, for a caterer to supply food to a yakuza group having a party. A yakuza member cannot open a bank account or get a cell phone—yakuza gangsters who come before Matsumoto District Court typically have cell phones in other people's names.

The laws put yakuza members in a very difficult position. If, for example, they are applying to rent an apartment from a non-yakuza real estate agent and admit to being in the yakuza on the application form they won't get the apartment, but if they say they are not a member they may be prosecuted for fraud.

Police in Nagano Prefecture introduced an anti-yakuza ordinance on September 1, 2011. Using a cartoon duck dressed up as a motorcycle police officer, the campaign was pitched as "all of society vs. the violent groups." Notices in train stations and post offices warn the public that the yakuza are the enemy. In Matsumoto City's tax office and post offices, for example, anti-yakuza posters feature cartoon figures: One represents housewives, saying, "Don't give them money, don't borrow money from them"; another representing the construction industry says, "Don't make contracts with them"; one from the service industry says, "Don't let them use golf clubs, hotels, or inns"; a schoolchild says, "Don't let them build yakuza offices near schools"; and another, in a suit, says, "Don't rent them office space."

It should also be pointed out that while arms of the Japanese state put up posters portraying the yakuza as social pariahs, the state is at the same time indirectly boosting yakuza coffers. An unknown but anecdotally significant number of yakuza-run companies are supplying labor for the publicly funded US$80 billion-plus nuclear cleanup around Fukushima Prefecture, after the meltdown at the Daiichi nuclear power plant following the earthquake and tsunami of March 11, 2011.

The supply of unskilled temporary workers via front companies, moreover, has long been a profitable sideline for the yakuza, which reportedly even provided laborers during the original construction of Fukushima's nuclear plants in the 1970s. In the post-meltdown cleanup, the yakuza-connected companies are found toward the bottom of a subcontracting pyramid. At the top is the Tokyo Electric Power Company (TEPCO), which owns the Daiichi plant and was effectively nationalized to save it from bankruptcy after the meltdown. TEPCO contracts with large companies such as Toshiba and Hitachi, who subcontract with other firms, who subcontract others, and so on. Yakuza-linked companies are generally at least five steps away from TEPCO in the subcontracting pyramid, supplying casual laborers who may work for a few months until their radiation exposure reaches the legal limit. Workers hired by yakuza-connected firms may be unaware of any gang links. I spoke to one decontamination worker in Fukushima who had no knowledge that his employer was yakuza-connected until he had a dispute with him over pay. Takeshi Katsura, a trade unionist who advises nuclear cleanup workers, told me that yakuza-run firms often don't have much sympathy for those with labor grievances. "I know of some cases where they assaulted workers who complain about conditions, and others where they threatened to kill them," he said.

Aside from the nuclear cleanup, the anti-yakuza drive—part legislation and part appeals to hearts and minds aimed at turning the gangs out of society and persuading citizens not to hire them in civil matters such as debt collection—is squeezing gangland revenue. The stated aim is social and economic exclusion—or, as the police term it, "annihilation of the *boryokudan*." *Boryokudan*, the official term used by state agencies to refer to the yakuza, means "violent group"; it is an appellation that the yakuza loathe.

In Matsumoto District Court, Mr. Kakiuchi expressed yearning for a time when it was easier for the yakuza to make a dishonest shilling. "When I was in the yakuza I was supposed to do *shinogi*," he said, using the word for all yakuza activities that generate money. "But with the new laws I couldn't open a bank account, I couldn't meet with presidents of companies, so I couldn't do business."

A key difference is that some company presidents who might have been pressured into making a monthly "contribution" to the yakuza in the past are now more scared of the police and the new laws—under which businesses that have dealings with the yakuza can be publicly named—than the gangsters. The laws also give companies a ready-made excuse for refusing to yield to extortion demands.

For Mr. Kakiuchi, however, leaving the yakuza didn't improve his fortunes. "I have given up the yakuza, but now I am treated like a former yakuza. So even though I have finished with them, I am discriminated against in business. I can't meet yakuza and I can't meet non-yakuza." All of which raises the question about what he will do in the future.

"You will probably go to jail, but when you get out, what type of work will you do?" his lawyer asked.

"I am missing a finger, so I won't be able to get manual work," Mr. Kakiuchi replied.

CUTTING TIES

During the months it took to try Mr. Kakiuchi, a former yakuza colleague, Takashi Kakefuji, also came before Matsumoto District Court, on charges of drug possession. He echoed the complaint that the laws were having a chilling effect on his group's ability to make money. He even went so far as to blame it for his own relapse into drug use. Mr. Kakefuji was a member of the Shinshu Saito Family crime group, also known as the Fujii-gumi, which had once employed Mr. Kakiuchi as a "general manager." Despite the use of the term "family," members are not actually related by blood. However, once admitted to the yakuza, loyalty to the gang takes precedence over loyalty to a member's biological family. The head of the organization is an *oyabun* (which literally means someone acting in place of a parent); the subordinates are called *kobun* (children) and *kyodai* (brothers).

Mr. Kakefuji, a portly, baby-faced father of three children who was missing the top joint from both of his little fingers, had dabbled in methamphetamine in the past, but gave up drugs once he was promoted to secretary-general of the Fujii-gumi crime group. His promotion meant he was in charge of handling group finances, so he couldn't be high on the job. Sounding a bit like a harried office worker, Mr. Kakefuji told the court, "I had to be at headquarters every day. I was too busy—I just couldn't be taking drugs."

Sadly, for him, he was in the finance job at a time when the new anti-yakuza ordinances had begun to bite into the gang's business model. "Once the ordinances came into effect, our income went way down, and it became hard," he said.

"So your psychological stress relating to the economy started after the anti-yakuza ordinances," his lawyer said. "Money became tight and life became harder?"

"It was really tough," acknowledged Mr. Kakefuji. He said he was approached by a member of another yakuza group, who asked if he wanted to do some part-time drug-dealing to make money. But Mr. Kakefuji said he had turned the man down because his own Fujii-gumi crime group was affiliated with the Kobe-based Yamaguchi-gumi—the biggest crime group in the world, with about 26,000 members—whose leader opposes drug dealing.

Mr. Kakefuji, however, no longer had to worry about the stress of making money for the yakuza. His lawyer submitted into evidence a declaration from his gang chief confirming that Mr. Kakefuji had recently resigned from the group. To neutral observers, it might seem bizarre to see a formal-looking paper certifying withdrawal of the defendant from a crime group being presented to the court. But there it was, a document known as a *zetsuenjo*, signed on May 26, 2014 by the yakuza group's leader Toshiki Kojima, being held up by the defendant's lawyer as evidence that his client would henceforth be on the straight and narrow.

This helped Mr. Kakefuji, as did testimony from his wife that after a 10-year separation—caused, she said, by his gangland activities—she was reuniting with him. Now that he was out of the yakuza she had arranged a job for him at a relative's construction firm. He was also helped by the fact that he had only one other conviction, dating back 12 years. So Mr. Kakefuji was given an 18-month prison sentence, suspended for three years.

CITIZENS FIGHT BACK

Mr. Kakefuji probably left the yakuza at the right time. Things look like they won't get any easier for the mob in Japan. In a July 2012 article in the *Asia-Pacific Journal*, UK-based academic and yakuza expert Andrew Rankin pointed to a 2008 amendment to the Anti-Yakuza Law as a key effective measure against organized crime. That change made yakuza bosses in certain cases legally liable to pay compensation to people harmed by their members.

A small but growing number of ordinary citizens have taken advantage of this amendment. Rankin quotes a lawsuit against the head of the Yamaguchi-gumi by the Thai owner of a bar who had refused to pay protection money to gangsters affiliated with the crime group. The owner sued after gang members seeking vengeance stole money from the bar, assaulted staff, and smashed up the interior. The fact that the Yamaguchi-gumi leader, Shinobu Tsukasa, had been in jail at the time wasn't sufficient to defend him in court, and Mr. Tsukasa was ordered to pay a fine of 15 million yen (US$150,000).

Other lawsuits against Mr. Tsukasa followed. As Rankin wrote, "In February 2011 a court ordered him to pay 4 million yen [US$40,000] to the owner of a bar in Gifu who had been assaulted by members of a Yamaguchi-gumi gang after refusing to pay protection money; in June, Tsukasa paid 42 million yen to a taxi firm in Hyogo from which gangsters had attempted to extort money; in July, a Nagoya man successfully sued Tsukasa for damages of 10 million yen after having his arm broken by yakuza debt collectors;

and in September, Tsukasa had to pay another 14 million yen in damages to a Tokyo man from whom gangsters had extorted money. One would think that the most powerful yakuza boss in Japan could easily silence potential plaintiffs with intimidation; apparently he cannot." Early in 2013 came another lawsuit against the mob leader, when a restaurateur in Nagoya sought repayment of the 10.85 million yen (US$108,500) in protection money she had paid over a 12-year period to gang members affiliated with Mr. Tsukasa's group.

These types of lawsuits and laws are contributing to a fragmenting of the yakuza. The 2013 police statistics show that the number of registered gang members fell below 60,000 for the first time since records began in the early 1990s. The police trumpet this as evidence that the battle against the yakuza is being won. But is it the success that is being claimed? Presumably some gangsters who leave the mob are gone from crime for good. Others, however, like Mr. Kakiuchi, the pimp before Matsumoto District Court, quit official gang membership but stay in the crime business. When Mr. Kakiuchi left, his gang would have notified police (as well as other gangs) that he was no longer to be treated as a gang member. "A lot of them have been leaving," a Suwa City businessman familiar with Mr. Kakiuchi's former gang told me, "but they are not leaving crime; they are just leaving the yakuza and setting up again in groups of four and five in other places."

LESS ORGANIZED CRIME

If the traditional yakuza is on the wane, does someone like Mr. Kakiuchi represent the future Japanese criminal—an unaligned and unregistered thug who remains involved in organized crime, but a type of organized crime that is harder to control and monitor than the yakuza? Mr. Kakiuchi has almost certainly retained some level of contact with the Fujii-gumi crime group, because it is inconceivable that they would allow an outside operator to set up a prostitution ring on their turf without permission.

Mr. Kakiuchi was able to draw on his experience from his

yakuza days in setting up his operation. "I had managed the sex-trade business years ago for the yakuza, and I'm good at it—it's something I can do. For years I was in charge of *kyabakura* [cabaret bars, similar to hostess bars] and *hakoheru* [brothels] and *deriheru* [call girls]." When he set up his prostitution business, however, Mr. Kakiuchi developed his own system. Prostitutes he hired would pay him 15,000 yen (US$150) per day, along with a small amount of money to their driver.

"Other places have a system where the pimp takes 50% of all a prostitute's income," he said. "With me, they pay a flat 15,000 yen, and anything they earn over that they keep. I wanted to make money and I wanted them to make money," Mr. Kakiuchi explained.

"So this 15,000 yen always went to you?" his lawyer asked.

"After work, one of my staff would let me know how business went. If the women didn't make any money, I didn't take the 15,000 yen." Mr. Kakiuchi's sex workers, who usually charged around 20,000 yen (US$200) per encounter, would do comparatively well if they had at least two clients per day.

Mr. Kakiuchi did much better. He had around eight women working for him in total, with about five working on any given day. If they each paid him their 15,000-yen fee per day, he would earn a tidy 27 million yen (US$270,000) per year, gross. Out of that came the wages of the three people who helped to run his operation and other expenses. One of Mr. Kakiuchi's henchmen estimated his boss was earning around 18 million yen (US$180,000) in profit annually—around five times what an unskilled adult of his age would typically earn in Nagano Prefecture.

The women worked in a set geographical area, not venturing beyond areas in and around Suwa and Shiojiri cities. Mr. Kakiuchi said he wouldn't, for example, send women to work in nearby Ina City, because that would provoke the local yakuza there. As he saw it, his success was built on an atmosphere where everybody made money and people were treated fairly.

"It was never forced. Everyone came and did it cheerfully. If they enjoyed it, they'd recommend their friends to work for me," he said.

"So between you and the women it was friendly?" his lawyer asked.

"Yes."

"Could they stop working of their own free will?"

"Yes," he replied, though he added that the work could be unpleasant because the clients included "weirdos, fetishists, and perverts."

"What type of people were working for you?" his lawyer asked.

"They were working to make money for their family, or they were using the money to go to host clubs," he said referring to the male version of hostess clubs. "I was like a parent. I took in the 15,000 yen, and they kept the remainder of the money; that was my thinking."

"What about their actual parents, did you ever meet them?"

"You'll be surprised, but I was friendly with some of the parents. I was even in their homes. Maybe it's a societal problem, but we were doing something for each other: I was hiring their daughter."

"So the parents knew they were doing this work?" his lawyer asked

"Yes, they did. I have been nine months in detention, and parents have contacted me and asked if I am short of money. They feel strongly that what I did wasn't such a bad thing."

Two witnesses testified before the court to defend Mr. Kakiuchi's character. The first was a friend from a yakuza group near Tokyo who had known Mr. Kakiuchi since they served time together in Morioka prison in northern Japan. It was difficult to see the value of Takeshi Suzuki's character testimony, given that he looked like an even more thuggish version of Mr. Kakiuchi, with a missing pinkie, visible tattoos, and a criminal record. Mr. Suzuki limped up to the witness stand.

"Today you came from Chiba for the defendant," Mr. Kakiuchi's lawyer said, referring to a prefecture about four hours' drive away.

"Yes."

"What type of person is he?"

"He is a great friend when you are in need. I want him to return to society quickly. My friends and I are waiting for him to come out. His return won't be a day too soon," he replied. I found it unlikely that the thought of a reunion between Mr. Kakiuchi, Mr. Suzuki, and his friends would encourage the judges to give the pimp a shorter sentence.

Mr. Kakiuchi's ex-wife Akemi also took the stand on his behalf. An attractive, cheerful woman, she told the court that they first dated when he was in the third year of junior high school and she was in her first year of high school.

"What is the defendant's personality like?" the defense lawyer asked.

"He is kind, he doesn't bully the weak, he looks after people. Even if he has no food or money he will share what he has."

"Did he give money to people in jail?"

"Every month when he was in jail I was asked to send money and he gave it to others."

"To people in jail?"

"To people in jail and people outside."

"The defendant's parents are dead?" the lawyer asked.

"Yes, he goes to their grave twice a month and lights incense. Even in the snow, he always goes."

Just as Mr. Kakiuchi was being sainted before our eyes, the prosecutor threw cold water on the canonization. "You know the reason he is here?" she asked, referring to his pimping of children. "What do you think about that?"

"It's difficult to say," the ex-wife replied.

"Is it that you don't think anything of it?"

"No."

"Are you shocked?"

"Yes."

The ex-wife's description of Mr. Kakiuchi as someone who didn't bully the weak is straight from the code of yakuza, who sometimes refer to themselves as *ninkyo dantai* (chivalrous groups). The hard-pressed guy with the noodle stand who is hit up every month for his yakuza "contribution," the foreign national trafficked by the yakuza into sexual slavery, or the Japanese woman coerced into prostitution to repay a debt to a yakuza loan company won't appreciate the "chivalrous" aspect of the yakuza or their alleged "don't bully the weak" principle. But it is true that the *yakuza* tend not to commit crimes that have a direct impact on the public's sense of safety. In general, they don't allow their members to engage in street robberies, beat up unconnected people, or commit the type of indiscriminate street crimes that plague many big cities around the world. This is one of the reasons why Japan's streets are so safe.

Overall, relatively few offenses are committed by yakuza members—in 2010, they amounted to just 6.4 percent of all crimes. But gang members committed around half of all detected crimes involving false imprisonment, drugs, and blackmail.

For those yakuza who are arrested, the golden rule is, unsurprisingly, that you never testify against your boss. Unfortunately for the pimp, Mr. Kakiuchi, his workers were never yakuza members. They hadn't gone through the admission ceremony that cements the criminal brotherhood. Had the monosyllabic Ms. Harada been a yakuza member—which was extremely unlikely because of her gender—she probably wouldn't have committed the ultimate transgression of squealing on the boss. It's true that she wasn't a particularly willing witness, as could be gauged by her inarticulate testimony. And it took her some time to turn against her boss. Likewise for her boyfriend Yuya Yamada and a third former lieutenant of the pimp, the similarly named Yue Yamada, who didn't testify in Mr. Kakiuchi's trial but did implicate him in testimony in his own related trial for prostitution offenses. The trio had been arrested by the police, but refused to speak during their initial period of detention. That was a feat in itself. Under Japanese law, suspects can be held in a police cell for up to 23 days without charge. If they are not charged by the 23rd day they have to be released, but they can be subsequently rearrested and held for the same period on a different charge. This is a hugely controversial police power that has been frequently criticized by the Japanese Federation of Bar Associations, the United Nations, and numerous other watchdogs. Aside from the length of detention, it is also notoriously difficult to get a proper night's sleep in a police-station cell compared to the relative serenity of a prison cell, a psychological inconvenience that makes suspects more amenable to confessing. Ms. Harada's boyfriend, Yuya Yamada, was held for 20 days, during which he maintained his silence. And then he was released. But just as he was breathing fresh air, he was rearrested. Facing another few weeks in custody, he decided to cooperate with the police.

When he testified as a witness for the prosecution in Mr. Kakiuchi's trial he was honest about his motive in squealing on his ex-boss. "I wanted to get out of detention." he told the prosecutor, giving evidence not via video link as his girlfriend had done, but from behind a courthouse screen.

And what about the girlfriend, Ms. Harada? Why did she decide to sing? She said she suspected that her boss "had betrayed us." Mr. Kakiuchi's former employees in the prostitution enterprise had fled the sinking ship. Mr. Kakiuchi could only glare as he listened to their testimony.

PRETTY BOY

The third turncoat employee, Yue Yamada, who implicated his boss during his own trial, was the kind of boy who probably wouldn't ever be recruited to any yakuza group. The yakuza like to recruit young thugs, people with a reputation for violence and lawlessness. It's generally easy to spot a group of young yakuza in Japan; they typically look tough, porky, and mean—true to their stereotype. Someone like Yue Yamada, who was sleek, cool, and effeminate, and had his mother testify for him in court, is the complete opposite. Mr. Yamada was a remarkably good-looking young man, and judging by the handful of immodestly clad young women that turned up for his trial, popular with ladies. Mr. Yamada had just reached adulthood, having turned 20 shortly before his arrest. While he didn't possess the necessary whiff of cordite, in some aspects he was a typical gang recruit: poorly educated and looking for cash. He had left school at 15, worked in a restaurant earning about US$8 an hour, but he soon gave that up. He was interested in making money but not so interested in sweating for it. He started a job hustling for a hostess bar, steering tipsy men into a poorly lit emporium where they paid handsomely for drink and conversation with a female. He gave that up because he didn't get on with the manager. But Kenji Kakiuchi saw his potential.

"It was through a friend that I got to know him. I had no job and I was asked to work for him." Mr. Yamada said.

"Did you know it was illegal work?" the prosecutor asked.

"At the start I didn't," he replied.

"Did you know he was a member of the yakuza?"

"Yes." Although Mr. Kakiuchi was no longer officially in the yakuza, he was still widely thought of as a member.

"Are you in the yakuza?"

"No." Mr. Yamada replied. He had been responsible for advertising the prostitution and also had duties similar to Ms. Harada's: collecting the cash from the prostitutes and driving them to and from the hotels. He started work around 4 p.m. and finished around 2 a.m.

"Once a customer had made an appointment, what would you do?" the prosecutor asked.

"I would tell the women about the details of the job."

"Did the women ever refuse?"

"Yes."

"When they refused, what did you do? Could you not order them?"

"I couldn't, it's between them and the customer."

"You took 15,000 yen (US$150) per day from the women. Did you sometimes take more?" the judge asked.

"No, it was a fixed amount."

Mr. Yamada's mother, Reiko, took the stand. She was pretty matter-of-fact in her testimony. Her relationship with her son had drifted. There was no big fight, they had just stopped communicating. He had moved out of the family home and she had no idea that he was working for a gangster. She had first learned of his arrest when she read about it in a local newspaper. She hadn't visited him in detention, which suggested deep embarrassment and an unwillingness to forgive, but she did write to him. He wrote back and said he had "learned from the experience." She didn't try to make eye contact with her son on her way to or from the witness stand, nor he with her. But his lawyer told the court that his client regretted causing his mother so much trouble. The defense lawyer promised the judge that once Mr. Yamada was released, he would return to live with his mother, would work hard, and wouldn't cause trouble again. Mr. Yamada received a suspended prison sentence.

BIG CATCH

While Mr. Yamada was small fry, Mr. Kakiuchi was quite an important catch for the police. This is partly because *enderi* pimps are very difficult to prosecute. It's not a visible crime: those who worked for him were not based in a brothel and there was no streetwalking involved; the entire operation was conducted using the Internet, mobile phones, and hotel rooms paid for in cash, making it difficult to track. But police relished his capture mostly because to them Mr. Kakiuchi was high profile and *mendokusai*, a pain in the ass. The police saw him as a freelance gangster who didn't show them deference. Once authorities decide to investigate a case, police and prosecutorial procedure in Japan is famously thorough; even minor cases before the courts in Matsumoto City generated substantial books of evidence that typically included scores of pages—sometimes hundreds—including statements, CCTV stills, photographs, and maps of the crime scene. US academic David Johnson, who spent 200 days with prosecutors in Japan researching his groundbreaking book *The Japanese Way of Justice*, wrote:

> Prosecutors and police routinely produce several hundred pages of statements during the pre-indictment investigation, even in cases that seem thoroughly mundane. My notebooks are filled with comments about the prodigious production of dossiers: 250 pages taken from a businessman who confessed to fondling a girl on a train; nearly 500 pages from two juvenile boys suspected of vandaliz-

ing several vending machines; and over 1,200 pages of statements from and about a seventy-year-old man who denied attempting to steal four books from a bookstore.

Criminals are supposed to play their part in this thoroughness. They are expected to confess, write letters of apology, pay compensation where appropriate, and promise never to offend again. But Mr. Kakiuchi didn't play by those rules—not initially, anyway. First, he failed to turn up for his arrest. Police often arrest by appointment; a warrant is issued and the person shows up at the appointed date. It's all very civilized. Rather than turn up on the chosen day, however, Mr. Kakiuchi went on the run. He and two of those who would later turn against him, Ms. Harada and her boyfriend, met late at night in a hostess bar in Suwa City. They then escaped across the prefectural border to Takasaki City in neighboring Gunma Prefecture and then down to Chiba Prefecture, bordering Tokyo. All three holed up in a love hotel; Mr. Kakiuchi, who by his own admission was probably a drug addict, made sure to bring his bag of speed.

His cheeky flight from justice really annoyed the police. On August 1, a nationwide alert was issued for him, and he was caught a week later. His own carelessness was one reason for his capture. He had fled in a car connected to him, and that car was noticed in Chiba Prefecture. Good police work helped, too: knowing he was in Chiba was one thing, but finding him in a prefecture of six million people was another. Police, however, figured that a man like Mr. Kakiuchi would probably stay in a love hotel, so they circulated the car registration to Chiba's love hotels.

A week after their alert, they got a call from the New Chateau hotel, and arrested Mr. Kakiuchi in the early hours of August 8. He tried to escape; police found him lying on the ground in the hallway on the third floor of a nearby apartment block, sweating profusely. In the panic of the escape, he had defecated in the hallway nearby. Mr. Kakiuchi, who has spent as much of his adult life in jail as out of it, didn't deny the prostitution and drug allegations against him, though his lawyer unsuccessfully argued that his arrest was unlawful over a technicality. His testimony, however, shed light on the dynamic between police and yakuza, and on his belief that the police had felt insulted because he had breached etiquette by not showing up for his arrest. "There are good cops and bad cops," Mr. Kakiuchi explained to the court. "You can swap information and talk with some of them." But during his latest arrest, he didn't find any goodness in the police. They "spoke rudely" to him and "bullied" him, he complained. He said they also delayed giving him water even when he said he was suffering a dangerous level of dehydration.

BREAKING PROTOCOL

It seemed peculiar that a hardened criminal like Kenji Kakiuchi would take genuine umbrage at the tone of police officers who had been forced to travel about 140 miles to arrest him. In fact, he complained repeatedly about it during his court appearance, in an almost childish fashion. "It was the way they spoke to me—it was different to any of the previous arrests. It got personal. I know I did wrong, and I'll take responsibility for it, but I want them to take responsibility for bullying me. It was like something from an elementary school," he said. He claimed that when he asked the police why they were treating him so rudely, one police officer replied, "You and your group are too defiant. You didn't come to be arrested when you should have." In other words, Mr. Kakiuchi had stopped playing by the rules—he had failed to adhere to decorum, so the police would do likewise.

Mr. Kakiuchi also told the court that police had previously encouraged him to return to his yakuza group. "The current Kakiuchi is not the real Kakiuchi," one officer allegedly said. "Why don't you rejoin the yakuza?" The annual reports from the National Police Agency may exhort the "annihilation" of the yakuza, but there is a strong faction which believes that, even now, some police at least prefer to coexist with the yakuza—albeit uneasily—because yakuza structures contribute to stability in the criminal world. Mr. Kakiuchi's testimony suggested a continuing closeness between the police and the yakuza, at least insofar as they exchange information. Anecdotal evidence indicates that cash rarely changes hands, but some police accept favors from yakuza such as free sex in their brothels or free drinks in their bars. Occasionally there is evidence of more serious bribery. For example, in 2013, details emerged in a trial of yakuza members of how the president of a chain of sex clubs in Nagoya City bribed four current and retired police officers with cash and Mercedes Benz cars in return for information on police investigations into his brothels.

The extent of the animosity that had grown between Mr. Kakiuchi and the police was clear when one of his arresting officers gave evidence. At times Mr. Kakiuchi shouted "Liar!" at the police detective during his evidence, and at others he growled insults while rolling his "r" in a way that Japanese gangsters do when they want to talk tough. This was the only time that I witnessed any verbal aggression in a Matsumoto courtroom. And it isn't that defendants of Matsumoto are especially mild-mannered. David Johnson wrote about "the radical differences in defendant demeanor" between Japan and the United States. "Japanese defendants are almost unfailingly polite, deferent and respectful," he wrote. "American suspects and offenders…are more inclined to shout obscenities at prosecutors and judges or wear shorts, caps and even 'fuck the police' T-shirts to court."

Mr. Kakiuchi wasn't shouting obscenities or wearing an offensive T-shirt, but he was being unusually rambunctious compared to the typical Japanese defendant. In his first four hearings he was warned about a dozen times by the judge over his behavior. He was petulant to the point of stupidity. If he had still been a member of the yakuza, his courtroom behavior would likely have been less erratic and more respectful. Yakuza defendants are not the same as most other criminals. While most ordinary defendants—the sexual deviants, the shoplifters, the traffic offenders, the common thieves—are extremely deferential to the court, yakuza are typically merely respectful, sometimes grudgingly so. For example, they bow much less to the judges than other criminals. Most ordinary criminals will bow to the judge even after the invariable guilty verdict. Many will thank the judge, even if he or she has just sentenced them to prison, and some will also bow to the prosecutor who has worked so hard to put them in jail. Yakuza criminals aren't as obsequious; they usually bow along with everyone else when the judge or judges arrive to court, or they may simply bend their body slightly to give something between a nod and a bow. They are much less likely to bow to a prosecutor. But what they typically do not do, at least in Matsumoto District Court, is interrupt the proceedings, as Mr. Kakiuchi did.

At one hearing, arm outstretched and finger pointing at the man, he accused a prosecutor named Taniguchi of swapping conspiratorial looks with one of the three judges. The judge, a female, seemed enraged and embarrassed by this interjection. After the day's sitting had finished and the three judges hearing the case had left the court chamber, Mr. Kakiuchi referred to the female judge in front of the court clerk as "Yuki-chan." *Chan* is a suffix usually attached to children's names or used casually among friends. It is highly disrespectful to use toward an adult you don't know, much less a judge, and doubly so in this case, as he called her by her first name.

"He is one of a kind," Mr. Kakiuchi's ex-wife, Akemi, said to me later, trying to explain his unusual courtroom behavior. "Though he is really honest, he hates lies." She had brought along her 15-year-old son from a previous marriage to see his former stepdad in the dock. "Why did you bring him?" I asked, expecting she would say she was giving the boy a life lesson, something along the lines of "I wanted to show him that bad things happen if you break the law." But that apparently wasn't her motive. "My son thinks Kenji is really cool, cooler than his real dad," was her surprising response.

By his fifth hearing, however, Mr. Kakiuchi's behavior made a U-turn. As he addressed the court at the end of his second and final cross-examination, the bluster, the desire to cock a snook at authority like a schoolchild talking back a teacher, was suddenly gone. "I want to say to the court that I was immature and stubborn. I caused you problems, and I apologize," he said. And just in case the judges thought this was a last-ditch attempt to curry favor before sentencing, he added, "I am not looking for a short sentence. I am looking for a long sentence so I can fix myself."

In the same breath, he admitted that jail would be uncomfortable for him. During his previous incarceration, he had been jailed as a senior ranking member of the Fujii-gumi crime group, which, though small, is well known in Japan's gangster circles; its former leader, Eiji Fujii, is a prominent yakuza and political rightist who went on to become a senior figure in the affiliated Yamaguchi-gumi. Mr. Kakiuchi had previously had the support of the organization behind him, the comfort blanket of yakuza membership. But now he would be entering jail as just another criminal. "The last time I was in jail, I could ask for money, 500,000 or a million yen (US$5,000–10,000); I could give people money to buy books," he lamented.

Then his lawyer asked something that prompted some soul-searching about his personal life. "You have a daughter, don't you?"

"I abandoned my family," Mr. Kakiuchi replied. "After I left them, I changed. My family is here to see me [his daughter, about three years old, was also in court along with his ex-wife and her 15-year-old son] and when I see them I realize I did a terrible thing. My boy is the same age as me when I was first caught by the police, and he's a year older than one of the girls who worked for me [as a prostitute]. In jail, I will reflect: I have to change, I want to change. Of course I have caused problems for my ex-wife and the guys I worked with. It's a sad memory for me, it's pitiful."

Finally, Mr. Kakiuchi was acting as defendants are expected to act. The humility came very late in the day, however, and it was hard to know whether it was genuine.

The prosecutor who did the summing-up was unmoved. "He was profiting from the exploitation of young girls," she said. "He exploited their immaturity. He damaged their minds and their bodies." She requested an eight-year jail sentence.

The defendant had the last word after the prosecutor and his defense lawyer had finished their closing statements. Speaking directly to the judges hearing his case, Mr. Kakiuchi continued his tone of repentance: "I am sorry that I involved so many people in my crime. Young girls have ended up in prison because of me. I exploited the influence I had over the youngsters who were working for me. If I told them to do something, they would do it; if I told them not to do something, they wouldn't. I have spent half of my life in jail. When I was out of jail I was doing something bad every single day, and when I was in jail I was thinking about how I could get to the top of the underworld and make money. I never thought very much about what exactly I was doing. I thought I was a great guy. This time, I've lost my business, but I've discovered the importance of my friends and family. You can give me a heavy penalty—I don't mind."

Mr. Kakiuchi was facing the judges for sentencing almost six months after his trial had begun. The court was well attended, mostly with Mr. Kakiuchi's supporters. His ex-wife, child, and stepchild were all there. He was sentenced to seven years, convicted on all charges that he had faced under the Anti-Prostitution Act, the Employment Security Law, the Act on Punishment of Activities Relating to Child Prostitution and Child Pornography, the Protection of Children Act, and the Stimulants Control Act.

OLD STYLE

With his unpredictable courtroom behavior, which veered from shouting in court and obstreperously interrupting proceedings to obsequiously showing repentance by requesting a long prison sentence, Mr. Kakiuchi was a most unusual defendant. Not so fellow gangster Masahide Miyazawa, a small but tough-looking 63-year-old. When Mr. Miyazawa came before the court on charges of attempted extortion, he bowed respectfully to the prosecutor as well as the judges.

Apart from being a yakuza member, Mr. Miyazawa was also the chief of a local right-wing extremist group. He would have known Mr. Kakiuchi, as he was a serving member of the Fujii-gumi yakuza group that Mr. Kakiuchi once belonged to. Unlike Mr. Kakiuchi, none of his former fellow gangsters testified against him. He had eight supporters in court, though, a slightly comical mix of the tough and the weird. One young man, maybe 22 years old, was dressed in a Spiderman T-shirt; another had an unfeasibly large Afro hairstyle, dyed brown; and another was dressed in spotless mechanic's overalls. There was another, slightly older, man, perhaps in his 30s, who despite the suit he was wearing—or perhaps because of it—looked like a typical yakuza thug: short hair, dark jacket and trousers, and skin that had seen more than its fair share of sharp instruments. Also, there was an elderly man, even wirier than Mr. Miyazawa, in white socks, black sandals, and a shirt with various horse designs that might have been fashionable in the 1960s. His attendance was obviously important to Mr. Miyazawa, because at the end of the hearing the defendant gave him an individual bow of gratitude for attending.

Mr. Miyazawa looked confident in the courtroom, but he was in big trouble. The short version is that he approached a director of a mid-sized building company, Horiuchi Kogyo, and asked him to make a donation to his right-wing extremist group. The prosecutor saw it as an attempted shakedown; Mr. Miyazawa denied the charge. The longer version tells a lot about how the yakuza use right-wing political groups as fronts for their criminal activities and the essential simplicity of their business model.

NOISY EXTORTION

The building firm first came into contact with Mr. Miyazawa on a construction site outside Chino City, south of Matsumoto City. Chino has city status, though it feels more like a small town, with a population of around 50,000 sprawled over a large area. It is Mr. Miyazawa's territory: his house on the outskirts of Chino was well known for its three *gaisensha*, or propaganda vehicles, parked to the side. Such vehicles are considered core to the propaganda armory of any self-respecting ultra-right-wing group. They come in different sizes, from small vans to large trucks, and their defining feature is the loudspeakers perched on the roof. They typically broadcast rousing imperial and militaristic tunes, as well as prerecorded messages attacking perceived enemies of Japan who don't concur with the ultra-right-wing narrative of Japanese history that denies, for example, the the involvement of the Japanese military in the sexual enslavement of thousands of women in World War II. North and South Korea, China, unions, liberals, the left in general, the media—specially the *Asahi Shimbun* newspaper—weak-kneed mainstream politicians, and those opposed to changing the current pacifist Constitution are the standard targets. If the Japanese right-wing activists get you in their sights, it can be quite literally a headache. Furthermore, propaganda trucks are not used solely to vilify political enemies and spread the rightist message; they can also serve a criminal purpose for those who, like Mr. Miyazawa, use their organizations as a front for illegal activity. The National Police Agency estimates that about a third of the 900 right-wing groups active in Japan are yakuza fronts. Their members are far more likely to end up in jail for common crimes rather than politically motivated incidents. The National Police Agency annual report for 2012 records arrests relating to only two cases of politically motivated attacks on property involving rightists. In one case, a disaffected rightist drove a car into the Social Democratic Party's headquarters in Tokyo; in another, a brick was thrown at the South Korean Consulate in Hiroshima, causing minor damage. On the other hand, in the same year, police arrested 408 rightists for finance-related crimes, including extortion and fraud. One crime described by the police in an annual report involved a relatively straightforward scam where a gang member buys a car using a fake driver's license. He then pays for the car via credit card, but fails to make the monthly payments. In the meantime, the car is resold or exported. Such a scam in Osaka involving multiple purchases netted a right-wing group 57 million yen (US$570,000), according to police.

Mr. Miyazawa's fundraising efforts were more old-fashioned. He preferred simple extortion, threatening to plague businesses with the hullabaloo from his propaganda vehicles if they didn't pay up. His three propaganda vehicles were painted entirely in black. One of them was a bus similar to a full-size 47-seater coach, with windows blacked out and imperial slogans painted on the body;

the other was a truck about the same size; and the third was a military jeep with four speakers on the roof. Mr. Miyazawa's propaganda vehicles carried the name of his group, Kokueikai, which translates as something like "Superior Country Association" (the superior country being, of course, Japan).

While the patriotism of Japanese rightists like Mr. Miyazawa is similar to that of far rightists in other countries, it differs in one key area. Whereas extreme rightists around the world often attack immigrants physically as well as verbally, Japanese rightwingers generally don't spend time beating up immigrants. In any case, finding foreigners to scapegoat or beat up in Nagano Prefecture wouldn't be easy, as just 1.5 percent of the population is non-Japanese; most of those are ethnic Koreans or Chinese born and reared in Japan, who blend more easily into the environment. Groups like Mr. Miyazawa's are generally known for their noisy and menacing verbal harassment. So when Mr. Miyazawa rolled up to the Horiuchi Kogyo building site in one of his big propaganda vehicles, the company paid attention. He had a pretext for his approach to the company, having spotted that the signage on the building site was inadequate. It was too small, he alleged. Whether it was or not didn't really matter; everyone knew it was just a pretext, one that could give Mr. Miyazawa an excuse to start circling the business with his propaganda vehicle, hurling abuse at the company through the loudspeakers.

What Mr. Miyazawa was counting on was that a cultural aversion to confrontation would persuade the building company to pay up. And he was correct. Japanese companies have a long history of paying for gangsters to stop bothering them. Though much less common now, as recently as the 1990s big companies were paying criminals to ensure they didn't interrupt their shareholder meetings. The list of well-known corporations which have paid off the gangsters known as *sokaiya*, or shareholder-meeting specialists, is a long one that includes the most illustrious names of corporate Japan—Nissan, Hitachi, Toshiba, Toyota, Japan Airlines, Nomura Securities, Mitsubishi Electric, and Dai-ichi Kangyo Bank, among many others.

Knowing that Horiuchi Kogyo would probably like to avoid trouble, Mr. Miyazawa made a proposal. He would be willing to ignore the signage problem for a small donation from the company to his group. The money would not be a bribe, but rather "co-operation money," he said; not a big sum, just 30,000 to 50,000 yen (US$300–500). Mr. Miyazawa invited the company director to come to his home. The director contacted the police, who told him not to go, and also asked others in his own company and in the construction industry what he should do.

One of them gave the director good counsel: any payment would give the rightists a foot in the door, he said. "If you pay them once, they will come back for more." The director ignored this advice, withdrew 50,000 yen (US$500) from the bank, and went to Mr. Miyazawa's house anyway. The company director had some knowledge of the group he was about to become entwined with. He told the court he had previously seen Mr. Miyazawa's propaganda trucks during a protest against a local gathering by the Japanese Communist Party, driving up and down and blaring out nationalist messages. During his testimony, the word the company director used most was "*osoroshii*," meaning terrible or frightening. "I was really scared, but if I didn't go he would come to the site again. I wanted to stop the propaganda trucks." On the way to the house, he stopped at a convenience store to buy an envelope. It is impolite in Japan to hand over "*hadaka*" (naked) cash (i.e., without an envelope).

"I wanted to leave as quickly as possible," he said of his arrival at Mr. Miyazawa's house, "but he brought me into a room. His wife brought me coffee and then she left, leaving just Miyazawa and me." Mr. Miyazawa pointed to a picture of himself taken with a man he named as Eiji Fujii, who headed the crime group to which the drug-taking Mr. Kakefuji and the pimp Mr. Kakiuchi also belonged. "Miyazawa mentioned Fujii's name many times in the conversation and said they had a 'long relationship,'" the director said.

Mr. Fujii is one of the tough guys of the Japanese mob. Born in Osaka just after the war, he came to Nagano Prefecture in the 1960s. By 2014, as mentioned earlier, he had risen to become a senior figure in the nationwide Yamaguchi-gumi crime group, with which his own Nagano-based crime gang was affiliated. The mention of his name should have been enough to intimidate the director. It transpired that he had no idea who Mr. Fujii was—although, as his testimony made clear, he was already sufficiently intimidated. Mr. Miyazawa told the company director, "We can bring out the propaganda sound trucks any time. Nobody can stop us, the police can't stop us." (The police can and do stop them: while they didn't arrest any rightists for merely driving noisy propaganda trucks in 2012, they arrested 48 of them for trying to block businesses from operating by using the trucks and other means.)

But the company director probably didn't want to take his chances. He left the envelope containing the cash with Mr. Miyazawa. "I wanted to get out of there! The conversation was scary. I left 50,000 yen (US$500) beside Miyazawa. I paid the money and I thought it would be finished." It was, however, only the beginning. As the director had been warned, Mr. Miyazawa, started to ask for more, like any professional extortionist. The next time it was six times more.

"He came back to the site and I thought, 'He's still looking for money!'" the company director told the court. "He told me the signage was still too small and that I should get 300,000 yen (US$3,000) ready."

"Was there a reason to pay him 300,000 yen?" the prosecutor asked.

"No."

"Did anyone ever before tell you to pay 300,000 yen in this manner?"

"No, he was the first."

"Did he force you to pay?"

"No, he didn't force me, but the atmosphere was that it had to be paid."

The prosecutor asked the director of the building firm, "If you didn't pay, what did you think would happen?"

"I thought he'd come back to the site and cause trouble, violence."

The court heard recordings of two subsequent conversations between the two men; the company director had concealed a digital recorder in his pocket during the face-to-face meetings. In sections of the conversations which were played in court, Mr. Miyazawa addressed the director as *omae*, a word that simply means "you" but when used toward someone you don't know is disrespectful and can sound aggressive. He later called the mobile phone of the company director. His wife answered, and Mr. Miyazawa told her; "*Ore uyoku, Kokueikai no Miyazawa.*" (I'm the right-winger, Miyazawa from Kokueikai [the name of his ultra-right group]). Neither the call itself nor the individual words used were threatening, though his use of *ore* was a very informal, and in this context was an impolite way of saying the personal pronoun "I." But merely getting a phone call from someone from an extremist group was enough to terrify the director's wife. "Her knees were shaking. Even when she remembers it now her knees shake," her husband told the court.

He went onto explain the psychological damage that Mr. Miyazawa had inflicted on him. "Since I first met him, I have felt mental pressure, and I am scared for my family when I think about it. I can't forget it. My wife is a nervous wreck and I am still frightened. He is a man who comes to businesses and tries to extort them. I want him punished."

"Did he threaten to disturb your business?" the defense lawyer asked the director.

"Yes, he said he could bring out the propaganda vehicles at any time."

"Did he say he would use the propaganda trucks to disturb your business if you didn't pay?"

"No, but that's the impression I got."

"Is that what he said?"

"Not in those words, but I felt scared."

Mr. Miyazawa denied he had tried to extort anyone. He told the judge, "I did not try to get money, so I am denying it." The judge didn't believe him, and he was sentenced to two years in jail.

DAMAGING

The jailing of Mr. Miyazawa was a big blow to the yakuza in Nagano, if only because the evidence against him was almost entirely generated by the company director who was brave enough to record their conversations as well as give evidence. The verdict showed the fallibility of the yakuza/rightist business model. If people stand up to them they start to appear weak. Despite his repeatedly expressed terror of Mr. Miyazawa, the company director still testified in court. And while he gave evidence behind a screen, the defendant obviously knew who he was and where he worked. He would be easy to track down.

Several months after Mr. Miyazawa was jailed, I visited his home, which is also the registered address for his extremist group. There was no sign of right-wing activity. "The propaganda trucks were gotten rid of soon after he was taken into custody," a neighbor told me.

The smallest of his three propaganda vehicles, a small black jeep, remained outside, but it had been stripped of its loudspeakers. I had been hoping to get an interview with Mr. Miyazawa's wife, but no one was at home. I also visited the Fujii-gumi yakuza headquarters, which occupy a three-story building on the edge of an industrial area overlooking a river in nearby Suwa City. Japan must surely be the only country in the world where organized crime groups have a publicly available postal address. The name of the veteran gangster Eiji Fujii was on a plaque by the door of the headquarters. If you didn't know who Mr. Fujii was (though people around Suwa do seem to know), you wouldn't know it is the local mafia headquarters. The only other giveaway signs that it wasn't a normal business were the tinted windows on the middle floor, the CCTV cameras at the door, and a vehicle decked out with crude advertising for bars and hostess clubs in Suwa City. Businesses in entertainment districts are invariably under the control of the yakuza, either being owned by them or—more typically—paying them protection money. There was also a man washing a white high-end Mercedes-Benz in the car park at the back—laughably stereotypical: the yakuza love foreign cars despite their avowed patriotism. I went to the front of the building and rang the bell. Two surly-looking men came to see me, but declined to open the glass doors to let me inside. I asked for an interview with a gang boss, but they refused.

Locals say the building had belonged to an electrical business until about two decades earlier, after the collapse of Japan's asset-inflated bubble economy, when the owner got into financial difficulty and the yakuza took it over. The building was apparently security for a loan that went sour.

"They keep a low profile," said a neighbor, who spoke in a hushed voice, and when I approached him initially even denied knowing that there was a yakuza office in the vicinity. "There used to be feuding between this group and other gangs, but not recently."

"Do they ever cause trouble for the local residents?" I asked.

"The new laws make it really hard for them to operate," he said. "If we call the police nowadays, they come immediately."

Another sign that times are getting tougher for the yakuza.

PERVERTS

The 39-year-old defendant's mother came to me at the end of the hearing. "Are you a journalist?" she asked. She looked very anxious.

"Yes," I said, "I am here gathering material for a book."

"Is it in Japanese?"

"No," I said.

"Oh that's a relief," she said, "He has children."

The "he" is her son, Shinji Horiike. He is a repeat offender from a middle-class family, and was before Matsumoto District Court on charges of trespassing in a toilet at a ski resort. He was trespassing to feed his obsession: watching strangers shitting—or, more precisely, watching female strangers shitting. His parents both testified at his most recent trial, embarrassed by their son's behavior but still sticking by him, hoping to help. It was the third time he had been tried by a court for a perversion-related offense, and he had already served a stint in prison. His mother's embarrassment, therefore, was entirely understandable. In fact, lots of mothers in Japan are embarrassed by the sexual antics of their sons, because—though I have never heard a convincing explanation for it—crimes involving perversion appear disproportionately common in Japan. Even in the courtroom of a small rural city like Matsumoto, roughly one in 12 of the cases I observed had some element of perversion, including groping, theft of ladies' underwear, child pornography, and child prostitution, not to mention the fecal fascinations of Mr. Horiike.

He started to take an active interest in female defecation when he was around 19 years old. Perhaps unsurprisingly, there is an array of websites that cater to those with a similar taste for female excretion. He was first apprehended by police as a peeping Tom when he was 26, and again a few years later. Those crimes were dealt with out of court, and he had to pay a fine. When he was 35 he was jailed for stealing DVDs of women defecating from a shop. He got out of jail two years later, in 2012, but soon returned to his obsession, filming unsuspecting women in toilets. A woman who had been using a toilet at the popular ski resort of Hakuba, north of Matsumoto City, told staff of suspicious activity in the cubicle beside her. This was how Mr. Horiike was caught for his fifth offense, camera in hand and footage of his targets on his phones. He had three phones for the purpose. His modus operandi was straightforward: he would find a suitable women's toilet and lock himself into one of the cubicles. When a woman came into a neighboring cubicle, he would put the camera under the gap at the bottom of the partition wall. For those of Mr. Horiike's bent, the traditional-style squat toilets, rather than the sit-down version, provide the best opportunities for filming.

"The places where you film: How do you choose them? Are they places that you can easily hide or that you can easily escape from?" the judge asked.

"I don't pick places based on whether they are easy to escape from. I pick ones where I won't be found. I avoid public toilets that are busy or that face out onto a busy street," Mr. Horiike replied.

"If you are discovered, do you have a plan?"

"No."

"Do you go into the toilet disguised as a woman?"

"No, I don't. I just make sure there is no one, around and then I go in."

Mr. Horiike's physique and appearance are suited to his chosen perversion. He is a fairly androgynous man, with long hair. And, of course, ski fashion is not gender specific. If the long-haired Mr. Horiike were seen entering a woman's toilet wearing sunglasses, a scarf, and bulky ski clothes, he wouldn't get a second glance.

His father was at a loss for his son's behavior. It's nearly a five-hour drive to Matsumoto from his home in Shizuoka Prefecture near Tokyo, and he made the journey with his wife for each of his son's three court hearings. "Why does he do it?" the father asked rhetorically from the witness stand, "I have been thinking for the last 10 years about that. There is no answer. What was it? His education at home? His school? His social life? Why has he done these things? It's all a mystery. I am 69 now; 70 this year, I have probably 10 years left in life. If he can fix himself I will die peacefully, but if he doesn't fix himself, how will I die? I don't know. I think about nothing else. It is a sickness, a sexual sickness. It's like a cancer. He needs to go to a hospital and have it removed. I think he knows he is doing something bad, but at the same time he lives in his own little world."

The defendant was a clever, educated man. He had a way with words and a facility for writing that his lawyer remarked on more than once during his trial. Like almost all defendants, he wrote a letter of apology and a letter of reflection to his victim. Both were submitted to the court by the defense lawyer; they were unusually well composed. Mr. Horiike had been the manager of a branch of a well-known electrical chain when he was in his early 30s, suggesting he was a man with ambition and a strong work ethic. He was once married to a woman who, his father told the court, had loved and respected him, and with whom he had had three children.

His father also told the court, "Before the judgment in the theft case in 2010, I was in court and the judge told my son: 'You work for a very good company, you have children and a wife and you are throwing it all away. Why do you throw everything away by doing something like this? I can't understand it.'"

That judge had sent Mr. Horiike to jail for three years, during which time his wife divorced him. The defendant's father gave some insight as to the shame the future holds for Mr. Horiike's children. "What he had done was written up in the newspapers. His name and address were in the article. The grandchildren are so good, and they are getting bigger. When they understand what their father did, the poor things, it will be so hard for them."

The defendant's mother then took the witness stand. "You wrote a letter of apology to the police," the defense lawyer stated. (Though the defendant will generally write a letter of apology to the victim, and sometimes a family member will do so as well, it's unusual to write to the police.)

"Yes," she replied. "He has caused so much damage to people and created so many problems." She wasn't as articulate as her husband, but she had the same question he did. "Why? Why? It swamps my thoughts. Why would he do such things?"

The defendant had an answer to that. "I'm a sex addict," he told the court (though he didn't have direct sexual contact with any of his targets, the pictures were taken for his sexual pleasure). "That's my problem. It's like drug or alcohol addiction. It's the same, but for sex. I have a compulsion do it."

"How do you cure it?" his lawyer asked.

"It is something you don't cure. It's something you recover from," he replied. He had been attending group sessions at a clinic for sex, drug, and gambling addicts, and said he identified with some of the feelings of others in the group. When Mr. Horiike had been released from jail having served his time for the 2010 conviction for stealing the defecation DVDs, he had regained contact with his now ex-wife. "We are not like man and wife, but we talk," he told the court at his first hearing. He also said that he hoped one day to explain to his children that the reason for his actions was a sickness—his "sex addiction."

At his first hearing, he also told the court that he remained on very good terms with his ex-wife and often consulted with her. He said he had written to her from his detention cell, telling her of his latest brush with the law, but added that he had yet to receive a reply.

By the second hearing, he had heard back from his ex-wife. She had contacted his lawyer with a conclusive message. "Tell him not to ever contact me again."

This news was taken badly by Mr. Horiike. "I am shocked, it's terrible," he told the judge, "She was the one who understood my sex addiction most."

"You have one less person to rely on. How do you feel about that?" the prosecutor asked.

"I can't say it's not painful, but I have my parents. I may not be able to contact my kids but I have my mother and father," he replied.

The judge did not appear convinced that Mr. Horiike's self-described sex addiction was an illness. "You don't do this in a place where you will be easily caught, so it isn't an addiction. If you think you may be caught you can control the urge. If you knew you were going to be heavily punished, would you still do it?" he asked.

"No, I wouldn't."

"So you are not thinking from the viewpoint of the gravity of your actions."

"No, I'm too lighthearted about it."

The prosecutor sought a jail sentence of 18 months in a correctional facility where Mr. Horiike could be treated. The defendant's final words to the judge were, "I have caused bother to a lot of people, as well as to the ski resort and the people who came to ski. I have caused damage to the hearts of the victims. When I return to society I will become a serious person." He was sentenced to one year in jail, with 30 days off for time already served.

An official familiar with Mr. Horiike's case said he expected to see him back before the courts at some point in the future. "It's the case not just for sexual crimes, but also repeat offenders who shoplift or take drugs. People get into a habit. They come to court and say they are sorry—and they probably are sorry at the time—but they still end up doing it again once they get out of jail. There is nothing that can be done."

STRANGER DANGER

Not everyone would agree that Mr. Horiike, still on the right side of 40, is incapable of reform, but for 64-year-old Tetsuo Ohira, rehabilitation seemed unlikely. He was an alcoholic and recidivist criminal, with a lengthy list of convictions for sexual and other crimes. He had previously been jailed for sexual assault and attempted rape. Past victims ranged in age from their 20s to their

40s. This time he was before the court accused of the sexual assault of a child.

He had found his quarry, an elementary-school student, at random on a cold February morning in 2013 in Ida City in southern Nagano Prefecture. Mr. Ohira lured the eight-year-old girl, whom he didn't know, into the empty basement of a commercial building. She had been on her way to school with another boy of similar age.

"What did you think when you saw her?" the prosecutor asked.

"I wanted to touch her private parts," Mr. Ohira replied.

"You could see that she was a primary-school student."

"Yes."

"Are you interested in children?"

"Yes."

"How did you get her into the building?"

"I told her there was a cat stuck in a narrow place and I asked her to get the cat. I grabbed her by the shoulder and dragged her in."

"Was there a cat?"

"No, it was a lie. She was with a boy. I told him to go to school."

"What did he say?"

"He left."

"Did the girl say she wanted to leave as well?"

"Yes."

"You put your hand in her pants."

"With my right three fingers."

"What did you do with them?"

"I put them in her private parts."

"What did the girl say?"

"Stop!"

"Did she cry?"

"She cried and said it was painful. She was standing when I put them in. She told me I shouldn't be doing it, and asked me not to kill her. I said I wouldn't. I knew I was doing something bad."

"Did you cover her mouth?"

"Yes. She bit my finger."

"How long were you touching her?"

"The police said 10 minutes."

"Are you interested in adult women?"

"Yes."

"So you are interested in both women and children. But women fight back."

"Yes."

"And young children don't fight back."

"They don't."

For Mr. Ohira, choosing his victim was a simple calculation of who he could most easily attack. It took the child a week to recover from her physical injuries. "Of course there is damage to her body," noted one of the judges, "but also damage to her mind. Do you understand that people are worried about the damage to her in the future?"

"Yes." His lawyer had told the court that a psychiatrist believed the defendant could be cured of his perversion. Inside the courtroom, however, there was little palpable belief that a man who had carried out such an appalling and calculated crime could be rehabilitated.

"You have come before the court many times," his lawyer said.

"Yes."

"When you are released from detention, won't you just do the same type of thing again?"

"I'll be OK."

"Why?"

"I'll give up drinking."

It was doubtful that anyone in court believed that. The prosecution sought five years in jail; Mr. Ohira was sentenced to four. Statistics suggest that the crime he committed—a random, serious sexual assault on a stranger—is rare in Japan. According to senior police official Kazumi Ogasawara, writing in the *Japan Medical Association Journal*, of the 82 arrests for child sexual abuse in 2008, 78 were of the father of the victim. The remaining four offenses were committed by others, including people not known to the child, as in the case of Mr. Ohira.

GROPER

Infinitely more common in Japan than this type of heinous child abuse is groping on trains, a term that can cover everything from a quick feel of a woman's body to a sustained silent attack, usually in a packed commuter train. Surveys suggest that there are tens of thousands of gropers in Japan, perhaps more. Hideo Kamijo is one of those, though he has also committed more serious crimes against women. Mr. Kamijo appeared before Matsumoto District Court charged under obscenity laws for groping a young woman in a shop at a retail mall. At his hearing, he described the lead-up to his crime. "I saw many cute women in short skirts. I wanted to feel their legs," he said.

The 39-year-old spoke directly and with apparent honesty about what he had done. "I had decided to never do it again," he said, referring to the fact that he was a repeat sexual offender. But on the visit to the shopping mall, he said, "Something came over me. I looked for a woman to touch. I came across one." His victim was wearing skimpy shorts and was showing a lot of flesh. "I saw those legs, I rubbed her thigh. I intended to touch her buttocks too, but she noticed me immediately. She chased me and I was captured by a male member of staff. I admit to touching her. I should have left the shop immediately when I got the urge, but I just couldn't."

Mr. Kamijo had two previous convictions, including one for breaking into a house and violently sexually assaulting a woman. He served six years in jail for that.

"What was the meaning of those six years?" the prosecutor asked him.

"In my head I reflected on my crime, but in actual fact my behavior didn't change," he replied. Mr. Kamijo said that he had never learned to look at his crime from the victim's viewpoint. His most recent assault, the groping, had happened just six weeks after his release from jail.

He was socially awkward, pudgy, and bespectacled, with a face that only a mother could love. He was not yet 40 but looked 50. If there were an image of an archetypical sex offender, Mr. Kamijo would be a prime candidate to fill the position. When he spoke, his words were of repentance, and he certainly didn't downplay his actions. But his expressions of regret sounded empty and formulaic.

The retail mall where the assault happened was not named in court, but we were told it was a fashionable place for young women to shop. The prosecutor didn't believe it was a likely place for the unfashionable Mr. Kamijo to be browsing unless he went there with the deliberate intent to fondle young women.

"Had you heard of the mall before?" the prosecutor asked.

"No."

"But it's well known as a popular place for young women."

"I didn't know that."

"You never heard of it?"

"No. I went there to buy clothes. I thought it was like a Jusco or Ito Yokado (two Japanese retailers), a place like that. I didn't know that it was place with a lot of young people."

"Did you buy anything there?"

"No. I saw the prices and they were very expensive."

His lawyer questioned him about his actions.

"What did you feel when you saw all those young women?"

"I got excited."

"Did you think about your family and what would happen if you did something?"

"Yes, I did think about my father. But I just couldn't hold back. I apologize fully to the victim for her shock. To be touched by someone must have made her feel bad."

When caught, Mr. Kamijo initially denied groping the woman but soon changed tack and admitted to the offense. Weeks before his court appearance, he paid her 200,000 yen (US$2,000) in compensation via his lawyer. Though his victim accepted the compensation—which would help Mr. Kamijo when it came to sentencing—she remained unforgiving. Direct oral evidence is not often given by the victims in Japanese courts. Their written statements are usually accepted as evidence by both sides, so they rarely have to testify. In her statement read out in court, the woman described her horror at Mr. Kamijo's action. "I was wearing short pants with no stockings at the time. He touched me on my naked flesh. I won't forgive this pervert; it's a terrible memory for me. Please punish him so there are no more victims like me."

"At your previous court appearance, you also said you'd never do it again. And you are also obviously sorry this time, too," Mr. Kamijo's lawyer said to him.

"Yes."

"So, what's the difference?"

"This time I really won't do it, this behavior."

"Your older sister has cancer. When your sister is fighting illness, you do something like this?"

"I am truly sorry. I feel ashamed ," he said.

Mr. Kamijo worked as a professional caregiver, minding some of society's most vulnerable: elderly people with Alzheimer's disease. "Looking after old people is difficult, but I have confidence in doing it," he told the court. "The job suits me. I want to help older people. I like to see older people enjoying themselves."

The judges of Matsumoto District Court often ask defendants what work they will do once they are released from detention. And it is pretty much a rule of thumb that the more unemployable a defendant is, the more likely it is that he will express an intention to seek work either as a security guard or caregiver for the elderly. Caregiving is close to the bottom of the jobs pyramid and it appears that employers don't waste much time on background checks. Mr. Kamijo's employer was unaware he was in court, because—unusually for a defendant before the district court—he wasn't being held in custody, as his crime was relatively minor. "I'll be fired if they find out. I want to continue working there," he said.

The defendant's mother sat in the public gallery and cried through the entire cross-examination of her son. At the end she gave a series of deep bows to everyone in the courtroom, including the handful of people in the public gallery. She looked like she was in her 70s. Her other child had cancer, and her husband was also ill after a brain hemorrhage. Her son was the most physically healthy in her family by a long margin. But he was a very sick man.

Although the mother looked utterly shamed and defeated, she hadn't yet given up on her son. She had enlisted her brother, also seemingly in his 70s, as a witness to show the court that there was a glimmer of hope for Mr. Kamijo. Wearing a grey work shirt, he had the tanned appearance and plain dress of a farmer. His sister had never spoken to him about her son's two previous convictions for sexual assault, but he had found out about the second one—the assault that had landed Mr. Kamijo in jail for six years. "I read about it in the papers, but I didn't like to ask the details; I didn't want to talk to my sister about that." It turned out that the uncle knew very little about his nephew. "The last time I saw him before this arrest was when he was in his second or third year of junior high school. I used to see him two or three times a year before that," he said, "I am here because I want to cooperate with his mother." And he was very sincere in his cooperation. Since Mr. Kamijo's arrest, on three occasions he had made the six-hour round trip to Tokyo with his nephew to visit a nonprofit organization (NPO) that specialized in the treatment of sex offenders.

The defense lawyer questioned the defendant about the organization: "What do you do at the NPO, specifically?"

"I meet with people who are the same as me; sex criminals and perverts. We talk and reflect on our individual crimes. I learn more about the feelings of the victim."

"Do you really learn about the feelings of the victim?"

"Yes, until now, I really didn't understand victims' feelings."

"Didn't you learn not to commit crime when you were in jail the last time?"

"In the jail I was with a group who were like me, sex criminals. This time I went out of my way to find the NPO. I talked to my mother and father and I really want to learn my lesson."

When Mr. Kamijo returned to Matsumoto District Court for a second hearing, his mother, who cried her way through the first hearing, didn't show up. Her daughter had advised her not to go to court because it was too upsetting, the defense lawyer told the court. His uncle turned up again, though. Mr. Kamijo's lawyer read from an assessment supplied by the NPO that Mr. Kamijo had been attending. The NPO acknowledged that Mr. Kamijo is a danger to women, but said that the likelihood of him reoffending could be reduced by keeping him away from "high-risk areas." Before the closing statement, the prosecutor asked Mr. Kamijo some additional questions.

"In order for you to never again commit this crime what is the most important thing for you to do?"

"I need to think about the other person. I have decided not to do it again. I think it is a sickness."

"So if it's a sickness, it doesn't depend on your own will?"

"Now that I have this feeling, I won't do it again," Mr. Kamijo replied. He told the judge that he believed the treatment would work for him. "I have negative empathy for women. I am trying to get educated about that so I can fix myself. I want to make sure I never commit another sexual offense."

The prosecutor used his closing statement to seek a six-month prison sentence, retelling Mr. Kamijo's dismal criminal history and emphasizing that there was a high chance he would reoffend. In his closing argument, the defense lawyer said that Mr. Kamjio had paid compensation, was reflecting on his crime, and would continue attending the NPO to seek treatment. Mr. Kamijo bowed twice to the judge. Again he promised to reform. At the end of the hearing he went to thank his lawyer and his uncle, who were talking together. His lawyer barely looked at him and his uncle ignored him.

A couple of months later Mr. Kamijo returned to court to hear the verdict. He was sentenced to four months in jail. Groping is considered a misdemeanor in most countries and it rarely lands perpetrators in jail. But in Japan, penalties range from a fine to a 10-year jail sentence, the upper limit reflecting the fact that men groping female strangers it is a very large social problem there. In bigger cities, where packed trains provide ample opportunity for anonymous hands, groping is particularly rampant. While it's extremely common to hear women complaining of having been groped, it's highly unusual to meet a victim who has reported the matter to the authorities. Police are now more sympathetic than they previously were, but it can still be an uphill battle to get them to take a complaint seriously. And of course it is a crime that is difficult to prove. Tokyo rush-hour trains are typically packed; sometimes the number of people in a carriage is double the capacity specified by the carriage manufacturer. It can be easy for an accused pervert to argue that his body was pushed against the victim by chance, or that another passenger was to blame.

While groping offenses around the world are typically committed by men between the ages of 15 and 25, men of all ages are perpetrators in Japan. The typical groper, according to a report by the *Yomiuri* newspaper, which compiled the ages of almost 700 men accused of groping, is between 20 and 49; men in their 30s are the most represented group. According to the newspaper's research, only four were teenagers.

The number of indecency cases known to police has been increasing in recent years, doubling between 1995 and 2011. In 2011, the number of indecency arrests was just under 5,000—more than those for robbery, homicide, rape, and arson combined. But the number of arrests doesn't even begin to reflect the reality of Japan's pervert plague. A government survey of almost 1,800 women of all ages released in 2000 revealed that slightly over half of respondents had been groped. For women in their 20s the rate was 60 percent; for women in their 30s, it was even higher, at 69 percent. In both those categories, more than two-thirds of those who had been groped were groped at least twice.

If we transpose those findings roughly onto the general population and assume that approximately half of all Japanese women will be groped an average of 1.5 times between the ages of 20 and 80, that is roughly 750,000 groping crimes per year. The groping phenomenon is not new in Japan, but the survey suggests it has grown significantly in the last two decades. Of women over 60, only 22 percent had been groped in their lifetime—a far smaller percentage than for women in younger age groups.

Train companies have responded by offering women-only carriages during rush hour. Surveys show that, while some use the carriages to get away from "smelly men" (there is a perception in

Japan that older men in particular smell bad), the most common reason is to escape gropers. The stereotypical offender is a white-collar worker frustrated by his career, with a pathetic emotional life. But he is not always a low-level employee. In December 2012, a 56-year-old executive at the West Japan Railway Company, Hidehiko Kinbira, killed himself in a public toilet in Osaka after he was arrested for feeling the buttocks of a high-school girl on a rush-hour train. Mr. Kinbira had allegedly repeatedly molested the same girl on the line over the previous two years.

In July 2013, the *Sankei* newspaper reported that a 49-year-old senior tax official had been arrested for placing a message on a *chikan* (pervert) bulletin board. He had posed as a woman seeking to be molested. He posted a description of "her" clothes and details of where on the train "she" would be. A 26-year-old man read the message, boarded the train indicated, and began to grope a 23-year-old woman in the mistaken belief that she had posted the message. Once the train reached its terminus, the victim grabbed her bewildered groper and handed him over to rail staff. The tax official who had set up the groper reportedly confessed to having posted over 20 previous messages posing online as a woman looking to be groped.

Gropers typically assault strangers in places such as shopping malls and crowded streets, as well as on public transport. Pervert websites offer tips on how to grope while avoiding capture. Recommended grope spots, for example, are on packed trains near doors that open beside station escalators, to facilitate escape.

The assessment from the sex-counseling NPO advised Mr. Kamijo to stay away from high-risk areas, but that won't be easy. Japan is a groper's paradise. Modest dress is not a feature of Japan's high-hemline fashion, so for those especially attracted to young women in miniskirts, there is ample opportunity to grope.

Something that helps sexual assailants in Japan is that people are culturally more likely to seek to avoid confrontation. While some Japanese women will shout at a groper and fight back, many will close their eyes and wait for the next stop, rather than simply smacking their attacker.

Not surprisingly, for those gropers who do not want to risk breaking the law, there are scores of venues where they can act out their fantasies entirely legally—many of which mimic the environment of a train carriage. In Kyoto, for example, a club called Mitsuran Railroad offers a 45 minute "course" to its customers that includes 15 minutes of *chikan taimu* (pervert time) where the client can grope three women in a replica carriage. The 10,500 yen (US$105) price also includes 30 minutes of *herusu taimu* (health time)—sexual contact exclusive of vaginal intercourse. For 34,500 yen (US$345), clients can grope four women on the carriage, and in addition to 100 minutes of "health time," they also get to keep the ladies' underwear. Tellingly, whereas sex clubs in Japan typically open in the later afternoon or evening, Mitsuran Railroad opens during the morning train rush hour, at 8 a.m.

UP FRONT

The unimaginable can be a disgusting reality, even in the apparently hokey conservatism of largely rustic Nagano Prefecture. This was the hunting ground of Yoshihisa Katsube, a 65-year-old who was not the average pervert. He didn't make plans for his escape or try to minimize the likelihood of capture.

Mr. Katsube walked into the waiting room of the Shinano Omachi train station near Matsumoto City and attacked his 18-year-old victim as she sat waiting for her mother. "He sat on me; he drew his face up next to mine and licked me on the face. It felt horrible. He kicked my right leg. It was only a minute in total, but it felt longer," the young woman said in a statement read out to the court.

Mr. Katsube's older sister took the witness stand. She had visited the victim to apologize on the defendant's behalf, and had paid her 100,000 yen ($1,000) in compensation. This may seem a small amount for the trauma of being attacked by a drunken stranger, but it was about the going rate for this sort of crime. "I don't think she will forgive my brother," the sister said. "What he did was disgraceful. It really saddens me."

"Do you know what your brother was thinking?" the prosecutor asked her.

"If he hadn't been drinking, it wouldn't have happened. I want him to stop. For years, I have implored him," she said in obvious exasperation. "He won't give up drink. I am really worried. He always turns to alcohol."

"In 2010, there was also an incident, and you said then that you'd try to get him to stop drinking, but in the end he couldn't give up," the prosecutor pointed out. "What did he say about alcohol this time?"

"Nothing," she replied.

"Did he say he'd give up?"

"No."

"Can you provide him with direction when he gets out?" the prosecutor asked.

"I will do my utmost."

The frail old woman returned to her seat. She looked to be in her mid to late 70s, significantly older than her brother. Mr. Katsube stared at the floor. He didn't make eye contact with his sister. He wasn't a typical pervert. Straddling a stranger, licking her, and physically attacking her in a train waiting room is not what the average anonymity-seeking pervert does. Also, he was much older than the average pervert and didn't have a job. But he was similar in one respect: he was a weak individual, a chronic alcoholic who lived in the house where he was reared and relied on his elder sisters to bring him food because, as his sister told the court, "if we didn't, he would live on cigarettes and beer." Mr. Katsube initially denied the assault; he kept denying it even after he was shown the CCTV footage of his crime and was told that his DNA was in spittle left on the young woman's face. He finally changed his mind and admitted his deed just before he went on trial.

"Before, you insisted that you hadn't done it," his lawyer said. "Was that because you didn't remember?"

"Yes, I was quite drunk."

"You admit to the perverted behavior now. Why?"

"I saw the CCTV pictures. I'm sorry for what I did, and I wrote a letter of apology."

"Is that why you asked your sister to pay the compensation money?"

No reply.

"Did you do this because you are, and I quote [from the letter of apology Mr. Katsube wrote to his victim], 'alone and don't have anything to do?'"

No answer.

"Is it correct to say that?"

"Yes."

"Will you drink when you return to society?"

"I will cut down."

The expression on the face of Mr. Katsube's lawyer suggested that this limited promise fell far short of the pledge of reform he had been hoping for.

"Do you remember the incident?" the prosecutor asked.

"I don't remember…there are parts that I remember."

"Do you remember what you did to the woman?"

"I can't remember."

"Isn't there something you can remember?"

No answer.

"Do you remember nothing?"

"I don't remember clearly."

"What does that mean?" the prosecutor continued, "You said that you didn't do it, but after the police showed you the footage, you said you did."

"At the start I didn't really know."

"Why did you do this? Why did you molest the girl and lick her face?"

Twelve seconds of silence. "It was like my body moved automatically," he finally answered.

"You were drunk at the time?"

Mr. Katsube nodded.

"Say it out loud for the record."

"Yes."

"Your biggest problem is alcohol. Do you want to stop drinking altogether?"

No reply.

"Can you stop?"

"Yes."

"Didn't you try to cut down on your drinking after going to hospital?" (The previous year, Mr. Katsube had spent five months in hospital being treated for alcoholism.)

"Yes."

"Can you promise not to be arrested again?"

"Yes."

"You know if you come here again, no one will believe you. Please give it up."

In his summation, the prosecutor asked for a six-month jail sentence. The judge sentenced Mr. Katsube to six months in jail, suspended for three years.

THE DIGITAL PERVERT

Mr. Katsube groped his victim, terrorized her, and licked her. But he didn't film the attack or swap information with like-minded people on an Internet bulletin board, or upload pictures online. He was an old-style pervert.

Nowadays, in the information age, many—perhaps most—of all perversion cases involve at least some online element. More assailants use the Internet to get tips on how to carry out their crimes or to view similar incidents. Or they may film the attack, either to share it online or simply for their own enjoyment. In one case reported by AFP-Jiji Press in 2014, a 41-year-old Osaka taxi driver was arrested for feeding female passengers crackers coated with a chemical that induces a desire to urinate. He would then refuse to stop his cab to allow them to visit a toilet, apparently motivated by a sexual desire to watch women wetting themselves in the back of his vehicle. He used his taxi's security camera to film the women and kept the footage in his DVD collection at home.

This was probably a unique crime. A more common practice

is up-skirting, which, as the name suggests, is the taking of digital images from beneath women's skirts, trying to capture a snapshot of their underwear, without the target's knowledge. Hideaki Shoji was an inveterate up-skirter. A slightly geeky-looking man reported by media as a temp worker in a travel agency, he was arrested in late 2013. Under the "Interested in" category on his Facebook page he typed in the single word "women." He is, of course, not the only male to profess women as a main interest, but few could match his obsession with them—or, more precisely, their underwear. He started filming under women's skirts in bookshops and on escalators in Tokyo around June 2011 before focusing mainly on women waiting on train platforms. He had come to the attention of police because of the volume of pictures he uploaded to a site called Nozokix. He had filmed around 500 women and uploaded about 1,000 up-skirt photos. Mr. Shoji told police he would spend five to six hours on train platforms on Saturdays. In 2013, someone called police about a guy acting strangely at a small train station called Kuhombutsu in a residential area of southeast Tokyo. There, Mr. Shoji was caught taking a picture up the skirt of a university student. He reportedly told police that he did it for the thrill and the feedback he got from those who commented on the website where he posted the pictures.

Like *chikan* train gropers, those who up-skirt come from all ranks of society. In 2012, Tokyo police charged a former president of IBM Japan, 63-year-old Takuma Otoshi, after he was caught using his iPod to film up the skirt of a woman on a station escalator. According to Japanese media reports, he told police that he had an interest in peeping photos. He had been the president of IBM Japan between 1999 and 2009, and was still working with the US computer-services giant as a consultant when he was charged. In 2013 he was fined 300,000 yen (US$3,000) for the offense.

Dedicated up-skirters use a variety of means to get their pictures. Police statistics show that of the 2,400 cases they detected in 2012, almost two-thirds were filmed with mobile phones, and 11 percent were filmed with a small hidden camera. Train stations are the typical venue of choice, because they usually have escalators as well as large volumes of people flowing through. Signs warning of up-skirting were put up on walls beside escalators in some train stations, including those at popular Tokyo tourist destinations Akihabara and Ueno. In 2012, just under a third of up-skirting happened in train stations, according to police statistics. DVD rental shops are another favorite, with 13 percent of detected cases happening there. A further 28 percent of cases took place in other shops and malls.

Favoring the latter locale was a man we shall call Takashi Nomura, a pseudonym necessary for reasons that will soon become clear. Mr. Nomura, a father of three young children, had multifaceted illegal sexual interests. He came before Matsumoto District Court charged with violating obscenity laws by taking up-skirt pictures. This crime is often regarded as victimless because the person affected usually doesn't know they have been violated, and the pictures, even if put online, do not readily identify the subject unless they show some singular characteristic such as a unique scar or tattoo on the inner leg. In the environs of a place like Matsumoto City, there are few train stations with escalators. Perhaps that was why Mr. Nomura liked to take up-skirt images in shops.

He traced his interest in up-skirting to a big argument he had with his wife soon after their youngest child was born. "Our sex life took a dive. We began to have sex only once every three months, sometimes once every six months. I wanted to do it once a week, but she didn't," he told the court. "I don't believe in having a mistress, so I took the pictures to relieve my stress. It was to satisfy me at the start, but I kept doing it. It was something like shoplifting; it was scary, but it was also a thrill."

He was also encouraged after seeing pictures on a website dedicated to up-skirting. "It looked like something I could do. I thought I could shoot the pictures from behind," he told investigators. So a new hobby was born. "I didn't think of the victims' feelings; it was for my own satisfaction," he told his lawyer under cross-examination. "I really regret it." Mr. Nomura took a lot of surreptitious pictures. By his own estimate, he photographed as many as 100 unwitting women in and around Matsumoto City, most of them up-skirt.

"Do you intend to delete the pictures?" the prosecutor asked.

"If it is for atonement," he replied somewhat equivocally.

"For atonement or not for atonement is irrelevant," snapped the prosecutor, "Do you promise to erase them?"

"Yes."

"What age were the women?" his own lawyer asked.

"Adult women and high-school girls."

"Any young children?"

"No."

Mr. Nomura's lawyer was anxious that the court understand that his up-skirting was not pedophilic, because Mr. Nomura was also charged with a far more serious crime—that of producing pornographic pictures of his own children. His road to court started when his oldest son, aged eight, was doing his elementary-school summer holiday project. Japan takes education very seriously. The typical summer break for elementary school students is around four weeks. And holidays are not a break from study: children arrive home with a summer holiday workbook on the day their vacation begins. They also have to do an "independent research" project during the holidays. The schoolchildren choose the topic of their research themselves; it may be about wildlife in their area, or a mini-science project such as checking how fast different foods go moldy, for example. But it should be original research, and it often involves the schoolchildren taking pictures to illustrate their investigations. For his summer research project on local infrastructure, Mr. Nomura's son took photographs.

The boy's mother—Mr. Nomura's soon-to-be ex-wife—gave evidence in court behind a screen. She was, according to the prosecutor, afraid that someone in the public gallery might recognize her and identify her family. She described how she discovered the pornographic photos of her children. "We went to print out the pictures at a machine in a chain store," she said. Once she inserted the camera's memory card into the photo reader at the store, she saw sexually explicit pictures of her eight-year-old son and five-year-old daughter sitting together naked on the family sofa. The pictures, taken by the children's father, showed the two children sitting with their legs apart, deliberately displaying their genitals to the camera. The couple's youngest son, a toddler, didn't feature. The images were shown to Mr. Nomura in court.

"Why were they naked?" his lawyer asked him.

"It was a hot summer's day, and it was bath time. I wanted to take the photographs as a memory."

"Were you sexually excited by the pictures?"

"No."

"Did you tell your daughter to pose like that?" the prosecutor asked.

"Maybe I did. Looking at it objectively, the photograph is sexual, but I took it with a lighthearted feeling at the time."

"What was your aim in taking the pictures?" Mr. Nomura's lawyer asked him.

"As a record of their growing up. I hadn't had the opportunity to take that kind of picture previously."

"As a parent, do you think pictures like this are OK?" the prosecutor asked.

"I didn't think about anything like that."

"So you did it without thinking?"

"Yes…but I suppose other parents wouldn't do it."

"Why do think other parents wouldn't do it?" the prosecutor pressed.

"Well, for others it's going too far, and it is probably not moral."

"Why?"

"Well, I don't have information, but, you know, I think it probably isn't good."

"Is that because you are taking pictures of their genitals?"

"Yes, that's it, I think."

"After you took the pictures, did you tell your daughter not to tell her mother?" the prosecutor asked.

"I don't remember."

"Does that mean that maybe you said it?"

"Yes," he said. He later added that "there is a high possibility that I said it."

Mr. Nomura had earlier told investigators that he didn't even think that what he was doing was a crime. "If the father thinks it's OK, then it should be OK." He also argued that if he had thought it was criminal he would have transferred the pictures from the digital camera, to which his wife had access, to password-locked storage on his computer that only he could open.

He explained his view to the court. "On the news, I see reports of people arrested for taking pictures of children in swimming costumes. So far, I've never seen news of any father arrested for taking pictures of his own children."

"So you think if a stranger is taking the pictures and putting them up on the Internet, or selling them, it's a crime?" the prosecutor asked.

"Yes."

"You said that if a stranger saw the pictures you took of your son and daughter, they wouldn't get sexually excited."

"Did I? If they had a chance to see them, certain types of people might get excited."

"What types?"

"A *lolicon* [the colloquial Japanese term for pedophile, derived from the phrase 'Lolita complex']."

Mr. Nomura's father gave evidence on his son's behalf. He had seen the photos of his grandchildren only a couple of days before he testified, and admitted that he had been shocked by them. "Even if he was only messing around," he said about his son, "it was really terrible." But like most parents, he was sticking by his son, who was, he said, a good father. The elder Mr. Nomura didn't explain why he thought his son might have taken the pictures, but he had more to say: "The defendant is more like an older brother to the children," he said. The practice in Japanese courts is that the accused is referred to as "defendant" even by witnesses. Most witnesses who are related to the accused usually slip up at some point, calling them by their first name, but Mr. Nomura's father managed to call his son "defendant" throughout. "The defendant would mock-fight with them. It was like watching brothers fight. The eldest boy would say stuff to him and he would give it right back."

"Did you ever see him make the older boy cry?" the lawyer asked.

"I never saw him cry because of kicking or punching, but I did see him crying on his bed because his father had bullied him verbally. He did say he didn't like his dad, but he didn't say he didn't want to be anywhere near him."

What the defendant's father characterized as brotherly-type roughhousing between an eight-year-old and his father was described differently by the child's mother. Mrs. Nomura said her son was terrified of his father, and that on at least one occasion her husband had made their eldest son drink toilet water as a punishment. She also said that ever since she and her children had fled the family home six months previously, her eldest son expressed fear that his father would track down the family and kill them.

Mr. Nomura was anxious to refute this point when it was his turn to testify. "It isn't like my wife said," he told the court. "My son smiles and chats when we eat together."

"Did you punch the oldest boy?" the lawyer asked.

"Yes."

"Did you stop if the child complained it was hurting?" the lawyer asked.

"No. If I saw it was actually painful, but that he could withstand it, I would continue, and the child would cry, but I wouldn't continue punching him to a level that would injure him. The boy's reaction was so cute, so that's why I did it."

"Did your wife ever say anything to you?" the prosecutor asked Mr. Nomura.

"She would say I was going too far, that I was being violent, but I didn't recognize it as such."

"Was your attitude toward your eldest son and your daughter a mistake?"

"I was trying to mollycoddle my daughter, but I was too hard on my oldest son, and I was too strict psychologically. In school and in athletics I wanted him to always be number one."

In public he was affectionate with his daughter in an unusual way—he typically kissed her on the lips. Mr. Nomura knew his behavior was unusual, but saw nothing wrong with it. "I think in other homes it's not done, but if the kids don't mind, then I think it's OK," he said.

In many ways, Mr. Nomura had the outward appearance of a model dad. He spent lots of time with his children. Unusually for a Japanese man, he didn't stay in his job after regular office hours to work for free (a common practice known as "free-of-charge overtime"), and he didn't socialize with colleagues. "Compared to other dads, I am more actively involved in child-rearing," the defendant said. "In common parlance, I am an *oya baka* [literally an "idiot parent"; one who is over-focused on his children and their achievements]. When I finish work, I don't go drinking with my colleagues. I work until the appointed time and go home straight away to look after the kids. I deal with the children's teachers and take time off work to go to sports days, kindergarten, piano performances, and class observations."

In Japan, parents are encouraged to visit their children's classrooms and observe classes as often as once a month in elementary schools and many junior high schools. Because they are usually held on weekdays, class observations tend to be attended by mothers only. If there is a male present, he is often a grandfather. Working fathers taking time off to attend a class observation is rare: even Mr. Nomura's estranged wife agreed that he was an unusually involved father.

Behind that model-dad image were other questionable aspects, apart from the pornographic pictures and violence. His daughter told her aunt that her father would touch her nipples in the bath, and that he told her not to tell her mother about this. Mr. Nomura told the court he was just "playing," and that he only did it after his daughter touched his nipples. Like the great majority of Japanese households with younger children, bathing as a family was a daily activity in the Nomura home. The defendant usually bathed with his daughter, and his wife bathed with their two boys. There is nothing at all unusual about this; Japanese children bathe with their parents until they are close to puberty. Even when they are older, Japanese adults will often go with their parents to public baths—though as adults, mothers will bathe with daughters and sons with fathers; few public baths are unisex nowadays. Compared to the Judeo-Christian–influenced world, people are less ashamed of nudity in Japan. The positive aspect of this is that children in Japan will talk of genitalia much more openly without shame, and are probably more likely to speak up if someone is abusing them sexually, as compared to a household where no one ever mentions penises or vaginas. The flip side of this open attitude toward bathing and nudity is that if a parent is a pedophile, the bathing culture offers ample opportunity for them to be naked with their children without arousing suspicion.

It wasn't clear from the evidence whether Mr. Nomura's bathroom behavior with his daughter was pedophilic. Touching his daughter's nipples was odd, but if the context was as he explained, it might have been relatively innocent. And there was no evidence provided to the court that any of the children were violently sexually assaulted. But when the disturbing sexual photographs were added in, it didn't look good for Mr. Nomura. His fetish for up-skirting suggested a sexually childish man, one who was willing to break the law to satisfy his fetishes. But his lawyer suggested that the up-skirting was also proof that his sexual interest lay in adults and not prepubescent children.

After about five months of detention, the defendant was released on bail. He moved to his parents' home and finalized his divorce. His wife gained full custody and legal guardianship over their children. Even if he were to be found innocent, it's unlikely that he would ever be allowed to see his children again. In Japan, only one parent is allowed to keep parental rights after a divorce, and whichever parent has those can effectively exclude access to the other if they so desire. In his final statement to the court before sentencing, Mr. Nomura argued that his wife's initial complaint to the police about the pornographic pictures of their children was motivated by her wish to obtain a divorce and ensure that he had no chance of gaining parental rights.

The defendant's father was asked by the prosecutor how he would make sure his son wouldn't break the law in the future.

"My wife will guide him on the small stuff. If it's a big problem, I will advise him."

"Did you ever reprimand him up to now?"

"I did up until he left high school, but after that, no."

"What advice will you give him from now on?"

"I will advise him to fix his attitude toward life. After he was detained I was asked by the defendant to go and collect his belongings from his home. He doesn't throw stuff out, and the room was a mess. He has to start managing his things better." Given the context, it was unusual advice to finish on. An untidy room was the least of his son's problems.

A few months after his father's testimony, Mr. Nomura became a convicted sex criminal. He was found guilty of breaking the Act on Punishment of Activities Relating to Child Prostitution and Child Pornography, as well as the Protection of Children Act. He was also found guilty of breaching a prefectural obscenity law for taking up-skirt photos. He was sentenced to 18 months in jail, suspended for three years.

MAMA'S BOYS

WEEK-WILLED

As Masaki Tsukahara stood whimpering in Matsumoto District Court, it was hard to imagine that he had once been a yakuza gangster. The former construction worker was telling the judge through his tears how much he loved his family and how grateful he was that they hadn't turned their backs on him once he got into trouble. He said he fell into criminal ways because of his weak personality. "I was always pampered by my mother and grandmother," explained the 32-year-old, who was in court charged with possessing speed, the most commonly used illegal drug in Japan.

When police raided the house Mr. Tsukahara shared with his mother and grandmother, they discovered a small quantity of illegal stimulants and some needles for injecting. "I couldn't even have imagined him taking stimulants," his mother told the court, as her son sat remorseful and sad-looking a couple of yards away, flanked by two policemen. She concurred with her son's view about the cause of his lawbreaking. "He was brought up by women, and we mollycoddled him," she told the court. She lamented that they hadn't made him develop a "bigger sense of responsibility."

Her son, she said, was "kind" and had "empathy" for people, but was "easily led." And he was easily led into drugs, apparently. By his account, the first time he took speed was in January 2011, soon after he had joined the yakuza. He was a driver for the gang boss, a typical low-level job that beginner mobsters are given while they are learning the bread and butter of the business—protection rackets, blackmail, intimidation, and drug-dealing. Mr. Tsukahara claimed a gangster friend had asked him if he wanted some drugs. "I couldn't refuse." He said he took speed about twice a week over a 10-week period and then stopped, and didn't touch drugs for three years. In the meantime, he left the yakuza and worked in different jobs. His mother got him a job at a construction company where her cousin worked, but he was made redundant a few months before his second bout of drug-taking. Unemployment, he said, had made him depressed and vulnerable by the time another offer of drugs came along. "My friend [a different yakuza gangster] offered it to me. I refused at first, but then I wasn't able to refuse. I couldn't find work, I was down. I had been called for many interviews, but I failed to land a job, I thought that if I did drugs my feelings would improve. My will was weak."

Neither was he able to refuse when the same acquaintance came looking to borrow money. "I bumped into him in a pachinko parlor, and he asked me to lend him money. I gave him some, but he kept asking for more and more, and I ended up giving him 2.5 million yen (US$25,000). He said it was for him to buy his way out of the yakuza and also to compensate a girlfriend that he had beaten up." There was no allegation that the former friend had extorted the money from the defendant—he was just very persuasive. "I didn't have the courage to refuse," said Mr. Tsukahara. Unsurprisingly, the defendant didn't have 2.5 million yen on hand to lend to his "friend," so he borrowed it from institutions specializing in lending to risky clients at high interest rates (many of which, ironically, are linked to the yakuza). And when his "friend" failed to pay him back, Mr. Tsukahara was left in a significant financial hole, with high interest payments racking up on the principal.

Fortunately, he was once again able to call on his mother for help. After he was arrested she repaid almost all of his loans. She also promised the judge that once her son was released from detention, she wouldn't allow him to hang around with "bad friends" any more. The prosecutor expressed doubt that even in the Tsukahara household maternal influence could extend this far, pointing out that she couldn't watch her adult son 24 hours a day.

Mr. Tsukahara, who was given a suspended jail sentence, represents a significant cohort of those who come before Matsumoto District Court. Whereas in other countries, defense lawyers often explain criminality by citing a defendant's dysfunctional background, low intelligence, or history of addiction, in Japan, mothers (rarely fathers) are commonly blamed for having spoiled or dominated their boys, making them, like Mr. Tsukahara, weak-willed and irresponsible, and ultimately vulnerable to the lure of a criminal life.

This is ironic, because Japan is a society that often places extraordinary emphasis on personal responsibility, along with the idea that everyone should pull their weight to work toward the greater good. The work ethic is instilled at an early age. Japanese elementary schools, for example, generally don't have cleaning staff; it is the job of the schoolchildren to clean. And not just the classrooms—they clean everywhere: the yard, the common areas, the toilets. In Matsumoto City, which is famed for the quality of its spring water, schoolchildren are also sent to clean up around water wells beside the streets. Sometimes teams of schoolchildren are sent to remove litter from some of the many small rivers around the city. For the schoolchildren, cleaning is an everyday chore, one that usually takes place after lunch. They gather their cloths, buckets, and gloves—depending on the task—and head for their designated cleaning area. At soccer clubs too, character-building chores are part and parcel of being on the team. When children play on a dirt pitch (grass is rare) they rake the dirt after a game to smooth it over. They also collect litter after games. Headline-making photographs of Japanese fans cleaning up the stadium after their team had played in the 2014 World Cup in Brazil reflect this type of inculcation.

Team talks by soccer coaches instill in the children lessons not just in tactics or ball skills, but also in the importance of greeting others in a confident manner, being courteous, and not causing bother to other people. Depending on the coach, punishments for failing to honor the latter in particular can be severe. I attended a soccer tournament where a soccer coach made one of his players do laps of the pitch for over three hours because he had been slow to tie his shoe laces. The boy was eight years old. After about 90 minutes his jog had turned into an exhausted walk. When I challenged the coach, it turned out that he was not just the coach but also the boy's father, though he maintained that this fact was irrelevant to the punishment. Soccer was "about preparation," he told me, and the boy was failing his teammates by being too slow in tying his shoe laces.

At home, though, it is a different story: boys in particular are often given little responsibility. If they live with their parents all their lives and then get married, they might never learn to cook. Measuring the extent of the "mama's boy" syndrome in Japan is an impossible task. But a 2011 OECD study of 26 countries showed that while women do on average 2.3 times more routine housework than men, in Japan, women did 8.3 times as much. The imbalance was more extreme in only one other country surveyed—Turkey—where women did 13.4 times more housework than men.

When it comes to sleeping times, however, OECD figures show that Japanese men are unusually well rested. Japan was one of only three countries among the 26 surveyed in which men slept more than women, managing an extra 16 minutes per night—more than any other. Mexican men slept for 10 minutes longer than women, and Estonians got one minute more. This type of research, combined with much anecdotal evidence, suggests that Japanese men are unusually reliant on the women in their life.

LOVE/HATE

One such man is Mr. Tsuyoshi Ishii, a 52-year-old former company CEO who was before Matsumoto District Court for his third arson offense, burning down his brother's house. Despite his ripe age, his 77-year-old mother remained the dominant force in his life. He hated her, though. And she was clearly sick of her eldest son as well. "I want him to stay in prison forever," she said in a statement read out in court. "I want him to die in prison," she added, for perhaps unnecessary emphasis. The person she wanted to die in prison listened to the statement, but didn't react. In his two-day trial, no matter what was said about him—and not a single word of it was flattering—he was unmoved.

He had recently been freed from prison after serving seven years for his first two arson crimes. Upon his release, his youngest brother, Tomoyoshi, had given him a place to stay. It was the biggest mistake of the brother's life. "I have a wife and kids, I didn't know whether I should let him stay or not, but if I refused, he had nobody to turn to. I had to look after him until he got a job," he told the court. The defendant shared a room with his mother, who was also living at the brother's house, even though Mr. Ishii loathed her and referred to her as his "enemy." The loathing had become mutual, as was obvious from the mother's stated desire for him to be jailed till death. That was a tragedy, because prior to his latest crime it seemed she was the only person in the world who actually cared about him. When he was in jail he relied on his mother for almost everything. He wrote letters to her regularly—mostly asking for things like books or clothes, according to his brother. She would write to him, asking about his life in jail or what he would do in the future, but he never answered those questions.

She went to visit him twice in prison—though both times he refused to come out to see her, for reasons that were unclear. But when he was released from prison in September 2013, she was waiting for him at the prison gates. After he got out, she gave him money—about 400,000 yen (US$4,000) over a period of four months, even though her own income was a miserly 50,000 yen per month, out of which she had to pay for her food and the nursing-care insurance that is obligatory for everyone over 40 in Japan. And, of course, she even let him sleep in her bedroom.

Mr. Ishii was a fit, handsome, and intelligent man with a remarkably articulate turn of phrase, but he was inordinately self-obsessed and apparently incapable of empathy, and had an acute victim complex. When his mother told him that he had to get a job and warned him she would stop doling out money to him if he didn't, he was enraged. His revenge was swift—and flammable.

Just after midday on January 15, 2014, he rolled up newspapers and placed them against a traditional-style sliding door made of light wood and heavy cardboard in the room he shared with his mother. He lit the papers and threw kerosene oil on the flames. The fire was not aimed at damaging his brother, he explained calmly. "I wanted to get back at my mother. My mother's things had to be burned. I didn't prioritize Tomoyoshi and his family. Tomoyoshi is a great guy. I wanted to get at my mother; I wanted revenge on her."

The journey to the sorry state of son-mother hatred was a meandering one involving perceived slights and alleged treachery over business affairs, as well as the impossibly self-centered personality of Mr. Ishii. It was an instructive tale of the lengths to which a man would go to take revenge on those he believed to have wronged him—even, as in Mr. Ishii's case, when the revenge was as destructive to himself as it was to his "enemy."

Mr. Ishii's life was once highly promising. As recently as 2004, he had been CEO of his family company, a charter shipping business. Within two years, however, he was sharing a six-bed cell in Yamagata prison, where food was scarce and heating nonexistent. Mr. Ishii spent 40 hours a week for the next seven years making rice bags. All of his many problems could be laid at the door of one person, he told the court: "It is all my mother's fault."

His woes began, according to his own rendition, in the late 1990s. The defendant, the eldest of three boys, took over his father's company; its chief assets were two charter boats operating around Tokyo Bay, mostly ferrying goods for construction companies. His father had made him company CEO when he was 28 years old. His younger brother, Tokyo-based Yoshitaka, was the second-in-command, while his youngest brother, Tomoyoshi, based in Matsumoto City, was uninvolved in the company.

But, as in many Japanese companies, the person running the company was not the one with the title of CEO. In the case of Mr. Ishii's firm, his father had made all the important decisions; after he died in the late 1990s, his mother called the shots. His title of company CEO was an empty one. Mr. Ishii fought with his brother Yoshitaka because he thought Yoshitaka was lazy, and accused him of spending his time sleeping instead of dealing with queries from clients. Things deteriorated sharply one day, and punches were thrown in full view of at least one of their customers. The fight, said Mr. Ishii, was about his brother's penchant for napping. "He told me he wanted to sleep in the afternoon, and I told him the afternoon was when he should be working. I got angry with him and he punched me."

The mother of the quarrelsome Ishii brothers decided, probably wisely, that the siblings should stop working together and the company assets should be divided up evenly, with each brother getting one of the company boats.

"Were you consulted?" his lawyer asked the defendant.

"No, even though I was the CEO of the company," Mr. Ishii replied.

After the company was divided, the defendant felt he was getting the brush-off as clients began to send more of their work to the younger brother instead of him. Japan's traditional hierarchy is age-based, and Mr. Ishii felt that he should have been highest in the pecking order. He complained, "They were prioritizing my younger brother when they should have been prioritizing me," since he was the older brother.

"How did you feel?" the defense lawyer asked.

"It felt as if the clients were making fun of me."

"Your brother caused the trouble, but you lost the work. What did you think about that?"

"I couldn't understand it."

Mr. Ishii decided to give up his job. He sold his boat, and after repaying debts he had about 3 million yen (US$30,000) remaining. He lived off that cash for a year, and when the money ran out he started delivering newspapers for a living. Delivering newspapers is not a particularly physically demanding job, but it hammers the body clock. The morning shift starts around 3 a.m. and continues until about 6 a.m. Workers then can get several hours sleep before it's time to deliver the evening editions. Mr. Ishii lasted about six months in the newspaper business, and in early 2006 he was offered a job back on a boat with one of his previous clients. But he was miserable. In his first month back, he only got four days' work, yielding just 50,000 yen (US$500) in pay. For the former CEO, it was a big fall from grace. "I thought the work was terrible, and I couldn't make any money," he said.

As he saw it, his life was heading in a downward spiral. He was humiliated, and he wanted to take revenge on his mother and brother because he believed they had conspired to break up the company he had once led. His revenge, though, like much of what Mr. Ishii did, was irrational. He hired a car on his credit card, and went for a long drive in the countryside, all the time mulling over his predicament, simmering with rage. He then set fire to the car. "I burned the car out of resentment for my mother and brother," he said. He presumably thought he could cause his family embarrassment by burning the car, though he didn't elaborate on this aspect. That was his first arson, and it gave him a taste for burning. The judge at the time gave him a 30-month jail sentence, suspended for four years: if he could go four years without committing a crime, he wouldn't have to serve the sentence.

Mr. Ishii's youngest brother, Tomoyoshi, whose house he later burned, had testified on his behalf at that first court case and promised to help him once the trial had finished. He was as good as his word, and used his contacts in Matsumoto City to arrange a job with a local transport company. "I asked a manager in the personnel department, and they said there was a vacancy for a job with accommodation and three meals a day, but just before my brother was to meet them for an interview he disappeared," Tomoyoshi said.

A week later he got a call from his Tokyo-based brother, Yoshi-taka. Their eldest brother had been in trouble again. "I turned on the TV and saw him in police custody," Tomoyoshi said. Just a week had passed since his first conviction for arson, and he had now committed his second offense, burning two boats belonging to a former client who had diverted work to the middle brother.

"I burned the boats," Mr. Ishii explained to Matsumoto District Court, "out of resentment for my brother and the former client."

When a judge gives a defendant a suspended sentence, it's always explained that if they commit a crime during the period of suspension, the jail sentence for the first crime can be added to the one for the second crime. The two sentences are usually not combined in full, as there may be a mitigating circumstance—for example, the second offense could be committed long after the suspended sentence has begun. But in Mr. Ishii's case, because the second offense occurred within days of his receiving a suspended sentence, there was little space for judicial flexibility. He was given four and a half years in jail for burning the boats; the earlier 30-month suspended sentence for the car arson was activated and added, making for a seven-year sentence in total.

Japanese prisons give early release if a prisoner behaves well and has shown penitence. But Mr. Ishii stayed in prison for the full seven years.

"Why was that?" asked the prosecutor.

"I was in a six-bed cell. The other prisoners considered me worthless, because I had no money to buy books and no one to bring me things. Prisoners without money have no value in the eyes of other prisoners. They picked on me, and said I was useless. They said my breath smelled. I was teased. So I had to leave the shared cell and go to a single cell. And because of that, the prison authorities said I was a problem so they didn't give me early release. The single cell was cold, and I didn't get much food. I didn't eat a single piece of candy for a year and a half."

Mr. Ishii seemingly had no friends and never contacted either of his brothers. In March 2013, however, his youngest brother received correspondence. "I got a letter from him that said he would be coming out of jail in September, and asked me to pick him up," he told the court. "He also asked if he could stay in my house until he could find a job." On the day he was released, Mr. Ishii had 250,000 yen (US$2,500) in his pocket—the proceeds of seven years' prison work—but he spent it quickly, and then relied on handouts from his brother and mother. Most of the cash came from his mother. But despite the assistance, he still hated her. "From morning to night, she would complain," he said. "She told me she thought my two younger brothers were great, and to look at myself." He also claimed she told him to "do [her] a favor and die." These harsh words, if spoken as Mr. Ishii described, contrasted with his mother's genuine attempts to help. For example, she gave him 240,000 yen (US$2,400) to pay for an intensive course so he could become a truck driver. But once he got the truck-driving license, he didn't apply for a driving job. "The ads were all looking for people with driving experience," he complained.

"Did you think of calling them and saying that you had a license but no experience, and ask them to consider hiring you?" the prosecutor asked.

"No, I didn't." Mr. Ishii said he traveled to Tokyo about every fortnight to look for work in shops making takeaway Japanese *bento* lunches. But in fact, he never did any actual job-hunting. He didn't make a single phone call to a potential employer; he didn't knock on any doors; he didn't even go to the nationwide state-run job agency Hello Work, which is the first stop for any job hunter. He told his youngest brother that he had to be choosy: "I have a sore leg, so I can't do a job that involves standing for eight hours."

Perhaps he was institutionalized after seven years in jail, or perhaps—as his mother said—he didn't want to work. Seeing no progress, his brother arranged for him to work in the ticket booth at a ski slope in the well-known resort town of Hakuba, about an hour's drive from Matsumoto.

The brother, Tomoyoshi, explained, "I thought if he could do it till spring he could save up several hundred thousand yen and then he might he able to do something else."

Mr. Ishii went for an interview, and got the job. But he told the court he found the work too confusing. "There were so many different types of tickets. Depending on the customer's voucher, there are over 20 tickets, and then there are different tickets for adults and children. So there are about 50 types of tickets altogether. I also found it hard to deal with foreign customers. The work manual had phrases written in Japanese on one side and

English on the other, but the pronunciation wasn't written. I didn't get any training." He was unable to cope as the lines of customers outside his ticket booth grew long, so after two days he gave up and fled the job.

"He panicked," said his youngest brother, who was furious at Mr. Ishii's refusal to stick it out. So Mr. Ishii returned to share his mother's bedroom on December 25, 2013. Before he had left to work at the ski resort, he had sensed that his welcome had worn out at his brother's house, and he had begun to eat alone in his mother's bedroom. His mother was a frugal woman, and since she was now bankrolling her son on her meager stipend, she demanded the same frugality from him. "My mother said not to spend more than 200 yen [US$2] on a single meal, so I ate cup noodles or 99-yen rice balls, and 180-yen hamburgers."

His anger at his mother began to grow stronger. He had blamed her for the demise of the business and for looking down on him. Now, another problem began to fester in his mind. He was desperate, he said, to rent his own apartment, but in Japan if you don't have a guarantor it is virtually impossible to find a place. A guarantor is usually an employer or an older relative, sometimes a friend who can be legally held responsible for any unpaid rent or damage that a tenant may cause. The defendant's mother declined, probably wisely, to be his guarantor. Her refusal—a measure of her total distrust in her son—infuriated him. "She was deliberately being mean to me, trying to annoy me," Mr. Ishii told the court.

She then annoyed her middle-aged son further by refusing to buy him a car. "If I had had a car, I would have been able to get a job in Matsumoto City," he said.

"Did you talk to your mother?" his lawyer asked.

"I said that it was possible to buy a car for 800,000 or 900,000 yen [US$8,000–$9,000]." (That amount would buy a very good second-hand car; Mr. Ishii seemed oblivious to the fact that his mother had very little income.) "I told her that if I had a car I could commute to work. She completely ignored me."

In early January 2014, his mother gave him another 40,000 yen (US$400) to buy a cell phone. She then told him, "This is the last money I will give to you." Mr. Ishii went to Tokyo for a few days of "job-hunting" and returned on January 11.

"What was your feeling when you returned?" his lawyer asked him.

"My legs were tired. My mother had refused to be a guarantor for me; she was being mean. I wanted to do something violent. I wanted to take revenge." It was then that he formed his plan to set fire to his mother's room. His mother didn't leave the house very often, but around midday on January 15 she went to the shops.

Soon after she left, he lit the rolled-up paper. "I threw on the kerosene, and '*fuuuu*,'" he said, making a gesture to indicate something going up in flames. His sister-in-law and his four-year-old niece were still in the house that would shortly be engulfed. "As I opened the door to leave my mother's room, I saw my niece, and our eyes met. I told her to escape, but she answered, 'See you later.'"

"The girl obviously didn't understand you," said a judge.

"Yes," Mr. Ishii replied. "In hindsight, I should have said to her clearly that she was in danger. That was an error."

Mr. Ishii told the court that before setting the fire he confirmed that there was nobody upstairs or in the back toilet where they could have been trapped. He said he was careful that no one would die in the fire. "I was worried about that, because if someone died I might get an indeterminate life sentence, or the death penalty, so I set the fire on a day without wind. I was trying to not kill people, because the death penalty would be terrible."

"Why didn't you warn your brother's wife directly?" he was asked.

"I knew she'd complain and I was afraid she would stab me or jab me in the eyes with her fingers," was his peculiar response.

His brother's wife had heard him saying, "Escape!" In her statement read out in court, she said, "I saw my brother-in-law putting on his coat and leaving the house." Noticing something strange, she went to her mother-in-law's room "I opened the door and saw the fire." That room, a traditional Japanese-style room, was beautiful and pleasant-smelling thanks to the abundance of wood and natural materials such as tatami reed. For the same reason, it was also highly flammable. Within minutes the house was an inferno. "I went back into the living room and called the fire station," said the wife. "I suspected he'd caused the fire. I said on the phone it was arson." In the middle of her call the flames burned through the phone cable and the phone went dead. "I took my keys and mobile phone and escaped with my daughter. One of my neighbors brought a fire extinguisher, and I went back to the house and tried to put out the fire, but I couldn't."

The fire took almost two hours to control. Twenty-six firefighters, eight fire trucks, 17 fire cars, and 192 volunteers from the local community volunteer fire-fighting group were at the scene. No one was killed or injured, though the fire cracked and broke windows and scorched walls in neighboring houses. Tomoyoshi was three hours away in Tokyo at a trade-union meeting at the time of the fire. He rushed back. "I never saw a house fire like it; the structure was still there but inside was really black." The 12-year-old family home that he and his wife had paid almost 16 million yen (US$160,000) to build was destroyed. "I felt appalled," he said.

"What did you lose?" the prosecutor asked.

"The Buddhist shrine dedicated to my father, my mother's kimono, pictures of the children, books. All our memories were burned."

His wife said in her statement, "I felt panicked throughout. I didn't feel sadness during the panic, but after a fireman spoke to me I began to cry. I love books, and we had around 200 belonging to my son and daughter, like a little library—all gone in a couple of hours."

Mr. Ishii's mother talked of the irreplaceable loss of her husband's ashes and pictures. Though Mr. Ishii didn't have many belongings, before he fled he stuffed a couple of sweatshirts into his backpack. He knew he would soon be in detention, probably somewhere without any heating, so he would need some warm clothes. As he ran from the house he passed someone he had been hoping to avoid. His mother was still waiting at the bus stop on her way to the shops.

"Where are you going?" she asked.

He said nothing but gestured towards the smoking house. "My mother shouted 'You!' and ran back to the house," he said, mimicking his mother's shocked tone. He appeared to be enjoying the retelling of his story, particularly the pieces that related to his mother's discomfort. "I had planned to stop a police car and tell them about the fire, but I couldn't see one, so I ran to the convenience store and told the clerk to call the police, because I had just set something on fire."

He then waited at the store for the police to arrive. He had told investigators that he burned the house so that he would be sent to jail, where he would be guaranteed three meals a day, but he was more equivocal about this aspect of his motive in court.

"You thought if you went to prison you'd have a place to sleep and eat," his lawyer said.

"Well, that's how it turned out, but I didn't want to go to jail." He admitted, however, that he "never intended to escape."

Mr. Ishii didn't seem genuinely bothered by what he had done. He spoke in court as if he were telling a story about an exciting event that he had caused, but he didn't seem to care about the victims. On the contrary, throughout the trial he talked as if he expected that others would sympathize with him. For example, when he complained emphatically in court about how his "uncaring" mother wouldn't give him the equivalent of 18 months' income so he could buy a car, he was apparently under the impression that he was speaking to an audience who would sympathize with his plight. Time after time he was cut off by his own lawyer midstream while complaining about the unlucky hand that life had dealt him.

The defendant's brother gave evidence for the prosecution. At the end of his testimony, he was asked by the prosecutor whether he had anything to say to the defendant.

"Not really to him. But to the judges and lay judges I have three things to say. My first point is that the defendant did many things that he shouldn't have done as a human being, and he doesn't show any signs he is going to reform. That is the first. The second thing is that it was attempted murder: my wife and daughter were in that house, and they could have died. If it had been 2 p.m. when he started the fire, my daughter would probably have been taking a nap, so it was a matter of luck that they were not murdered. The third thing is that it has been 140 days since the incident happened, but the effects are ongoing. My wife has lost has seven kilos [15 pounds] since the fire, and we are still living in a temporary apartment. Also, my mother can't use a stove or a heater because she has become so afraid of fire. My children lost their toys, some of which are irreplaceable. Sometimes my daughter wonders aloud about a particular toy that was lost in the fire, and my son finds the fire so painful to remember that he won't even let us talk about it. So there is still anger in our family. I came alone today, but I am carrying the anger of five people."

He finished his comments by asking the judges to ponder a question. "What kind of trial is this? Is it to help the victims or the perpetrator? I want you to figure it out. To be honest, there is no possibility of rehabilitation, and no way of rehabilitating him. I lived with him for four and a half months, and we helped him, but it was no use. I want him to repent for the rest of his life."

The defendant made no attempt to rebut any of his brother's criticism; in fact, it appeared to have no impact on him at all. The following day in cross-examination he repeatedly praised his brother's character.

"Are you sorry?" his lawyer asked Mr. Ishii.

"Yes."

"What about the people in the house, your sister-in-law and the children?"

"I am very sorry," he replied in an offhand tone.

"Are you worried about going to jail?"

"I won't have any money, my mother won't send me food, it's cold, I can't stand the cold, so I will have to go to a shared cell."

"Didn't you admit to your crime because you like being in jail?"

"No, that would be stupid."

"So you don't want to go to jail?"

"No. I burned the house to get back at my mother, but it has affected other people too and I am sorry for that. But my mother made this problem; she belittled me, she induced me to do it. It's hard to explain to others, but…" Then he added with considerable understatement, "In the future, when I get out, I don't think that my family will support me."

"Will you promise not to go near your family?" his lawyer asked.

"Yes, I promise." Two days later he was back in court to hear the verdict. The prosecutor had sought a 10-year term. The judges decided on nine years, with 60 days taken off in lieu of the more than five months Mr. Ishii had already spent in detention.

It was a heavy sentence for a crime which had caused no physical injury. Mr. Ishii smiled. As he had told the court, if it was a choice between living with his mother and living in prison, he would choose prison. He seemed genuinely scared of the thought of ever meeting his mother again and enduring her blame face-to-face.

MAKE-BELIEVE

Forty-eight-year-old Koji Miyashita was the opposite of Mr. Ishii. He obviously dreaded the thought of going back to jail and appeared not to be scared of his mother at all, though she was furious at him. He was in court on charges of stealing four gallons of heating oil from a building company and two packs of cigarettes from a convenience store. He had already been jailed twice for theft, so another spell behind bars was a certainty. He was also being charged as a habitual offender, so he could expect a stiffer sentence than before. His mother, who looked close to 80 years old, was called as a witness. She bowed in three directions—to the prosecutors, to the judge, and to the people in the public gallery—before she reached the stand. Like many Japanese people her age, she was small and dignified. She was mortified by her son's behavior. He looked mortified, too, at the sight of his mother heading to the witness stand. He furrowed his brow and sucked in his lips.

His mother ripped into him. "I have never felt anything like it. I am in such a rage with him that I can't even look at him. He has done this type of thing so many times now I have lost count. On top of that, he has deceived me again and again and again. I'm furious...I can't forgive him."

Before his recent spells in jail, Mr. Miyashita had trodden the familiar path of mankind: he had gotten married, had a family, and worked steadily. But then he lost his job and got divorced. "His family hit hard times," his mother said. "His wife came to me for help. I helped them—not with money, but with vegetables and rice."

"Why did he commit these crimes?" the lawyer asked.

"After the divorce he started to gamble," said his mother. "He now has a habit, I think, of stealing, and he is addicted to gambling."

The gambling to which she referred was in pachinko parlors, which are gambling halls masquerading as game arcades. Pachinko is played by putting small silver metal balls into a machine and hoping that they fall in particular ways to yield a prize that can be exchanged for cash. The pachinko parlor has become an institution in postwar Japan. The Japanese equivalent of the Irish Sunday morning pub queue I remember from my childhood is the morning pachinko line of gamblers who hope that early arrival will guarantee a seat at their favorite machine. The attractions of the pachinko parlor are not immediately obvious to outsiders. The interior is usually a wall of noise and a cloud of cigarette smoke; there is virtually no social interaction, and the game itself appears thoroughly uninteresting at first glance.

In the weeks before he was arrested, Mr. Miyashita had been spending his days in pachinko parlors. But that only partly explained his mother's rage. She was mostly furious because the money he was gambling there was cash that she had given him while he was waiting to get payment from a phantom "job." Mr. Miyashita had pretended to his parents that he had gotten a full-time job at a company, and asked them for money to help with the costs of traveling to work until he got paid. So his mother gave him cash to tide him over. Also, for weeks, she had dutifully been preparing a *bento* lunchbox every morning for him to bring to his make-believe work.

"I made him the *bento*, but somehow, from the start, I felt he wasn't being truthful. He never talked about his job, but when I asked about it, he gave me the company phone number," she told the prosecutor. The number and the company name were real, and she didn't want to make a fuss by phoning to check up on her son. "I couldn't call to ask if he was there. He left home and came home every day at the same time. So I came to believe it."

On the day the police came to her house to arrest Mr. Miyashita, who was living with her, her daughter and grandchildren were visiting. Arresting someone in Japan is a big event. Whereas in the United States and other countries arrests are often made at an early stage in an investigation, in Japan they are a last resort. Police are usually unwilling to arrest until they believe they have enough evidence to convict. Probably more than in other countries, in Japan the sight of police at your doorstep coming to take away a member of the family is shocking and shameful in equal measure. "I have never felt anything like it. I thought I would die of terror. I had told my daughter about my son's crime, but I hadn't said anything to the grandchildren," the mother said. She told the court she and her husband may "break off relations" with their errant son, adding that "he has no honesty." That provoked tears in her son. During his detention, Mrs. Miyashita had paid 10,000 yen (US$100) in compensation to the construction boss for the theft of kerosene oil, which was worth less than 1500 yen (US$15); and she paid 30,000 yen (US$300) to the convenience store—a handsome amount of compensation considering that the two packs of pilfered cigarettes would have retailed for a mere 880 yen (US$8.80). Lest her actions be interpreted as a sign of indulgence toward her son, she told the court, "I didn't do it for him. I did it for the other person; I feel sorry for the victim."

Paying the compensation, however, would help her son. Proof of receipt of compensation is submitted to the court by the defense lawyer and can contribute toward a lighter sentence. The convenience-store owner remained enraged at the theft, so he had to be mollified with a higher amount. Though he accepted the compensation—which not all victims do—in his statement he nonetheless called for a "severe punishment" for Mr. Miyashita. At times during her testimony, the defendant's mother's anger eased, and it seemed she hadn't given up on her son yet. She admitted that, when it came to him, "My heart and my head are always separated." Later, during questioning by the prosecutor, she said, "He is important to me, and I intend for us to live together in the future." She had also visited him in custody, though only once.

"He will go to jail, I think, but when he gets out of jail, will you look after him?" the defense lawyer asked.

"Yes, I think so. We will learn to communicate better, we'll listen more to each other," she replied. But she seemed to contradict this tentative truce offering later on when the prosecutor questioned her.

"This is your fourth time giving testimony before the court, isn't it? Will you live together when he gets out?" he asked.

She waited about 10 seconds before she responded. Maybe she was stung by the reminder that her son had turned into a repeat offender, or maybe the delay was because she had reached the end of her tether. "My heart is undecided and my husband is the same. When he is in jail we will talk. It would be a difficult task to repair our relationship," she said.

When the defendant, Mr. Miyashita, took the stand, he gave tearful but mundane testimony. He came out with the standard platitudes—he was sorry, he would try his best in the future, and he promised not to do anything bad again. He was still reliant on his mother, and told the court that whatever happened he would "go forward together with my mother."

The prosecutor sought three years in jail; Mr. Miyashita was given two. After his sentencing, he bowed to the judge and to his lawyer. He was handcuffed by his guards and led out the courtroom back door to serve his sentence. He didn't turn to acknowledge his mother. She left the court with tears in her eyes.

LOVER BOY

Natsuki Takenouchi, 24, was a different type of defendant from Mr. Miyashita—though, like Mr. Miyashita, he was attached to his mother. Very handsome, cool-looking, and formally attired, Mr. Takenouchi waited in handcuffs with a guard on either side of him for the judge to enter Matsumoto District Court. Being in detention usually has a significant bearing on a defendant's fashion style or lack thereof. There is a limit on the amount of clothes detainees are allowed, so most opt for comfort over style and arrive at court in a jogging suit. But Mr. Takenouchi, who was charged with robbery, didn't look like the type who would be seen dead in sweatpants; for him it was a black suit and white shirt. Another unusual thing about the young man was that he gave his birth year in the Western fashion—1989—rather than saying *Heisei gannen* (the first year of the emperor Heisei's reign). After sitting through cases for about nine months, this was the first time I had heard a defendant give his date of birth according to the Gregorian calendar.

In the 1920s, Japan experienced a wave of moral panic as young men in big cities started to do outrageous things like spend money on Western clothes, drink coffee, and pass love letters to strangers on commuter trains. Such young men were termed "modern boys"—*modanboi* in Japanese-English, further shortened to *mobo*. Their female equivalent was the modern girl—*modangaru* or *moga*. Mr. Takenouchi struck me as a 21st-century *mobo*, interested in fashion and fashionable cars, loose with money, and willing to break the rules to win the heart of the woman he loved. The woman he loved, though, was apparently not a *moga* and didn't share his devil-may-care "modern" outlook. Her response to his marriage proposal was eminently old-fashioned and grounded. "Let's take a break from each other and wait for one year," she said. "If you clear off your debts and get some savings during that time, we can marry." The problem was that her beau had debts amounting to around 3 million yen (US$30,000), a large part of which had been incurred to pay for a fancy second-hand car costing the equivalent of eight months of wages. His girlfriend had suggested he get a new job, but jobs are not that easy to come by for young men with little work experience. Mr. Takenouchi was earning 180,000 yen (US$1,800) per month at his current job, and his boss had told him that there would be no chance of his getting paid overtime. So even if he could use every single penny of his gross salary to pay off his debts, it would take 17 months. Take food, rent, general living expenses, and taxes from his salary, and it would take years. By then his girlfriend would probably have found someone more solvent.

Apart from his love problem, Mr. Takenouchi was also getting harassed by his landlord, who was seeking to embarrass him into paying his unpaid back rent. "He didn't call me on my mobile phone, but on the office phone, so I had to talk to him in front of my colleagues. And I was just a new employee," he said, describing his embarrassment. "I was stuck in a cycle; as soon as the money came in at the end of the month it was gone to pay for things." Mr. Takenouchi even turned to gambling in pachinko halls as a way to make money, and pachinko losses soon added to his financial woes.

He then devised an even sillier and extremely dangerous get-rich-quick scheme. Central to his plan was the object in the 12-inch envelope lying on the prosecutor's courtroom desk—a large kitchen knife. The prosecutor took the knife out of the envelope and showed it to the defendant to confirm that it was the weapon he had used in two attacks, both of which were on a 59-year-old colleague who was rumored to be cash-rich.

The first was on a dark cold December evening. Mr. Takenouchi lay in wait near the car park of the company where both men worked, clutching the kitchen knife, which he had bought a few days earlier. He also wore a newly purchased mask. He pounced on his victim just as he was getting into his car and ordered him to drive.

"Is your life important? Are your relatives' lives important?" he barked at his victim from the passenger seat as he held the knife to his throat. (Though the men worked for the same company, they had never spoken to each other.) Mr. Takenouchi then took his victim's wallet.

"Did you think of stabbing him?" the defendant was asked by his lawyer.

"No, I wasn't thinking of hurting him. If he fought I was going to escape. From the start, I was never thinking of hurting anyone, though now that I am asked there was always the possibility."

His victim was understandably terrified. "I am still scared," he said in a statement read out in court three months after the first assault. "I can't sleep properly, just two or three hours and then I wake up. Why did Takenouchi come after me? He saw my driver's license and knows my address. Maybe he will come after my family. I don't want him to do it ever again, I want him to reflect."

The first attack netted Mr. Takenouchi 140,000 yen (US$1,400) in cash. (It is not unusual for people in Japan to carry large amounts of cash in their wallets, as many restaurants and shops do not accept credit cards.) Despite his hitherto profligate lifestyle, Mr. Takenouchi was unusually fiscally responsible with his illicit takings. If the cases of Matsumoto District Court are anything to go by, the typical Japanese thief who steals money uses the proceeds of their crime in either of two ways: responsibly (cash gifts to family or debt repayment) and/or hedonistically (restaurants, gambling, prostitution and drugs). But Mr. Takenouchi went straight from the crime scene to his car, which was parked nearby. He then drove to a convenience store, where he used a bank ATM to transfer some of the stolen money to his landlord's account to pay his back rent, and virtually all the remainder to cover the repayments for his car loan. He used 2,000 yen (US$20) out of the 140,000 yen to buy food.

Stupidly, he threw his victim's driver's license in a bin in the convenience store. He was so sloppy that capture would be a near certainty. But as he was lodging his money to repay his immediate debts, he wasn't thinking of being captured; he was reveling in the fact that he had just made almost a month's salary in minutes. He was beginning to discover the power that a kitchen knife could give him. Next time he would be more ambitious.

Eighteen days later, on January 7, he struck again—the same man, same car park, same tactic. He hid and jumped on his victim just as he approached his car. "I have just killed someone," he said. "The corpse is in the back of my car. I know you don't have much money in your wallet, so tomorrow go to the bank and take out 4 million yen (US$40,000). If you don't, I will kill your children. If you don't get it ready, you'll be a criminal. You will be responsible for the death of your children. It will be your crime." Four million yen would have been just enough to cover Mr. Takenouchi's debt and his planned wedding ceremony.

But the defendant never got the money. A week after that attack, he was arrested. In the familiar pattern of the "mama's boys" cases outlined in this chapter, the mother was left to clean up the errant son's mess. Akemi Takenouchi approached the victim with an offer of 300,000 yen (US$3,000) in compensation, which he rejected. "I have no intention of accepting compensation," he said. "I want him to go to jail." All he would accept was 140,000 yen, to replace the money that had been stolen from him. Even though the defendant had no previous criminal history, he was bound to go to jail for a violent offense of such magnitude, and the victim's refusal to accept compensation would make his prison sentence longer.

"You wanted to be together with your girlfriend; that's why you wanted to repay the debt?" his lawyer asked.

"Yes," replied Mr. Takenouchi.

"Not just the debt, but you needed money for the wedding ceremony?"

"Yes."

"But if you'd gotten the money in that manner, she wouldn't have been happy," the lawyer continued.

"No, she wouldn't. But I was thinking not only about her, but also about repaying my debts."

Mr. Takenouchi also gave his assessment of the main reason for his crime. "The worst thing is my financial management," he said.

"But there are many people with debt, and they don't rob people. What you are saying is really strange," his lawyer said.

"Yes, it is strange," the defendant acknowledged. "Since I was arrested, I've been thinking about what I should do. From now on

I will talk with my family about financial matters." He then went on to blame his parents, however, for his inability to manage money. "They really spoiled me," he said.

The defendant's grandfather took the stand. Sadayuki Oi was the boss of a small business that manufactured electrical parts. The business was strictly family, employing just five people in total— Mr. Oi, his wife, two sons, and a son-in-law. He said that the family plan was to groom Mr. Takenouchi to take over the family business.

"When he returns to society, will you hire him?" the defense lawyer asked the grandfather.

"Yes." The defendant broke down in tears upon hearing about his grandfather's faith in him.

"But he caused this incident. Is there not someone in the family who will object?" the lawyer continued.

"No, we have discussed it."

"What will he do?"

"I want him to continue the family business, in the job that I am doing. He knows the gist of the technology already; he just needs to learn the skill of dealing with and negotiating with other people."

The defendant's mother, Akemi, a serious-looking woman, then took the stand. "What was your reaction when you heard about the crime?" the defense lawyer asked.

"I couldn't think about it. I wondered about the victim; I wondered what could I do as a mother."

"You think you have responsibility?"

"Yes."

"As a mother, how have you taught him?"

"I didn't teach him properly, this incident has shown me that. In various ways, I feel I evaded my responsibility."

Asked by the defense lawyer whether she had "mollycoddled" her son, she admitted it was so. "I have to change as a mother," she said, and promised to teach her son to be more independent and responsible when he was released from detention.

In his closing statement, the prosecutor sought a seven-year prison sentence. It was Mr. Takenouchi's first offense, but it was a grave one. The defense lawyer looked for mercy, pointing out that the defendant was still a young man. As always, the final words were left to the defendant. "Every day I will reflect on this," he told the judge, before adding a formulaic apology about there being no excuse for his actions—one that judges have heard word for word perhaps hundreds of times.

Three weeks later, Mr. Takenouchi was back in Matsumoto District Court for his sentencing. There was a relatively heavy journalistic turnout; half a dozen newspaper reporters were in court, their readers presumably interested to hear about the punishment for the masked, knife-wielding lover and mama's boy. The judge sentenced the young man to four years and four months in jail. The defendant stayed expressionless; his only reaction was a very deep bow to the judge. His mother didn't look too surprised, and remained composed as her son was taken away.

DRUG INTOLERANCE

LOST AND FOUND

I f only 43-year-old Yuichi Ishiijima hadn't had those few drinks and a joint before he went for a soak in the hot-spring bath. If only he hadn't forgotten his belongings in locker number 9. If only the hot-spring employee who came to check the lockers for forgotten goods hadn't found the tiny bit of marijuana in the small bag along with Mr. Ishiijima's wallet and phone. And if only the worker had looked the other way instead of contacting the police. After all, the marijuana—which the prosecutor would later show in Matsumoto District Court in a small see-through plastic bag—was barely enough to make a single joint, just 0.3 g in weight. And it was for this pitiful amount that Mr. Ishiijima was arrested, charged under the Cannabis Control Law for possession, and detained for several months in a cell at Hakuba police station in Nagano Prefecture, four hours' drive from his Tokyo home. While in detention awaiting trial, he lost his job as a supervisor at an architectural firm, he was about to lose his home, and he had made his common-law wife very, very angry.

"Looking back, why were you smoking marijuana?" his lawyer asked.

"I was under a great deal of pressure and stress. I was doing a lot of work on my own; I should have consulted with my boss," he said.

He first smoked marijuana in the US state of Oregon 20 years earlier, because, as he told investigators, he wanted to "experience hippie culture." He developed a love of weed that he just hadn't been able to shake off. Since then, he had deliberately chosen Holland and the United States as travel destinations, because he could easily smoke the drug there. In other countries, smoking pot is considered a relatively harmless activity, but not in Japan, where mere possession of marijuana can land you in jail for five years. Selling it carries a maximum of seven years, and cultivating or importing it for profit, 10 years.

Mr. Ishiijima wasn't facing five years in jail, but he was in serious trouble. The problem was that it was his third marijuana offense. On the first occasion he had received a suspended sentence. The second time he was caught, he managed to stay out of jail again, even though he was still within the suspension period. His second sentence was one year in jail, suspended for four years. He wasn't yet two years into that suspension when his small bag of dope was found by the hot-spring employee.

His mother was dumbfounded by the stupidity of her university-educated son. She told the court, "I was so surprised and angry when I heard what he did. He had a suspended sentence hanging over him. What he did was pathetic."

"Did the defendant write to you often from detention?" the defense lawyer asked.

"Yes, about five times."

"What did he write about?"

"He reflected on what he had done and said that he had really messed up. He said he wouldn't do it again."

The defendant's common-law wife, Ms. Suzuki, was also before the court to testify on his behalf. A tall, slim, elegant woman who worked for a leading financial institution, she was perplexed.

"What did you think when the police showed you his drugs?" the lawyer asked.

"I couldn't believe it. He was on a suspended sentence," she said, echoing Mr. Ishiijima's mother's disbelief.

She said she felt responsible for not preventing the offense. She had testified at the trial for his second offense about 18 months earlier, and at that time she had promised to watch her common-law husband carefully and search his personal effects to make sure he wasn't slipping back into his marijuana habit.

"I was looking in his bag at the start, but maybe I got complacent. After a while I stopped checking and stopped asking him whether he'd been smoking. I really regret that," she said. With her partner in detention, she was struggling to pay the mortgage on their apartment in an upmarket area of Tokyo. "Without his income, I can't afford the mortgage," she said, adding that their apartment had been put up for sale or rent; she and the defendant would live with his mother when he "returned to society."

"You gave evidence the first time the defendant was in court and the second time," the defense lawyer said. "How is this time different for you?"

"It's the end of the line…I can't do it again," she said.

On the previous occasions Mr. Ishiijima had been in court, he and Ms. Suzuki had not told their friends or most family members about his encounter with the law. This time, with a jail sentence looking extremely likely, she spread the net wide and gathered statements from a variety of friends, who testified that her partner was a good man and promised to watch him vigilantly to make sure he didn't break the law again. Ms. Suzuki also asked the defendant's best friend, a Mr. Kitaoka, if he would be willing to testify. He was, and the defense lawyer put him on the witness list. Mr. Kitaoka, who runs a mid-sized company in Tokyo that sells eyeglasses, promised in court that he would give his friend a job planning retail shops and displays. The promise of a job would encourage leniency in sentencing—but how much leniency was the question.

Mr. Kitaoka's testimony was a brave act. The antipathy of the average Japanese adult toward illegal drugs, including marijuana, and those who take them is strong. Most businesspeople would run a mile from the whiff of any drug scandal, much less take the stand on a defendant's behalf. Mr. Kitaoka also went a step further, promising—as the defendant's partner had done—to watch over him to make sure he wasn't secretly carrying any weed.

"Will you check his pockets?" the defense lawyer asked.

"Yes, I will. He's my best friend, I've known him for 27 years," he said. "He won't be like my other employees."

"They will be going through your belongings," the defense lawyer said to his client. "How do you feel about that?"

"I never want to take marijuana again, so they can check."

"Some friends came to visit you in detention and some wrote to you. What did they say?" the lawyer continued.

The defendant replied that Mr. Kitaoka had written to him saying, "This is the last time; do it again and we are no longer friends."

"And other friends?"

"They encouraged me, but they also warned me never to do it again."

"You have visited countries where you can smoke marijuana legally, where it is seen as a small thing. Because of that, did you look at it lightly?"

"Yes, I think so."

It is of course nonsensical that an adult's life and career could be threatened over possession of a small amount of a plant that was fully legal in Japan until 1947 and which, despite its dangers, is widely considered to have some therapeutic value. Furthermore, while the Japanese state punishes those who roll joints, it remains the largest shareholder in one of the world's biggest cigarette makers, Japan Tobacco. The Japanese Ministry of Finance holds one-third of Japan Tobacco's shares, and by law it can't reduce that holding. Not only does Japan Tobacco dominate the domestic market, selling around 60 percent of the cigarettes smoked in the country, it also has a major international presence, producing the Camel and Winston brands of cigarettes for markets outside the United States, as well as the Benson & Hedges and Silk Cut brands for the United Kingdom, where the company has a market share of about 40 percent.

According to the World Health Organization (WHO), Japan took in just under 2.4 trillion yen (US$24 billion) in tobacco taxes in 2012. That figure comes close to matching the nearly US$27.3

billion equivalent spent on salaries and other personnel expenses for the nation's 294,000 police officers. Yet with all of this tobacco income, the WHO points out that in 2012 the state employed just two full-time staff in its national tobacco control program, with a total budget for the program of under US$3 million. While marijuana is undoubtedly damaging to human health in some aspects, it has low toxicity, and there are no recorded deaths from overdose worldwide apart from a handful of people who also suffered an underlying medical condition. Tobacco, however, is responsible for one in nine Japanese deaths annually, according to the Department of Health. Although the Japanese state holds controlling shares in a company whose products kill tens of thousands every year, it puts people who dabble in marijuana, like Mr. Ishiijima, in the dock.

Like most defendants before Matsumoto District Court, Mr. Ishiijima did not make excuses for his behavior. He was very serious, spoke in very respectful language, and bowed a lot. He was eager to show his repentance in a practical, somewhat self-flagellating way, by not seeking release from detention pending trial.

"You didn't apply for bail?" his lawyer asked.

"No."

"Why not?"

"I should take responsibility for what I did." As a sign of repentance, it was more effective than any words.

But for all his contrition, one thing that Mr. Ishiijima didn't do in court was to name those who sold him his drug. Most drug defendants refuse to reveal names, citing the potential threat dealers could pose to their loved ones. But for those who answer, by far the most common explanation given in Matsumoto District Court is to say they bought it from a (choose one from each category) foreigner, black person, or Iranian in Nagoya, Osaka, or Tokyo. If the drugs were allegedly bought in Nagoya, the defendant is more likely to say his dealer was an Iranian; if they were bought in Tokyo, he is more likely to say the dealer was *kokujin,* a black person.

Mr. Ishiijima told the court his first purchase of marijuana in

Japan had been 13 years earlier, when he bought it from a "foreigner at a live music venue." And his last one was from "a black man in Roppongi" (Roppongi is one of the livelier night spots in Tokyo). He said he had paid 10,000 yen (US$100) for that deal. Based on the testimony of drug defendants in Matsumoto District Court, you might have the impression that foreigners ran Japan's drug trade. That would be incorrect, however: the great bulk of all drug arrests, over 95 percent, are of Japanese nationals.

Before the judge adjourned to consider sentencing, he had some questions for Mr. Ishiijima.

"Can you taste food better if you smoke marijuana?" he asked.

"Yes," said Mr. Ishiijima.

"If you use it on top of alcohol, is the effect more profound?"

"No, I have never felt that."

And then the most salient question, and one to which the judge undoubtedly already knew the answer. "When you got a suspended sentence the last time, was it explained what would happen if you committed another offense in the period of suspension?"

"Yes."

It looked ominous for Mr. Ishiijima, a three-time offender with no extenuating circumstances beyond some workplace stress, which is so common in Japan that it hardly qualified as an excuse.

In his closing statement, the prosecutor emphasized that because marijuana is sold on the black market, buyers such as Mr. Ishiijima are effectively "supporting organized crime." In his closing, the defense lawyer made the usual points—the defendant was reflecting on what he'd done; he had been fired from his job; he had committed the crime due to stress; and his partner, Ms. Suzuki, would supervise him when he was released. But he also mentioned that Canada, Holland, and the United States had relaxed their laws on marijuana, implying that possessing the drug was not such a dreadful crime.

When the day came to announce Mr. Ishiijima's verdict, it had been four months since his arrest and he was still in custody. Ms. Suzuki was in court to support him, having traveled from Tokyo. The defendant looked nervous, but a little hopeful. His hopes, however, were quickly crushed as the judge read the sentence: eight months in jail, with 60 days off for time already spent in detention. Distressed, he tried to mouth something to his partner as the guards put his handcuffs back on, but failed. The job offer from his friend had been contingent, the court had previously heard, on him staying out of prison, so he would have to look elsewhere for employment once released. Finding white-collar work as an ex-con isn't easy. It would be tough for Ms. Suzuki as well: having a jailbird as a partner wouldn't go down well in her workplace; there would likely be deep apologies to bosses and possibly pressure to quit. All because of Mr. Ishiijima's love of weed.

THE OBAMA CARD

Mr. Ishiijima played the courtroom game—lots of repentance and a guilty plea. He didn't try to politicize the trial by arguing that the laws in Japan were unjustly harsh, and his lawyer—apart from a fleeting mention in his closing argument—did not allude to the growing trend of countries liberalizing marijuana laws.

Not so Naofumi Katsuragawa, who is probably Japan's proudest marijuana smoker. Sitting on the floor of his house in the small town of Ikedamachi in Nagano Prefecture, where he was born and raised, the 63-year-old was talking about marijuana, jail, and what he sees as the brainwashing of Japanese against the leaf he loves so much. Retired from his family's printing business, Mr. Katsuragawa looks like an academic and is obviously very clever, but he is better known as an inveterate pothead and a man on a mission to convert Japan to the benefits of cannabis. He has been smoking marijuana for 30 years; he has been jailed for it; he campaigns for pot legalization; and he had just started a business importing medical-use cannabis oil, which, he and his business partner had recently discovered, was allowable in Japan due to a legal loophole.

His home, about a half-hour drive north of Matsumoto, looked like a student crash-pad from the 1980s. His living-room wall featured a giant gecko lizard that lighted up. It didn't look like much during the day. "It's more impressive at night," Mr. Katsuragawa assured me. When I met him, he was in the middle of a lengthy trial before Matsumoto District Court, charged with cultivating cannabis plants (he had nearly 100 in his garden) and possession of 200 grams of weed. In Japan, as in other countries where marijuana is illegal, people can apply for a license to grow cannabis plants for industrial-use hemp. These industrial-use plants are usually low in THC, the chemical in cannabis that make you high.

Mr. Katsuragawa was arrested after hosting a party at his home for people who wished to smoke the fruits of his marijuana garden. It was supposed to be aimed at those who had medicinal needs for marijuana, though, as he pointed out, "It is difficult to distinguish between the people who smoke it for medical reasons and those who smoke for their own pleasure." Regardless, any type of marijuana smoking in Japan is illegal. Cancer patients can be legally prescribed opium, but not cannabis.

Unwisely, as he now admitted, Mr. Katsuragawa advertised his party openly on the Internet. Around 100 people showed up from as far away as Tokyo and Osaka, the latter about a five-hour drive away. As the party was in full swing, a dozen police officers showed up. Mr. Katsuragawa believes they were tipped off by someone with "mental health problems" who had visited his house to smoke marijuana on previous occasions, but who had been barred due to his "strange" behavior. Whether Mr. Katsuragawa was actually betrayed or whether the police had stumbled across his Internet invite, he found himself being prosecuted. It was set to be a long trial—mostly because Mr. Katsuragawa pleaded not guilty, and also because he was mounting a defense that was more political than criminal. While admitting to the cultivation and supply of cannabis, he intended to plead innocent on the grounds that Japan's marijuana law breaches Article 13 of the Japanese Constitution, which offers the following guarantee: "All people shall be respected as individuals. Their right to life, liberty, and the pursuit of happiness shall, to the extent that it does not interfere with the public welfare, be the supreme consideration in legislation and in other governmental affairs."

Japanese judges are not known for judicial activism; that is, interpreting the law to reflect personal views or the changing views of society. They see their job as implementing the law, so it was virtually certain that Mr. Katsuragawa's constitutional argument would not win. He acknowledged to me that a not-guilty verdict was unlikely, and that his best hope was for a suspended sentence.

But prison was also a strong possibility, because it was a second offense. His first offense had landed him in prison for five years—an extremely harsh sentence for a first-time drug offense. That had been for cultivation of marijuana as well as possession of small amounts of methamphetamine and magic mushrooms, he said. Mr. Katsuragawa claimed that only the marijuana belonged to him, and that the other drugs had been left lying around his house by guests at one of his parties. He had served his time in Kyoto prison, which he described as Japan's second-toughest prison after the infamous Nagoya prison.

In one respect, Mr. Katsuragawa had been a prisoner of conscience. He could have gotten out of jail early if he had renounced marijuana, he said to me. That would have shown prison authorities that he was remorseful for his crime, indicating rehabilitation. "They kept coming to me and asking me to say that marijuana was bad and that I wouldn't smoke it in the future, but I refused to do either. In the end, I couldn't get early release. If I had apologized when they first asked, I would have gotten out immediately." So Mr. Katsuragawa served his full five-year term, equivalent in length to some manslaughter sentences.

"It was obviously tough in prison, so why didn't you criticize marijuana, just to make the prison authorities happy?" I asked.

"Psychologically, for my own conscience, I couldn't say that. When I left I was able to tell people that I hadn't said that marijuana was bad. That was important."

Mr. Katsuragawa told me his lawyer was the son of a family friend from Tokyo, who was taking the case for a fee of 1 million yen (US$10,000), about one-fifth the normal cost. Core to the defense was that Mr. Katsuragawa's marijuana was given to people with a medical need, and that by maintaining a rigid prohibition,

Japan was lagging behind liberalizing tendencies in the United States and elsewhere.

In the latter context the lawyer evoked the name of US president Barack Obama. Even after President Obama's glitter had long faded in his home country, in Japan he was still regarded as a superstar politician, though this was probably the first and last time his name would be mentioned in Matsumoto's district courtroom. Decades after the end of the United States' postwar occupation, Japan remains transfixed with American culture and society. Despite Japan's geographical and cultural proximity to China, the United States is the typical reference point for Japanese. When it comes to coverage of issues related to national image, the most powerful newspaper in Japan is neither of its two best-selling dailies (which are also the two best-selling dailies in the world)—the *Yomiuri Shimbun* and the *Asahi Shimbun*—but the *New York Times*. There is surprisingly little bitterness against a country that carried out what were undoubtedly the two greatest atrocities of the Pacific War—the nuclear bombings of Hiroshima and Nagasaki.

Japan is a country steeped in influences from other cultures. It took Buddhism from India, via China and Korea; its writing came from China; the martial art of karate may have originally come from India but certainly arrived in Japan via China; and its medicine and education were first heavily influenced by China, later by Germany, and then by the United States. Japanese law was initially borrowed from China, then from Germany and France until the second half of the 19th century; finally, after World War II, the United States became the major legal influence. The hold the United States has on Japan goes well beyond its political importance as a "hard power" ally with about 50,000 US military based on Japanese soil.

Many of the most progressive changes to postwar Japan have been due to the influence of the US occupiers who wrote Japan's Constitution, which guarantees freedom of speech, freedom of religion, workers' right to unionize, and various rights for criminal suspects, including the right to silence. The 1948 Cannabis Control Act under which Mr. Katsuragawa was charged was also the product of US influence. The cannabis plant used to be widely grown in his hometown of Ikeda, as well as in other parts of Japan, for textiles and other commercial uses. "Behind us is Miasamura, which means 'the village of beautiful cannabis,'" he said, gesturing from his living room. "They could have smoked it, but they didn't; no one smoked it in Japan then."

Cannabis was prohibited across the United States starting in the 1930s. Popular feeling against the drug had been heightened by the 1936 film *Reefer Madness*, which showed people turning variously into brutish, murderous, sex-crazed, amoral, and gibberish-speaking loons after smoking a joint. For those US postwar administrators who wanted to re-fabricate Japan in an American image, an anti-cannabis law was a logical step. Mr. Katsuragawa's basic point is that because Japan's intolerance of marijuana was imported from the United States, Japan should now consider importing America's growing acceptance of the drug.

Hence President Obama's entry on behalf of the defense. The US president—himself an admitted former pot smoker—had given an interview in which he talked about marijuana. He wouldn't recommend it for his own daughters, he said, just as he wouldn't recommend alcohol, but he said that alcohol was more dangerous than marijuana.

In addition to citing Mr. Obama's opinion, the defense introduced at great length other examples of how thinking toward marijuana was changing in the United States. Usually the reading of evidence from a defense lawyer only takes a few minutes. But Mr. Katsuragawa's lawyer spent about two hours summarizing evidence into the court record. The focus was mainly on the United States and the number of states that had legalized marijuana in certain situations, or had decriminalized possession of small quantities to make it a civil offense (like a parking fine) rather than a criminal one. Montana, Delaware, Hawaii, Colorado, Alaska, and more than a dozen other states were referenced as having liberalized their regulations. It was the "Look, they're doing this in the United States, so it must be OK" defense. And that has a resonance in Japan.

Mr. Katsuragawa's lawyer's strategy was clear. If US state legislators were changing their attitude based on a growing body of research showing the beneficial properties of the plant, then surely Japan must follow suit at some stage. If that was the case, then his client deserved to be dealt with leniently. It made for a very boring defense, however; details of state after US state where pot laws had been relaxed. And then the lawyer moved onto other countries such as Romania, Uruguay, and, of course, Holland, long known for legal pot smoking. People nodded off in the public gallery as the lawyer built up his intended battering ram of evidence.

The lawyer was also hoping a young American girl called Charlotte Figi would nudge the battering ram through the judicial door. Figi's upsetting and uplifting story was the focus of a 43-minute CNN documentary called "Weed." The documentary was played in full on a Friday afternoon in Matsumoto District Court. Ms. Figi was born as healthy as her twin sister, but from the age of about three months she began to suffer from seizures that left her in great pain and unable to speak. At its worst, her life had become a torture of around 300 seizures per day. Her parents were at their wits' end: No medicine seemed to work, and they were even beginning to hope for an early death to save their daughter from her suffering. Then they decided to give her some drops distilled from a cannabis plant with low level of THC. The effect was close to miraculous. Her seizures didn't stop, but they were reduced to as few as one a day. Their child began to speak, socialize, and enjoy life.

Ms. Figi's story appeared to be a clear case of the medical benefit that cannabis can offer in some cases. But it looked unlikely that Judge Toshihiro Honma would be moved enough to offer unusual leniency to the defendant. The judge would know that while marijuana laws had been relaxed in more than 20 US states, it remained, at the time of the trial, a so-called Schedule I drug, defined by the US Department of Justice as a drug "with no currently accepted medical use and a high potential for abuse. Schedule I drugs are the most dangerous drugs of all the drug schedules, with potentially severe psychological or physical dependence." The judge would also know that while the rate of marijuana addiction is lower than that for cocaine, dependence on the drug is a serious social problem.

Both sides of the marijuana debate are aired in the United States, but much less so in Japan. By using his trial to raise wider issues about marijuana rather than sticking to the specifics of his case, Mr. Katsuragawa hoped to effect a change in his country's solidly anti-marijuana public opinion. Public opinion on this issue is, in fact, malleable. According to polling by research firm Pew, in 1991, 17 percent of Americans supported marijuana legalization and 78 percent opposed it. By 2013, that had changed to 52 percent in favor and 42 percent against.

Whether Mr. Katsuragawa's trial will eventually make a difference in legislation remains to be seen. While some local journalists attended his hearings, Mr. Katsuragawa told me there had been no mention of his case in any of the papers and, for the present, at least, the status quo remains intact. Mr. Katsuragawa was sentenced in November 2015 to four years in prison, nothing suspended.

SPEED

Although a veteran criminal and yakuza member with a decades-old alcohol and drug problem, Akira Nakano made his appearance at Matsumoto District Court not as a defendant, but as a witness for the prosecution in a case against his drug dealer. The drug in question was speed (also known as methamphetamine, or meth), which is not only widely imported and sold by the yakuza (as is marijuana), but is also the drug of choice for gangsters. They're not the only ones, however; while roughly one in five drug-related arrests in Japan are for marijuana, the remainder are almost entirely for speed and amphetamine-type stimulants.

There are historical reasons why speed is the dominant recreational drug in Japan. Masayuki Tamura, of Japan's National Research Institute of Police Science, notes that at the outbreak of the Pacific War the drug, which was then sold under the name Philopon, was generally restricted to psychiatric practice. He further adds:

But during the Second World War, the military, considering stimulants to be useful for aeroplane pilots, the signal corps, and civilian military workers on night shifts, proceeded to increase production markedly. After the war, pharmaceutical companies sold stockpiles of stimulants to the local population. It was believed that stimulants met the needs of war veterans and juveniles affected by dramatic postwar social change.

This sparked an epidemic that grew even after sale was restricted in 1948 and banned in 1950. Harsher laws and a reorganization and centralization of the police pushed arrests up and led to a sharp decline in use. Arrests for stimulants hit 55,000 in 1954, but then fell rapidly to 32,000 in 1955; 5,000 in 1956; and fewer than 300 in 1958.

Today, however, Japan is Asia's most lucrative market for speed. While a tiny proportion is made in Japan, most is smuggled from countries and regions like China, Mexico, Peru, Brazil, and West Africa—fully 82 percent of all West African-produced amphetamine-type drugs seized at Western European and Japanese airports from 2009 to 2013 were bound for Japan, according to the United Nations Office on Drugs and Crime. The drug remains in demand, partly because, just as it helped the weary wartime factory workers laboring flat out to produce more armaments, it keeps people awake. In other words, it's a drug that fits busy Japan more than sleep-inducing marijuana. Japan is, after all, the country that gave us the word *karoshi*, meaning death from overwork.

Mr. Nakano came straight out of yakuza central casting. For a start, he had lost his little fingers—both of them gone from above the lowest joint, which suggested four separate amputations, one joint at a time. By some accounts, the yakuza practice of finger-cutting originated because the little finger is crucial in gripping the hilt of a samurai sword. If a samurai's little finger is mutilated, he cannot hold his sword as well, and is therefore less able to defend himself. That makes him less useful to the group as a fighter, but increases his loyalty to the group because he needs their protection more than ever. Other accounts say the grotesque practice originated as a punishment for those who couldn't pay their debts: if not a pound of flesh, the unsatisfied creditor at least got a fingertip. Finger-cutting is carried out by the yakuza member himself, either to atone for his own mistake or, in the case of more senior yakuza, for a serious mistake by an underling.

But Mr. Nakano didn't look like the kind of yakuza who had underlings. Poorly and garishly dressed, with a shuffling gait, he looked to be at the bottom of the yakuza food chain; if his absent finger parts were anything to go by, he wasn't very good at his job. He was apparently conscious of his self-inflicted digital deformity. He wore a large silver ring on the stub of the finger on his right hand, presumably to mask the sight. He told the court that he worked as a "collector" for a real-estate agent who was enforcing property liens. His boss would register a claim on a property as security for a loan, and if the borrower defaulted, Mr. Nakano would arrive at their doorstep to persuade them to hand over the property. Going through the courts to enforce a lien is a long process—the arsonist couple described in chapter 1, Mr. and Mrs. Hara, managed to live in their house for more than five years after they had stopped repaying their mortgage. But a visit from Mr. Nakano, with his four-fingered hands, nasty scar along the back of his bald head, garish jewelry, and gruff manner, would surely speed up the eviction process.

Even with a full set of fingers, Mr. Nakano's speed habit meant he would probably be unemployable in a regular industry. The drugs, he admitted, "make me strange. They make me forget things." Unlike the pot-smoking Mr. Ishiijima, who had kept mum about his drug supplier, Mr. Nakano was in court to name his dealer—Kenichi Ota. Mr. Ota delivered Mr. Nakano's drug supply by post, mailing a small bag of the requested amphetamine powder inserted between the pages of a magazine. Their relationship was not strictly commercial; the two men had been friends as well. Sometimes Mr. Nakano would "forget" to pay, but Mr. Ota continued to supply him anyway.

Mr. Nakano had an arrangement with his local post office. When a package arrived for him, the staff—innocent as to its contents—would call his cell phone to let him know it had arrived. But the police had found out about Mr. Ota's postal drug service. On the day of his final, fateful delivery Mr. Nakano had been drinking at home, so he asked his wife to pick up the package. She collected it and brought it home, and within minutes there were eight police officers knocking on the Nakanos' door. "I was caught red-handed," Mr. Nakano told the court.

He was arrested immediately. And after a spell in detention, he decided to spill the beans on Mr. Ota, who pleaded innocence despite a quantity of evidence, including CCTV footage of him posting the envelope at the post office and records of drug-related emails sent to him by Mr. Nakano.

After initial questioning by the prosecution, it was time for the cross-examination of Mr. Nakano by Mr. Ota's lawyer. Defense lawyers usually question witnesses in a courteous and soft manner while standing several yards away at their own table. Not so with Mr. Ota's lawyer. His questioning was aggressive, and he also moved from his table to stand close to the witness, as defense lawyers often do in US courtroom dramas.

"You are yakuza, you have many convictions," the lawyer stated sternly. "You have been using drugs since you were 25."

"Before that, actually, since I was around 15," Mr. Nakano replied.

"You have a mental problem, don't you?" the lawyer accused.

"I am an alcoholic."

"And your wife has a criminal past."

"No, she doesn't. Why do you speak in that tone? And why don't you speak from over there?" grumbled Mr. Nakano, gesturing to the lawyer's desk.

The lawyer ignored him. "Why did you name the defendant? Did the police force you to name him?"

"No. It wasn't like that. When I was in detention, my wife wrote to me, and that got me thinking. I decided to change my mind about my involvement in all of this."

"There was about a gram of the drug in the package. How much would it cost?"

"I don't know."

"Would it be 20,000 yen [US$200]?"

"When we met, he said 20,000 yen."

At the end of his testimony, the witness addressed the defendant, his former friend whom he had now betrayed. "Both you and I are involved in this business. I think you should admit to it, and once you are out of jail I want you to do your best."

Mr. Ota didn't reply. When he took the stand himself for cross-examination, almost one year and several hearings later, he refused to answer any questions. "I have a lot to say," he said, adding cryptically, "but I can't say it now." He was jailed for five years.

FESSING UP

DEMOLITION MAN

Forty-seven-year-old Asahiro Hashimoto wasn't caught by the police for drug-taking: he caught himself. They would never have known about his crime if he hadn't confessed. He looked like a quiet type—mouse-like, even—and was very respectful in court. He had, however, a colorful past, as suggested by his shortened pinkies on both hands. He told the judge that he had previously been a member of a yakuza gang in his home city of Osaka. When he left the gang at age 23, his boss had made him cut off the top section of his right finger as punishment for disloyalty. In addition, his left pinkie was down to a stub, missing two joints, which indicated two other previous gang-related "transgressions" for which he had to atone by tying a string tight around his finger and using a knife to slice off the digit down the next joint. It is specifically outlawed under the 1991 Anti-Organized Crime Law to pressure a gang member to cut off a part of his finger, but it remains the quintessential yakuza demonstration of atonement.

Mr. Hashimoto had joined the yakuza as a teenager and initially worked in construction, an industry in which the mob has a strong, albeit declining, involvement. He was still a minor (under 20) when he was apprehended for his first offense, and was in and out of jail until he was around 30. Then he got married, had a child, and turned his life around. But he got divorced after eight years of marriage for reasons that he didn't explain, and started living in Tokyo on his own. He later got very depressed.

"Why were you depressed?" his lawyer asked.

"I was working in house demolition, and I started to notice that I just wasn't able to do as good a job as when I was younger. I was no longer pulling my weight. I was really worried about that, and I couldn't sleep properly at night."

"Were you treated for depression?"

"Yes, I saw a doctor. I have felt depressed for a long time, but it really got bad last autumn. I was thinking of going to the hospital, but that costs money." He told the judge he was also feeling suicidal. With his life in crisis, Mr. Hashimoto drove from Tokyo to Matsumoto City looking for moral support from his ex-wife. Though they had been divorced for almost seven years, they had remained on good terms, and he was a regular visitor to see their 14-year-old daughter. His wife advised him strongly not to give up work. Apart from anything else, he was paying child support for their daughter, so he needed cash for that. She also asked him to think realistically about the likelihood of finding alternative work. The job market for men in their 40s with a criminal record and two self-mutilated fingers would not be buoyant. He understood her reaction, he said, but added that it wasn't what he wanted to hear.

It seemed like he was stuck. He hated life and was seized with an urge "to escape reality," as he told investigators. He jumped into his car and drove five hours from Matsumoto to Osaka to buy drugs. As a yakuza member based in Osaka's Nishinari Ward, he had taken methamphetamines, and he remembered the happy rush that the drug once gave him. So he returned to his old stomping ground, looking for some white powder to inject into his veins.

Nishinari Ward is home to the Airin district, also known as Kamagasaki, which is the closest thing that Japan has to a ghetto. In Japan it is rare to see people living on the street outside the major cities, and begging is virtually nonexistent. However, a visitor is more likely to see rowdy street behavior and poor people (as opposed to white-collar workers) slumped on the street in an alcoholic stupor in the Airin district than anywhere else in Japan. The area, whose population is predominantly male and transient, is speckled with cheap flophouses where day laborers can get a tiny room for as little as 750 yen (US$7.50) per night. But even the grubbiest parts of Nishinari feel more down-at-the-heel and less like a ghetto. They are very safe by the standards of any Western ghetto. Assaults on visitors to the area are very unlikely; street robberies even more so.

Airin has, however, experienced infrequent rioting, fueled in one form or another by anger against the state. In the 1960s and '70s, the area often experienced several outbreaks of rioting in a single year. In the 1980s major unrest became more sporadic but there were still periods of intense disturbances. Stephen Weisman reported for the *New York Times* on a week of rioting in October 1990:

> For five nights last week, 2,500 police officers battled as many as 1,500 rock-throwing rioters in Airin, a seedy neighborhood of Osaka. Several buildings, including the rail depot, were burned, at least 55 people were arrested and about 200 injured in the worst rioting in Japan in nearly 20 years. The violence has subsided, but residents say it can recur because nothing has been done about the police harassment and corruption that is at the heart of their grievances. "The police treat us like garbage," said Masaru Kikuchi, a 46-year-old part-time construction worker. "Whenever someone gets drunk, he gets slapped in the face or arrested. They pick us up for gambling, but they never arrest the gangsters who are running the gambling dens."

Though the most recent riot, in 2008, was a relatively harmless affair, parts of Nishinari retain an edgy, socially deprived atmosphere. The yakuza remain strong, and drugs can be bought easily on the street. When Mr. Hashimoto made the journey back to his home turf, he knew he would quickly find a dealer. He told the court that he paid 30,000 yen (US$300) to an Iranian dealer for three bags of methamphetamine powder, which he dissolved and injected. "I took one bag, then another, and then another." The drug didn't have the desired effect, though: instead of making him feel happy, it just gave him a headache. And it gave him a surge of guilt. He got into his car and drove back to Matsumoto City. On the return journey he began to dwell on what he had just done; he hadn't been involved in criminality for almost two decades.

"I really regretted it," he said. "I went into the Matsumoto police station and told officers that I wanted to consult with them." He confessed that he had taken the drug and was immediately arrested.

"I knew I would go straight into detention," Mr. Hashimoto said during his trial a couple of months later.

"Didn't you think of your wife and daughter?" his lawyer asked.

"It wasn't an easy decision. I sat in the police-station parking lot for about an hour, mulling it over. I thought about not being able to see my ex-wife and daughter, but I also believed handing myself in was the right thing to do." There was, he claimed, no other motive for his decision; "I just thought I should go to the police."

However, under the Japanese Constitution, the courts cannot convict a suspect "where the only proof against him or her is his or her own confession." The police sent a urine sample to be tested, and that showed positive for stimulants. Mr. Hashimoto told the court that he hoped his current situation would be a turning point in his life and that, in the future, he wanted to do "fatherly" things. "I first want to fix the depression and get mentally well. I don't want to do drugs."

His younger brother, who was also involved in housing demolition, had promised to give him work. Demolition is big business in a country where the average house is expected, according to government estimates, to last a measly 30 years, compared to 55 years in the United States and 77 years in the UK. The fear of earthquakes—about one in five of the world's larger temblors occurs in Japan—fosters a notion that houses are not going to last, and they lose value quickly. Furthermore, earthquake-proofing standards for housing have been revised roughly every 20 years in the postwar period, encouraging the belief that houses predating a particular set of revised building regulations are less safe and therefore less worthy of preservation. According to the Nomura Institute, the average house in Japan has zero value 15 years after construction. Thus, once a house is past 16 years old, it typically has a negative value. A buyer of an older house is, in effect, paying solely for the land it sits on and should receive a discount to reflect the cost of knocking the house down and disposing of the debris. Because of these circumstances, Japan is a country of relatively new homes. Government figures from 2008 showed that only 6 percent of Japan's housing stock had been built before 1960. In the United States, the figure was 31 percent in 2011, even though the US population had grown at over twice the rate of Japan in the previous fifty years, fueling demand for new houses. The construction and relatively rapid destruction of houses in Japan may be a ludicrous and environmentally destructive waste of resources, but it keeps people like Mr. Hashimoto and his younger brother in jobs.

In court, the defense lawyer was anxious to show that the offer of a job from the younger brother was not evidence that he would indulge any future failings by his elder sibling.

"If you do drugs again, will your family cut you off; is that possible?" his lawyer asked.

"Yes," replied Mr. Hashimoto. His ex-wife had visited him three times in detention, indicating her continued interest in his welfare. She testified that she would help him to find a solution to his depression, and even said she would give him a temporary place to live once he was freed from detention.

"How does your daughter feel about him moving in?" the defense lawyer asked the ex-wife.

"She is ambivalent about it, but I think it should be OK."

In their closing speeches, prosecutors invariably ask for a jail sentence and usually get it (either suspended or actual), so it was no surprise that the prosecutor asked the judge to give Mr. Hashimoto an 18-month prison term. But by the standards of prosecutorial closing statements it was soft, emphasizing that the defendant had shown remorse and admitted to his crime. Indeed, it was a measure of the harsh stance that Japan has against drugs that such a case even came to court.

Mr. Hashimoto received a jail sentence, but it was, predictably, suspended. By the day of sentencing he had already spent eight weeks in detention. The judge noted when she sentenced him that if the defendant hadn't confessed to the crime, it would never have been detected.

UNDER THREAT

In contrast, when 23-year-old Takashi Sato bellowed, "Hand over the cash!" while waving an 18-inch bar in the face of a 79-year-old worker in a Circle K convenience store in Shiojiri City, near Matsumoto, the likelihood was high that he would be caught by police. CCTV cameras captured him coming into the shop and attacking the worker, so there was a good chance that police would have been able to identify the young man. Nonetheless, as soon as he went out into the shop's parking lot, he saved them the bother. He took out his mobile phone and called the police himself. He was later charged with attempted robbery. He told investigators that he had tried to rob the store because he had run out of cash after leaving his job just days earlier. He was hungry, he said.

Mr. Sato didn't manage to get any money from the shopkeeper. Elderly Japanese men are often hardy, and can be expected to take aggressive umbrage at young men like Mr. Sato trying to terrorize their way to some quick cash.

"He was holding the bar over me, and I began to struggle with him," the shop worker said in a statement. "He fell to the ground. He looked as if he was about to hit me, but I grabbed the iron bar from him and he ran out of the shop." A daredevil response from a man just a year under 80! I learned later while making enquiries in the shop where he worked that he had been employed in convenience stores for 30 years, and had rehearsed in his mind for a moment such as this. He would, he had told coworkers, size up dodgy-looking customers in his head and categorize them into three types—those he wouldn't be able to beat; those he might take with a struggle; and those who he could beat easily. Unfortunately for Mr. Sato, the septuagenarian shop worker reckoned he was in the latter category. For his part, Mr. Sato ascribed his failure to overpower the elderly man to weakness brought on by hunger. He said he hadn't eaten for a couple of days before the attempted robbery.

The prosecutor showed Mr. Sato the bar the old man had taken from him. "Is this yours?" he asked. "It belongs to someone I know," Mr. Sato replied, acknowledging that he had used it in the crime.

The metal bar wrapped in plastic with a handle like a walking stick was then passed to the judge, who inspected it. Events leading up to the robbery represented a catalogue of misfortune for the defendant. He had been working for a small construction firm that specialized in public works such as building roads and sidewalks. But the boss, according to Mr. Sato, was a bully who had beaten him with his fists and even kicked him with steel-capped boots. Indeed, the defendant also claimed that his fear of the boss was the trigger for his decision to rob the convenience store. Days before the robbery attempt, he ran out of diesel while driving the company truck. He had no money to put anything in the tank, having spent much of his previous month's wages on the pleasures offered by hostess bars.

He called his boss, who, according to the defendant, was enraged that he wasn't able to bring back the truck. He claimed the boss roared down the phone, "I will kill you!"

"Did you take the death threat seriously?" his lawyer asked him.

"Yes," Mr. Sato answered. After he received the alleged threat he didn't return to his job or the place he had been staying. For the next couple of days, he said, he lived in fear that his boss would come after him. He had no money to buy food, and his stomach was growling. He began to get suicidal.

"I had to escape. I had a rope and a bar in the truck. I was thinking of killing myself. I couldn't think of any other way." Mr. Sato then decided to rob the store. He described entering the shop. "I had the bar up my sleeve. There was an old man there." The old man was the 79-year-old worker, who was outside the counter restocking the refrigerated shelves with rice balls. The defendant came behind him, steel bar in hand. Sensing that he was about to be attacked, the old man continued to stock the shelves, but said aloud, without turning to face Mr. Sato: "If you assault me, the punishment for you will be severe." The defendant ignored this good advice and tried to attack the elderly shop worker.

"I fell down," the defendant explained to the judge. "The bar was taken and I ran out of there. I called the police just after I left the shop, I knew what I had done was wrong."

In the absence of any family members to take the stand on his behalf, a previous employer of the defendant gave testimony, praising him as a "hard worker." He also gave his view on the boss who had allegedly threatened to kill Mr. Sato. "He is good at his craft, but he's like someone from olden times; he raises his hand to his workers, he punches and kicks them. He is so short-tempered. I heard he hit the defendant with a wooden or aluminum rod and threatened him."

"Would it be possible for you to hire the defendant when he gets out?" the defense lawyer asked.

"Yes, I will do that," the former employer replied. He also promised to pay Mr. Sato a wage of 200,000 yen (US$2,000) per month upon release—not a bad salary for someone his age with a criminal history.

Mr. Sato's was an extreme case, but bullying in the workplace is a huge problem in Japan, as is bullying in schools and sports clubs. Shin Naito, of the Japan Institute for Labor Policy and Training, wrote in a research paper that in 2012 fully 17 percent of counseling by prefectural labor bureaus was related to bullying and harassment, compared to less than 6 percent in 2002. In 2012 bullying became "the most common" reason for complaint to the labor bureaus for the first time ever, according to Mr. Naito. Another survey, from the Ministry of Health, showed that about a quarter of workers reported having been a victim of workplace bullying in the previous three years.

Japan has coined the phrase "power harassment" (*pawahara-sumento*, usually shortened in conversation to *pawahara*) to describe the phenomenon of senior workers picking on those of

lower rank. Bullying in Japanese workplaces is usually psychological, and may include exclusion from meetings, "requests" to do
silly errands, and verbal abuse in front of other staff. But Mr. Sato's
former boss, as the court heard, allegedly preferred the physical
version, more reminiscent of the bullying of the Japanese Imperial
Army—which not only tolerated physical abuse, but encouraged
seniors to thrash new recruits—than a modern private enterprise.

The prosecutor, however, was unpersuaded about the link
between the bullying and the attempted robbery, pointing out
that the defendant had received a suspended jail sentence for
another crime, the theft of a television, just eight months before
the latest attack.

He showed the defendant a still from the CCTV camera—evi-
dential item number 42. "This is a picture of you threatening the
victim, when you were shouting that you would hit him. The last
time you were in court for stealing, you said you regretted your
crime. You said you were sorry for the trouble you'd caused. You
said you wouldn't do it again. What about this time?"

Mr. Sato had no cogent answer, but in his final words he
repeated something similar. "I won't commit a crime again. I will
look for work and will try to lead a regular life." It was too late; the
fact that he had called the police on himself would obviously stand
in his favor, but as his lawyer had suggested earlier in the hearing,
he was going to go to jail. The prosecutor sought five years' imprisonment, and Mr. Sato was sentenced to three.

The precise type of honesty shown by Mr. Sato and Mr. Hashimoto, the ex-yakuza drug taker, is unusual. Few criminals in Japan,
or anywhere else, confess to a crime before the police even know
that it has been committed. But honesty by defendants—once they
have been caught—is a striking feature of the Japanese courtroom.
Instead of admitting to as little as possible, most defendants use
the opportunity provided by the court to get things off their chest.
In the 119 cases that I followed through to sentencing in Matsumoto District Court, only two defendants used their right to be
silent for virtually the entire cross-examination, and two others
did so for a handful of questions. Of the remaining 115 defendants,

only a few tried to duck or dodge courtroom questions. Defendants usually seem to accept that an honest description of their crime is part of showing remorse.

So why are Japanese defendants so honest? It would be ridiculous to suggest that they are genetically honest—about as ridiculous as the suggestion in this American song from 1916 that Japanese are genetically sneaky:

> They meet us with a smile
> But they're working all the while
> And they're waiting just to steal our California!
> So just keep your eyes on Togo
> With his pocket full of maps
> For we've found out we can't trust the Japs!*

The reason for the courtroom honesty is surely more structural. Once a prosecutor decides to pursue a case against a criminal, it generally means that the evidence is compelling. Because the conviction rate is a shade under 99.9 percent, the accused has virtually no chance of acquittal. The main route to a lighter sentence is to show remorse. The defendant is expected to confess, write a letter of apology and a separate letter of remorse, and pay compensation to the victim as part of a *jidan* (settlement). Some defendants go further than simply showing remorse for the crime they have been charged with; they admit to other crimes as well.

SELF-SERVICE

Kazuo Chiba was an androgynous-looking divorced 58-year-old man with a sad face. He was before the court on charges of fraud after he had ordered food in two restaurants and then left without paying. It turned out, however, that his dine-and-dashes in those eateries represented only the tip of his food fraudulence.

---

* William Helmreich, *The Things They Say Behind Your Back: Stereotypes and the Myths Behind Them* (New Brunswick: Transaction Publishers, 1984), 105.

"I did the same thing in about 18 other restaurants," he confessed to the judge. He then tilted his head back and began to reel off a list of locations in and around Matsumoto City where, in the months before his arrest, he had carried out his well-practiced scam.

"Sometimes I do it in an *izakaya* (Japanese pub), but usually it's a family restaurant," he said. He would order, eat up, and then make an excuse to nip out of the building. "I sometimes say I have to get my money from the car, or I pretend to have just received a phone call."

Mr. Chiba promised the court that he would repay the restaurants, though as he said this he wondered aloud if he would be able to remember where they were all located "because there were so many." When Mr. Chiba ate for free, he ate in style. At a Skylark family restaurant, he ordered the all-you-can-drink option for soft drinks and for soup, along with some fried noodles, scallops, a hamburger, and udon noodles. It was quite a feast; he stayed in the restaurant from 3 in the morning until 7 a.m. before he went out to "make a phone call." An employee spotted him driving out of the car park, bill unpaid.

He was charged for that crime, and for another a couple of months later when he ran up a bill of over $100 at a small *izakaya* before slipping away. Obviously a believer in the "may as well be hung for a sheep as a lamb" school of criminal thinking, Mr. Chiba enjoyed 12 dishes that night, including oyster stew, squid, and sashimi, as well as beer.

The owner's mother-in-law, who had been on duty that night and saw him leaving, was understandably angry. "I don't forgive him," she told police. "If you catch him, punish him."

At the time, Mr. Chiba was working at a steel company, but complained that he didn't have much money left from his 270,000 yen (US$2,700) monthly salary. He had a smattering of previous convictions for theft and fraud between 1982 and 2008 but was fortunate never to have been jailed. He knew that his luck was about to run out. After he was arrested, he told investigators, "I think I will go to jail, I have already had two suspended jail sentences."

"You have a type of personality that gets bored easily," the defense lawyer said to his client, suggesting he didn't have the stereotypical Japanese adversity to risk-taking. "You have an indulgent personality. You like to get drunk, you don't dislike gambling."

The trigger for Mr. Chiba's recent crimes was his separation from his wife the previous year. He had moved out of the family home in northern Japan. The judge was worried about his rootlessness. "Do you have somewhere to live?" he asked. At that moment, the only other person in the public gallery apart from me, a woman who looked to be in her 50s, put up her hand.

That judge asked aloud if she was the ex-wife.

She was. "He has somewhere to live, I have decided to move out of the home where he used to live," she said.

"You can't talk [from the public gallery]," the judge said.

"Oh, is that bad? Sorry."

The judge asked Mr. Chiba, "Did your wife visit you in detention?"

"Yes."

"Did you talk about a place to live?"

"No. This is the first I've heard of it."

Mr. Chiba's lawyer, who had already finished questioning his client in the witness box, asked to make an additional comment. "You can't think of the easy option," he scolded his client. "Places to live and work shouldn't be thought of as "easy-come." You can't think of relying again on your wife. You can't act spoiled, hoping she will help you. You have to do things properly yourself." The defendant said that he would.

The prosecutor sought two years in jail, while the defense lawyer argued for a suspended sentence. It was hard to say whether the judge found the defendant's honesty in admitting to the 18 other crimes refreshing, or whether he was dumbfounded at the frequency with which he defrauded businesses. In any case, he imprisoned Mr. Chiba for a year and six months. The restaurants would have to wait for him to repay them.

STEALING TO SURVIVE

Mitsuru Ota was another who surprised the court with his admissions. The tall, thin 60-something, hair streaked with grey, looked more like an avuncular academic than a common thief. Like Mr. Chiba, he was in court on a food-related charge. Unlike the gourmet Mr. Chiba, there were no dinners of sashimi, beer, and oyster stew for Mr. Ota. He stole basic foodstuffs from shops: he was thieving to survive. Over the previous decade he had been jailed twice for shoplifting. He was before Matsumoto District Court to answer a single charge of stealing 620 yen (US$6.20) worth of pickled vegetables, potato salad, and rice balls from a supermarket, five months after his release from prison.

"How many times have you stolen since you got out of jail?" his lawyer asked him.

"About 40 times. I resisted at first, once I got out of prison, but then I just got used to it."

"Why did you steal?"

"I was hungry."

Shoplifting is the most common form of theft in Japan; among the cases before Matsumoto District Court, the most common item shoplifted was food. Food theft, as mentioned elsewhere in this book, is not necessarily a consequence of poverty. For example, in another case before Matsumoto Summary Court, a 53-year-old divorced professional caregiver, Fumiko Suzuki, was earning 220,000 yen (US$2,200) per month, and had another 6 million yen (US$60,000) in savings when she was arrested for stealing 3,000 yen (US$30) worth of supermarket food. She told the judge she had wanted to keep her money so she wouldn't be a burden on her adult children when she got older. Similarly, neither of the two elderly food shoplifters featured in chapter 2 had financial problems.

Mr. Ota, however, stole because he had no income at all. He had tried to apply for welfare, but couldn't get past the bureaucracy, principally because he had no fixed address; he also had a problem with the requirement that welfare applicants submit a statement of assets. If you have shares or other significant assets, such as a car or even a drum kit, you will usually be told to sell those before you can claim welfare. In Mr. Ota's case, it appeared that he had assets in his name but wasn't able to access them for a reason that wasn't explained.

"Have you family or friends you can rely on?" he was asked.

"No; not now." There was obviously more to Mr. Ota's family background than met the eye, but he wasn't asked—nor did he volunteer—how he had reached his stage in life apparently without a single friend or relative he could count on. He had already served time in prison for theft.

"How was jail the last time?" his lawyer asked.

"I don't ever want to return."

"How was homelessness?"

"It was tough."

The judge was visibly sympathetic. He advised the defendant on reapplying for social welfare once he was released, but added, "This time you will have to go to jail; it can't be helped." Mr. Ota was sentenced to 14 months.

When it comes to honesty, Japan is a contradictory society. Honesty is a prized social virtue in everyday business and social life, in the sense that if a person makes a commitment to do something, they are expected to honor it without delay or excuse. Aside from ample anecdotal evidence, there is also much field research testifying to the honesty of the average Japanese.

For example, in his book *Law in Everyday Japan*, US academic Mark West describes a research project in which he dropped 100 phones and 20 wallets with the equivalent of $20 inside in Tokyo's Shinjuku commercial district. Fully 95 percent of the phones and 85 percent of the wallets, with cash intact, were handed in. The same experiment in midtown Manhattan in New York resulted in a 77 percent return rate for phones and a 30 percent return rate for wallets with US$20 intact (a further 10 percent of the wallets were handed in, but the cash had been taken). Professor West repeated the experiment in front of a New York grocery store catering mainly to Japanese expatriates; this resulted in a commendable 84 percent return rate for the phones and a 60 percent return rate for the cash.

TOLERABLE DISHONESTY

While Japan may be an extraordinarily honest society when it comes to personal integrity, at a wider level, intellectual honesty and straight talking are often neither expected nor demanded. Neighboring China and the two Koreas frequently lambaste senior government figures for attempting to underplay or even deny wartime atrocities such as the sexual slavery of thousands of foreign women sanctioned by the Japanese military during World War II—even though Japan has officially apologized for the forced wartime prostitution.

There are many recent examples of an establishment apparently comfortable with its own brazen intellectual dishonesty. Take whaling, for example: Although Japan signed an international moratorium on whaling in 1986, it continued to hunt whales. For years, Japan's government argued its case internationally, and with a straight face, that it wasn't breaching the moratorium because it was killing whales for "research purposes." But it turned out that there wasn't much research involved in whaling research. The International Court of Justice ruled in March 2014 that the "research excuse" was just an excuse, and that during a six-year period from 2005 to 2011, when Japan killed 3,600 Minke whales under its Antarctic research program, the country could point to only two papers published in academically respected journals arising from the whale haul. And even those two papers, the Court of Justice noted in its judgment, did not relate to the whaling program's objectives.

Then there is the lie of Japan's army. Under its constitution, which was written by American occupiers after World War II, Japan isn't allowed to have an army. It's there in black and white— Article 9 baldly states:

> Aspiring sincerely to an international peace based on justice and order, the Japanese people forever renounce

war as a sovereign right of the nation and the threat or use of force as means of settling international disputes. To accomplish the aim of the preceding paragraph, land, sea, and air forces, as well as other war potential, will never be maintained. The right of belligerency of the state will not be recognized.

It couldn't be clearer: it is unconstitutional for Japan to keep an air force, or land and sea forces. Yet Japan, without amending its constitution, has very strong and expensively assembled armed forces, including F-15 fighter jets, Aegis destroyers, Hawk missiles, and around 230,000 soldiers. The Supreme Court has never ruled directly on the constitutionality of its army, but in a 1959 case relating to an extension of a US airfield, it said, "It is indisputable that, as an act of exercising its proper powers as a nation, Japan is allowed to take self-defense measures that are necessary for maintaining its own peace and security and ensuring its existence." Officially, Japan calls its army the Self-Defense Forces (SDF), though Prime Minister Shinzo Abe controversially slipped up in 2015 when he accidentally referred to the SDF as Japan's "military." Even many ordinary Japanese bristle when the term "army" is used to describe the SDF—even though that, for better or worse, is patently what it is.

There is also the gambling lie. Most types of gambling are illegal in Japan. In 2011, 903 people were arrested for the crime of gambling—more than the number of arrests for rape or arson. In addition there were 211 men (no women) serving time in Japanese prisons who were punished for gambling while incarcerated. Both frequent and infrequent gamblers can be punished under the law.

Article 186 (1) of the Penal Code says that "A person who habitually gambles shall be punished by imprisonment with work for not more than 3 years." Article 185 says, "A person who gambles shall be punished by a fine of not more than 500,000 yen or a petty fine; provided, however, that the same shall not apply to a person who bets a thing which is provided for momentary entertainment." Momentary entertainment is interpreted as light gambling not involving cash payment. Legal exceptions to the no-gambling laws are state-controlled lotteries, as well as state-licensed cycling, boat racing, and horse racing. But the law doesn't allow for gambling using pachinko machines (which, as mentioned earlier, are something of a cross between pinball and slot machines, which punters sit in front of, putting in silver balls that they have bought). Pachinko machines are controlled so a player can't lose too much in a short space of time. According to government estimates, pachinko generated around 19 trillion yen (US$190 billion) in gross revenue in 2012, and has 11 million regular players. Another six million are infrequent players, meaning that about one in eight Japanese plays pachinko. According to figures from pachinko-machine manufacturer Sega Sammy, there are more than 12,000 pachinko parlors nationwide, with over four and a half million machines. Even in food-crazy Japan, people spend more on pachinko than they do on dining out.

Pachinko parlors get around the gambling ban by offering token prizes that can be cashed in at a shop that is either attached to the pachinko building or very close by. Just as official Japan pretends its whaling is "research" and its army is not an "army," it pretends that pachinko is not gambling.

These unrelated examples show that, despite the striking honesty of the Japanese people, it can be considered acceptable to say one thing and do another. In that sense the description of Japan as "honest" is arguable. But at an individual level in everyday Japanese life, honesty is valued and expected across all levels of society. Here is one example. In late 2013, I traveled to Namie district in Fukushima Prefecture. Of the 22,000 who once lived there; only a local farmer remained, defying the evacuation order issued after the meltdown at the nearby Daichi nuclear plant in March 2011. Residents were not permitted to live in Namie town but it could be accessed during the day through a cursory checkpoint. The houses and main street were as they had been left on the day of the earthquake and tsunami that flooded the nuclear plant: cars and bicycles remained outside buildings, and some buildings remained knocked down by the earthquake. While locals had been back to collect valuables from their homes, it was clear that there were still things worth stealing in Namie. In any other country there would surely have been a visible security presence to protect the homes from looters. But there was neither security nor looting.

Namie wasn't the only tsunami-hit town in Japan left apparently unmolested by opportunistic thievery. Five months after the tsunami, police reported that 5,700 security safes containing a total of 2.3 billion yen (US$23 million) in cash had been handed in to police by citizens, all of them apparently washed away with the buildings that once housed them. One safe held 100 million yen (US$1 million) in cash. The return of the safes was widely reported by a surprised and impressed foreign media, whose reaction was in turn reported by a Japanese media pleased to see foreigners reporting on Japanese honesty.

Research shows, however, that this honesty doesn't necessarily come from altruism. If Japanese are honest, it is because they are kept honest by law as well as custom. As Professor Mark West points out in *Law in Everyday Japan*, picking up lost property and failing to hand it in to police—or, if found in a building, a security guard—within seven days is a crime punishable by up to one year in jail. After larceny, he notes, such property embezzlement is the most prosecuted crime among under-20s. The law is the stick; the carrot is that if the lost property is claimed, the finder gets a fee of 5 to 20 percent of the value of the goods. "If no one claims the object in six months and two weeks," the law states, "the object is returned to the finder." The agreed finder fee for claimed items is usually 10 percent, so the person who handed in the $1 million in the safe mentioned above should at least get a $100,000 windfall—or, if the owner can't be found, the full amount. If the person hadn't handed it in and was found out, he or she could face criminal prosecution.

Likewise, there is a real incentive for courtroom honesty. Several lawyers estimated to me that where a defendant shows no remorse he can expect his prison term to be lengthened by approximately 15 percent.

LOW DOWN

Even those who do the most despicably dishonest things, such as taking a child's pocket money, can have moments of courtroom honesty. Forty-five-year-old Hiroshi Ueda stole four rice balls, two sports drinks, a cola drink, and two pieces of fried chicken from a supermarket. He appeared before Matsumoto Summary Court charged with one count of theft. The goods he stole were worth 720 yen ($7.20). But he was anxious to admit to much more. Unprompted, he told the judge that he had in fact shoplifted more than 15 times in the two months before he was caught. In fact, the judge would have already known this, because in his statement to prosecutors after he was arrested, Mr. Ueda confessed to a litany of crimes, including the theft of clothes on one occasion, a radio cassette player on another, and an umbrella on still another.

The now-unemployed former newspaper deliveryman cut a lonely and pathetic figure, with no family member present in court to support him. His sister had previously given him a place to stay when he was down on his luck, but she had ordered him to leave the house after he had stolen her child's pocket money. Mr. Ueda was quite overweight by Japanese standards, and had a peculiarly shapeless form. He looked and sounded entirely socially inept. He sat in court wearing checked green trousers, nervously clasping and unclasping his hands during the court session.

If Hiroshi Ueda had paid for the basket of food items that he was caught red-handed stealing, it would have been a bargain. Japan has an undeserved reputation for being very expensive. The fact is that low-end hotels are reasonably cheap (around US$50 for a single, even in Tokyo); public transport is affordable (though bullet trains are expensive); and food in most restaurants is very cheap.

Like Mr. Ota—who, as recounted earlier in this chapter, was jailed for stealing 620 yen worth of food—Mr. Ueda hated prison. "The food was bad," he told the judge. He shared other things in common with Mr. Ota, as well: his social isolation and an absence of friends. And like Mr. Ota, he was unable to apply for social welfare because of his lack of an address. He sometimes slept in Internet cafes.

"Why did you steal?" his lawyer asked.

"I was hungry."

"How long had it been since your last meal?"

"Around three or four days. I didn't have anything to eat at all during that time. I only had 43 yen (43 cents) in my pocket when I was caught."

"You knew it was wrong."

"I was so hungry I couldn't stand it anymore."

"Did you have anywhere to live?"

"No."

"Did you look for a house?"

"I went to City Hall; they said there was no place."

"Can you return to your younger sister's?"

"No."

"Why did you leave?"

"I took the eldest boy's pocket money."

"Why?"

"To buy food and cigarettes."

"Did you repay the money?"

"Yes."

The judge asked Mr. Ueda, "Do you have any hobbies?"

"Idols," he replied.

"Like [pop group] AKB48?" the judge asked.

"Yes," Mr. Ueda answered.

"You like them," the judge said.

"Yes."

AKB48 is a mass-marketed pop group with a pool of over 100 members (it was originally 48, hence its name) from whom acts are chosen. They are all girls—mostly teenagers, but some as young as 12—who prance coquettishly on stage singing uncomplicated pop songs, appealing simultaneously to an audience of older men as well as young girls. They are a phenomenon in Japan, managing over a half a billion dollars in revenue from DVDs and CDs between 2011 and 2013. The band is famous for its level of interaction with fans, especially its "handshake meetings"—events where fans line up for a seconds-long audience with a member. Tickets for certain events are included along with the band's CDs, so to meet an AKB "idol," fans often have to buy a CD. Some buy multiple CDs so they can line up repeatedly at the same event. In May 2014, Asahi TV featured an interview with a 38-year-old self-employed male who had bought boxes of AKB48 CDs solely for the meet-and-greet tickets. He estimated he had so far spent about 20 million yen (US$200,000) on CDs alone. When he spoke about AKB48 he used the word "we," as if he is part of their success—and in a way, he is. It wasn't difficult to imagine the lonely and friendless Mr. Ueda similarly enjoying his AKB48 fantasy, taking some comfort in watching a group ever eager to promote a message that their fans really matter.

The prosecutor called for a 14-month jail sentence. The defense lawyer called for mercy, saying that the theft of 720 yen worth of goods shouldn't merit a heavy penalty. But Mr. Ueda was jailed for one year—a less severe punishment than it could have been, considering he had been jailed on two previous occasions. His honesty in admitting to 14 other crimes besides the one he was charged with had most likely helped, rather than hindered him. The judge noted Mr. Ueda's remorse in sentencing.

Like most of those convicted in Matsumoto courts, Mr. Ueda accepted his fate with equanimity. He bowed to the judge, the guards put his handcuffs back on, and he was taken downstairs, out a back door and away in a prison van. No one from his family was there to see him off.

MOTHER KILLERS

KANAKO MIBU

Who knows what 86-year-old Kanako Mibu was thinking as the blows rained down on her on the afternoon of August 26, 2013? Was she wondering what she had done wrong? Was she thinking, "Why does my son hate me so much?" Did she beg him to stop as she tried to block the blows with her frail wrists? Did she curse him? Did she believe he wasn't going to stop until she was dead? He did kill her, but she didn't die that day. She passed away nine days later.

He beat her everywhere on her body, using his fists and an aluminum crutch. Though her son, Mitsutaka Mibu, was a one-legged 56-year-old man in very poor health, he was still much stronger than his octogenarian mother, who measured just 141 centimeters (4 feet 7½ inches tall) and weighed 31 kilos (68 pounds) at the time of death. The autopsy report said she had suffered fractures and external and internal bleeding, with some bruises measuring over 20 centimeters (9 inches) in length. She had wounds on her legs, back, arms, chest, knees, and head. She had lost 40 percent of the 2.4 liters (2.5 quarts) of blood that should have been circulating in her tiny body.

Seven months later, in Matsumoto District Court, her only son was on trial for injury causing death. He offered excuses for his behavior, but he also spoke honestly, painting a portrait of himself that was repulsive and self-incriminating, but also human. He wasn't, it seemed, in any way mentally unstable. He was known as a sociable man, with a big ready smile; his interests were animals and singing—he had been in chorus groups since he was a youth. But in the months before he killed his mother, the former restaurant manager changed from a man with no history of domestic violence into a serial abuser of the woman with whom he had lived for all of his 56 years. Mr. Mibu admitted to his crime. He said there were mitigating circumstances, but he didn't flinch from describing the brutality of what he had done.

His trial would be brief. The average district court trial in Japan in 2010 took almost three months and 2.5 hearings. Mr. Mibu's trial case, however, was to be heard by six lay judges as well as three professional judges, which meant that it would be held over a short period; lay judges can't be expected to surrender weeks or months of their lives to decide on a defendant's fate. The first hearing was on a Tuesday and the judgment and sentencing delivered the following Tuesday.

There was only one witness: Mr. Mibu's wife, Setsuko, also 56 years old. Called by the prosecution, she looked an unassuming person, understatedly dressed. She spoke with a small voice, but she gave her testimony with rare eloquence. She was sympathetic to her husband, offering insight into the stresses of looking after an elderly person without minimizing what he had done.

She had known that her husband was beating his mother. She saw the evidence of his assaults when she changed her mother-in-law's diaper. "She was often bruised. The bruises would come and go," she said. On a couple of occasions she heard a commotion in her mother-in-law's room but arrived after the fact. She was an eyewitness to only two beatings.

"How did he beat her?" the prosecutor asked.

"He hit her with his fists on the face and shoulders and pulled her hair."

"What did you do?"

"I stopped it."

"How?"

"From behind. I pulled him back with both of my hands."

The second beating she witnessed was in August, weeks before her mother-in-law's death. "He hit her with a crutch," she said.

"Where?" asked the prosecutor.

"Around the face and chest."

"How many times?"

"Three times."

"What did you do?"

"I stopped it."

Mrs. Mibu told the court that to prevent further attacks, she tried to not leave her husband alone with his mother. But there were times when this wasn't possible, because she had other responsibilities. Aside from looking after her disabled husband and his mother, known as Okaasan (Mother), she also looked after her own 92-year-old mother, who lived in the same house and was never assaulted by Mr. Mibu. Mrs. Mibu was the sole carer for all three.

"Who did the cooking in the home?" the prosecutor asked.

"I did."

"Did your husband help?"

"No."

"Who cared for the victim?"

"I did."

"Did your husband help?"

"No."

Mr. Mibu was at home all day; he didn't work because of a list of medical problems. He had diabetes and heart disease, and had to undergo kidney dialysis three times a week. If he didn't get dialysis, he would die within a week, doctors had told him. He also suffered from an eye disease that would eventually make him blind. On top of that, his left leg had recently been amputated just below the knee after an infection. Apart from an extraordinarily healthy head of hair, and a relatively large physical frame for a Japanese man of his age, Mr. Mibu was a wreck—his skin had a jaundiced pallor and he looked like he hadn't had a decent night's sleep in years. His appearance was more like that of an unhealthy 66-year old than an unhealthy 56-year-old.

Mr. Mibu had not only lived with his mother all his life, but had also worked with her in the family fishmonger's shop since the age of 15, after his father had been diagnosed with terminal cancer. Once he graduated from high school, he worked full-time at the shop, which was located in the city of Ida, south of Matsumoto. Years later, Mr. Mibu and his mother ran a restaurant together, selling basic Japanese meals. "They didn't have a particularly bad relationship," the defendant's wife claimed in court. But they didn't seem to have a good one, either. Mrs. Mibu said that when they were running the restaurant together they had barely communicated beyond relaying customer orders. "It was a mother-son relationship," she said, by way of explanation.

The defendant, however, told the court that his relationship with his mother was loveless. "My mother saw me as an obstacle. There was no kindness, there was no affection."

"Concretely, what do you mean?" his lawyer asked.

"Well, I have a body that tires easily, and when I used to come home from work, my mother would ask me to do the shopping or some other chore. But I'd often be very tired, and would tell her to let me rest for a while, that I would do it later. She wouldn't like that and she would say something like, 'Don't bother to do it, then,' in a snarky tone."

"But isn't it natural that someone you live with will ask you to do work around the house?" his lawyer continued.

"Yes, but honestly, my body would really get tired quickly, and when I asked my mother to consider my fatigue, she didn't do it."

Presumably not persuaded that a mother who reacted sharply when her son refused to do some shopping showed a significant lack of love, a judge pushed Mr. Mibu to give another example of what he meant when he said that his mother lacked kindness.

The defendant replied with one example. "My mother often opened mail that was addressed to me."

"Were you violent toward her then?" the defense lawyer asked.

"No," Mr. Mibu answered.

The violence came later, years later. The reason may have been deep-rooted, but the trigger was straightforward. The old lady had difficulty controlling her bowels and had a hip problem that meant she needed a walker to get around. She was very slow in moving to the toilet, and sometimes she didn't reach it in time. She began to soil her clothes, and after some family discussion, she began wearing adult diapers in April 2013, five months before she died.

The problem was that she hated wearing the diapers, and she sometimes took them off. She could have been suffering from undiagnosed Alzheimer's disease or some other mental illness, but to Mr. Mibu his mother was merely being selfish and irresponsible, creating a fecal mess that his wife had to clean up. He was infuriated. One day he confronted her. He usually didn't go anywhere near his mother's room. But his wife had told him it smelled, and that Mother had been leaving out fewer clothes for her laundry than usual. Mr. Mibu suspected, correctly, that his mother hadn't been wearing her diaper as she had promised, and was hiding soiled clothes in her wardrobe. He went to her room, opened the wardrobe door, and pointed to a heap of smelly garments.

"I said, 'What's this?'" he told the court. "She answered that it wasn't hers, and that she didn't know anything about it."

"How did you respond?" his lawyer asked.

"I told her she couldn't say she didn't know, and asked her why she didn't know. Then she said, 'It's nothing to do with you.'"

"When did it change from words to violence?" the lawyer asked.

"Just then. I got angry; I raised my hand and slapped her. Then I punched her and I pulled her hair." That was May 2013, the first time that Mitsutaka Mibu had battered his mother.

"Why did you do it?"

"She was telling lies."

"How was she telling lies?"

"She promised to wear a diaper and she didn't," he said. "I thought violence would make her understand. She was peeing in her clothes, and they were dirty. She was hiding them in the wardrobe, all piled up and smelly."

The prosecutor reminded the defendant that his mother was, in a way, correct. It had "nothing to do with him" because he contributed nothing to the care of his mother: his wife did everything.

"Who washed the dirty clothes in the closet?" the prosecutor asked.

"My wife."

"If you were worried about your wife's burden, why didn't you help with cooking and cleaning?"

"My head was strange at the time."

It is undeniable that sexism is alive and thriving in Japan. Any number of surveys show that females have very few powerful positions in politics and business. For example, the Inter-Parliamentary Union's 2014 index of women in national parliaments showed that Japan ranked 127th—52 places below Saudi Arabia and 103 below Uganda. Corporate Japan is an equally unwelcoming place for women with ambition, especially those with children: fewer than one in six department managers are female.

In the home, Japanese women typically do virtually all the housework, spending more hours on it than the OECD average for females, according to a 2011 survey of 26 OECD countries, while their husbands do 68 percent less than the average OECD man. But although the man usually has his meals served and his socks washed—it's somewhat unusual to meet a Japanese husband who cooks regularly at home, or does laundry—he has little say in how the house is run and little control over its finances. Wives typically rule the domestic roost. A man's salary is handed over to the wife, and the husband gets *okozukai*, or pocket money, each month—an average of 38,457 yen (US$384), according to a 2013 survey by Shinsei Bank, from which he has to pay for his incidentals.

Roles, then, are strictly defined. Wives run the home and often work at a part-time job, which usually pays at or close to the minimum wage (this, at time of writing, is 664 to 869 yen, or US$6.64 to 8.69 per hour, depending on the prefecture). The men are the money makers, and they are expected to work—no excuses.

In the Mibu household, however, the man did not work either inside or outside the house. He had been unemployed for close to a decade, though he believed that he was capable of some sort of work. He told the court that once the justice system had finished with him he planned to set up a home for unwanted cats and dogs.

His wife, on the other hand, came across as a self-sacrificing Trojan. At one point she was working full time by day and also had a part-time job three evenings a week. Mr. Mibu needed her far more than she needed him. Despite the imbalance in their relationship, she was utterly loyal to him. And her husband obviously respected and appreciated her—probably even loved her. He cried a lot during his trial; sometimes his words were hard to understand because he was crying so much. But his tears were almost invariably not for his mother—he merely hung his head during the prosecutor's description of the wounds he had inflicted on her— but for his wife, who had had to clean up his mother's feces and urine. He frequently apologized to his wife in court for having left such a dirty job to her.

After Mr. Mibu's first attack on his mother in May 2013, he began to beat her regularly. "How often did you hit her?" his lawyer asked.

"Every four or five days. I usually used a crutch," he said. "She often soiled her clothes. She wouldn't listen to me, so I went to her room and used one of my crutches to hit her."

The prosecutor emphasized repeatedly that when the defendant attacked his mother, he went to her room using crutches that were for outside use. The implication was that Mr. Mibu was deliberately insulting the old woman: in Japanese culture it's considered disgusting to carry outside dirt into the house, whether it is stuck to the soles of one's shoes or the base of a crutch. That's why Japanese houses have slippers at the entrance for visitors and residents to change into.

"Where did you strike her with the crutch?" the prosecutor asked.

"On the arms and legs, mostly. August 26 was the strongest attack yet; until then they weren't so strong," he said.

The defendant's wife didn't witness that beating because she was outside cutting the grass, but she arrived on the scene soon afterwards.

"I heard my husband shouting. I went into the house and found my husband sitting in the kitchen. I went to Mother's room. She was on the bed; her wrists were swollen and her left wrist was bleeding. I went to get the first-aid kit. I asked my husband what he had done."

"What did he say?" asked the prosecutor.

"He didn't reply. I bandaged her up and put a cooling patch on her wrists."

"How was her leg?"

"There was a big mark on her thigh, though I only noticed it in the evening when I was changing her diaper. I asked my husband why he hit her. He told me that he didn't know. I told him to never hit her again and not to go near her room. He said he understood."

The defendant's wife told the court she had advised her mother-in-law to go to the hospital, but the old woman refused. She then consulted with her husband, who said that if Mother didn't want to go to the hospital, she didn't have to go.

The old woman had a longstanding dislike of hospitals, but she was also protecting her son: a visit to a hospital by a battered elderly woman would trigger a police inquiry. The tendency for elderly victims and their family members to remain silent about abuse is as common in Japan as it is elsewhere. Of the 25,636 reports of suspected elder abuse in Japan in 2011, only 11 percent came from the person who was experiencing the abuse, according to the Health Ministry; only 12 percent of whistle-blowing calls came from relatives. Mrs. Mibu admitted to the court that she had thought about calling the authorities, but when she considered how difficult it would be for her husband in prison, her resolve, she said, faded.

The old woman's decision not to go to a hospital for treatment probably contributed to her premature death. She had been in good health, apart from the hip problem, and she was an exceptionally good eater for a woman her age. But after the beating on August 26, that would change.

"Let me ask about the day after the severe beating. Did she eat?" the prosecutor asked Mrs. Mibu.

"No, she said she didn't need anything."

The day after that, she only consumed half of her normal intake. Within five days of the beating, she was eating just a fourth as much as usual.

"How was she?" asked the prosecutor.

"She had no energy. She had no appetite, and just ate one or two spoons of custard pudding, a couple of spoons of miso soup, and a small bit of tofu and egg."

"So she wasn't really eating?"

"No."

The old woman was already on the path out of this life, but her son hadn't finished with her yet. On September 1, 2013—six days after the attack that he described to the court as "the strongest yet"—he went back to her room.

"Why did you go?" the prosecutor asked.

"Maybe it was worry," he said. He knew from his wife that his mother hadn't been eating much. He asked his mother how she was feeling. Who knows what he was thinking at this stage? Did he think his mother would respond breezily, kindly, as if he hadn't savagely beaten her less than a week before?

"It's none of your business," she said. "Get out, get out."

They exchanged some unpleasantries, culminating in one of the most hurtful phrases in Japan's armory of insults. "Go away and die," the son said. The mother, according to her son, replied in kind. "You die," she said.

"I was angry," he told the court.

"So you went to the entrance area of the house to get the crutches?" asked the prosecutor.

"Yes."

"You left the wheelchair that you normally use inside the house by the main doorway and went back to her room on the crutches, which are for outside use."

"Yes. I went into her room and hit her hands, her thighs, her shins, her chest, her back. She was sitting; she fell to the side when I hit her on the chest, then I hit her on the shoulder," he said.

"How many times did you hit her on the shoulder?"

"I don't remember. At least once, but I don't remember."

"After she fell, did you hit her on the thigh with a crutch?"

"Yes."

"How many times?"

"Several times."

"Does several mean two or three times, or four or five times?"

"Around two or three times."

The honesty was striking. The defendant answered the questions in an apparently truthful fashion. Not all defendants in Japan do likewise, but as mentioned elsewhere in this book, the equivocation and denial by the guilty that are commonplace in Western courtrooms are generally absent in Japan. Defendants like Mr. Mibu know that judges will punish them more unless they repent and take responsibility for their crimes, and mostly they do. Mr. Mibu gave details of incidents that were self-incriminating, which the judges would otherwise not have known about. If he hadn't told them, for example, that he beat his mother every four or five days over a period of months, the judges might never have known anything about it. Mr. Mibu described the manner of his attacks in detail, adding nothing to leaven the grim narrative of a son who became addicted to beating up a mother who couldn't fight back. Before the trial, he went with investigators to his home and reenacted the attacks in his mother's room, using a crutch similar to the murder weapon and a mannequin as the victim. Investigators supervised him beating the mannequin with the crutch and measured the power of his blows. The crutch weighed less than 2.2 pounds, but the force of one of his blows was measured at 185 pounds of pressure, and another at 121 pounds.

Throughout the trial, the crutches—the weapons that had been used to beat Kanako Mibu—were left leaning against the court clerk's wooden desk. The prosecutor took them and showed them to the defendant.

"Are these the ones you used?"

"Yes."

"On August 26 and September 1?"

"I can't tell which one it was, but it was one of them."

The defendant accepted responsibility for his mother's death, but said he hadn't meant to kill her. "When I got the crutches after my leg amputation, I thought they were well made and strong. I thought if you got hit with one of these it would hurt. And so I hit myself, but it didn't hurt at all. The crutches are strong, but if you hit someone they don't hurt. That's why I began to hit her using a crutch."

"Your wife testified that the bruises on the victim were very big," the defense lawyer said, "but you're saying it's not painful to be hit with the crutch?"

"Yes, I thought they were light. I didn't think I would bruise her with them."

Mr. Mibu didn't see his mother again after the final beating on September 1, 2013. But his wife went about her caring duties as usual. "I got up and went to Mother on September 4, like always, to change her diaper, and she was unconscious," she said. An ambulance was called, and the woman was taken to the local hospital. Within an hour she was pronounced dead.

"Why did she die?" the prosecutor asked Mrs. Mibu.

"Because of the beating on August 26, and because of the stress from that; she just got weaker."

"Did she speak to you about that attack?"

"No."

"The beating came from her own son. What do you think about that?" the prosecutor asked.

"It must have been such suffering for her."

"Did she ever criticize her son to you, even after the incidents?" a judge asked.

"No," replied Mrs. Mibu.

Given the circumstances, the family didn't publicize the old lady's death. Only eight people came to her wake, and four to her funeral. It was the saddest of deaths and the saddest of send-offs. Few people in the small town of Matsukawa (population 13,374), where the Mibus lived, appeared to know the family. None that I spoke to knew them well, presumably because they were relatively new to the area. But people were not without sympathy for the defendant. "It's really difficult taking care of someone that age," said one woman. "He must have had a lot of stress." A man from the town said, "He really bullied her, but he had his own problems, too, his own health problems."

There is much understanding of the difficulties of caring for the elderly in a country that has traditionally fostered a sense of obligation toward old people. Living with older relatives is a proud tradition in Japan, where about one in every six households is made up of an elderly person or persons living with their adult children and/or grandchildren.

One's duty to the elderly is reinforced in schools and through children's stories. Around 25 miles from Matsumoto District Court is a mountain known locally as Obasuteyama, which literally means "mountain where old women are disposed of." According to folklore, when an old woman had become a caregiving burden she was carried up the mountain on her son's back and left there to die. Different versions of the story are told in other parts of Japan, and its roots are in a practice that may have existed but was not widespread. Nonetheless, the retelling of this morality tale in picture books provokes children to think about how the elderly should be treated.

In modern Japan there may be no granny disposal, but the question of what to do with older relatives is much debated. Whether the issue is rural depopulation, increased immigration, public finances, crime, future market opportunities, the pension system, the future of the housing market—or indeed, the future of the entire economy—*koureikashakai*, the aging society, is often a central issue in the debate. The OECD's estimate that 39 percent of Japan's population will be over 65 by 2050 is frequently quoted in the media; less quoted is its estimate that 16.5 percent will be over 80 years old. A country where one person in six will be an octogenarian has focused government minds, entailing—as it will—enormous public expense.

"The biggest item of spending used to be infrastructure such as roads; now it's welfare," a senior health official at Matsumoto City government told me. "Thirty years ago, 10 percent of our budget was spent on welfare, but now it's 40 percent." The city's two public nursing homes are full, so the city encourages people to care for their elderly relatives at home if possible.

Dealing with dementia is a national priority. The Department of Health reckons that about one in 10 over-65s suffers from senility. One of the department's initiatives is to deploy dementia specialists to more than 4,000 nursing-care teams to work with family caregivers as well as the elderly. "Appropriate diagnoses" and "support" are some of the buzzwords the Health Ministry has used in its drive to help the senile and those who care for them. Very worthy stuff, but too late for Mitsutaka Mibu and his wife, who got no public help dealing with an elderly woman who was likely in the early stages of senility. There was apparently no respite care available, and the old woman didn't wish to attend a day service for the elderly.

Toward the end of his trial, the defendant was asked by a judge, "You said in your testimony that you should have shown your mother kindness. What did that mean?"

"I should have talked to her; maybe she was lonely. Conversation is number one for old people, isn't it? It's the time they enjoy most," Mr. Mibu replied.

In his closing statement, the lead prosecutor said that the defendant had committed a crime of hideous violence. He called for a five-year prison sentence. The defense lawyer argued as best he could for his client, pointing out that the defendant had no prior criminal record, he was sick, he was sorry, and he had cooperated with the police. He asked the court to consider a suspended sentence. His wife, the very embodiment of marital fidelity, who was married to a sick, unemployed man, added her support. She said she wouldn't divorce him. Once he got out, she told the court, they would live together. "We will rebuild our lives; we will repair relations with the neighbors [that had been soured by the killing]; we will make amends for the wrongdoing; we will continue together."

As always, the defendant had the final word before sentencing. "I am deeply sorry for a profound crime," he said. "From my heart, I feel sorry for my mother. I am full of remorse. And for the damage I have caused to those around me. I am very sorry."

He was in tears as he made his final statement, but the judges didn't betray any emotion. Nine judges in total—four females (three of whom were lay judges) and five males (three of whom were lay judges)—all just looked at him.

Five days later, Mr. Mibu was pushed in his wheelchair into Matsumoto District Court for sentencing. The presiding judge, Toshihiro Honma, walked into the courtroom. Moments later the lay judges arrived in order, from one to six, and finally, two younger assistant judges entered. Mr. Mibu struggled out of his wheelchair to stand and bow to the bench, but the judge gestured for him to sit. He read the verdict: four years and six months in jail. The crime was of a type that could have warranted double that penalty, the judge said, but they took into account the defendant's remorse, his lack of criminal record, his cooperation with investigators, and his disability.

In 2005, Japan's parliament passed a law to combat elder abuse. As its title suggests, the Act on the Prevention of Elderly Abuse and Support for Attendants of Elderly Persons also represented a recognition that caregivers do a difficult and stressful job and are themselves in need of support. Many carers are in a challenging position because social and cultural pressure, especially outside of the major cities, means that the eldest son and/or his wife are generally expected to care for his parents, whether he gets along with them or not. The eldest son may have received most or all of any family assets in a usually unspoken deal: "You get the family home, but you also get the granny," which means that siblings may be less willing to help him out. And sisters in particular are often less able to assist, because once they marry they "belong" to their in-laws' household in a manner that doesn't exist in the West.

Mr. Mibu's case was unusual because his violence resulted in his mother's death. The number of elderly actually killed by relatives is low, fluctuating between 21 and 32 in recent years, amounting to 3 to 5 percent of all homicides. But in many ways, his story is unexceptional. Of the more than 25,000 cases of reported elder abuse in 2011, two-thirds involved physical abuse. Psychological abuse allegedly existed, often along with physical assault, in one-third of cases, and economic abuse—family members helping themselves to an elderly person's cash without their consent—was a factor in one-quarter of allegations. Just one in 200 cases involved sexual abuse. The typical abusers were sons, responsible in 41 percent of reported cases. Husbands made up 17 percent of abusers; 16 percent were daughters, 5 percent were wives, and 2 percent were sons-in-law. Most victims were over 80 years old, and just over three-quarters of them were female. The representative picture of elderly abuse in Japan is of a son beating and psychologically abusing a mother who is over 80. A man just like Mr. Mibu—and also like Takeshi Tomioka.

TEFUKO TOMIOKA

Takeshi Tomioka was just one year junior to Mr. Mibu, and lived only about seven miles away from him. It was extraordinary that in a country of 127 million people, with an average of about 25 deaths from elder abuse each year, two such crimes should have happened in one small and beautiful corner of southern Nagano Prefecture within the space of nine months.

Mr. Tomioka killed his mother because he hated her; he had for decades. His mother, Tefuko, was 91 years old when she was killed. She had lived through three imperial reigns, survived the chronic food shortages of the final period of World War II and early postwar Japan, and experienced the economic go-go decades from the 1950s through to the 1980s while remaining, according to her son, semi-literate and unwilling even to learn how to use a phone. She lost her husband in 2005; she then had her own life pummeled out of her on January 16, 2013. On a snowy night in a place called Nanakubo, which is known for the quality of its apples and pears, her only son punched and kicked her so ferociously that her bones were fractured or broken in 33 places.

Her son was a hardworking and hard-drinking man who had trained as a carpenter. As a young man, he worked in different prefectures before moving back to Nanakubo to raise a family. He got married at 21 to a woman with whom he had little in common.

Every evening he drank *sake*; when he was drunk, one of his daughters told the court, he liked one-way discussion.

"He is hard to understand when he is drinking," she said, "He talks about economics and things that we don't know about."

A fondness for "lecturing," his wife called it. She had a poor relationship with her husband. "We really have nothing to talk about, so we stopped bothering," she said, adding that they slept in separate bedrooms.

Like Mr. Mibu, Takeshi Tomioka didn't speak with his mother if he could help it. Both men were the youngest child and the only boy in the family. Both were spoiled, and did no cooking or cleaning at home. Both said they had felt unloved by their mothers since they were young. And both were left looking after a mother whom they detested.

Mr. Tomioka's biggest problem with his mother, it seemed, was a lack of a bond. "My mother's love for my sisters was strong, but her attitude to me was that she never accepted me. It is my great sadness," he said. He also told the court that although he found much about his mother, who was senile, irritating, there was one particular reason why he hated her.

"I had kidney disease in fourth grade," he explained. "The doctor said that I shouldn't have salty food, but my mother still gave me miso soup, which is salty. My mother said that if she diluted the miso soup it would be OK, but it wasn't, and that's why I got sick."

This story was apparently a familiar one at home. "He hasn't liked his mother since he was a child," his wife told the court. "He said he had to go to hospital because she made him eat something."

And his daughter was asked by the prosecutor, "Did your father and grandmother get on well?"

"No. My dad tried to avoid her."

"Did you ever hear why?"

"I heard about the time he had to go into hospital when he was in elementary school."

The defendant's older sister, however, dismissed his suggestion that their mother had deliberately sought to make him sick. "The defendant says that your mother fed him salty food as a child and that damaged his kidneys," the prosecutor stated to the sister.

"It's so stupid. Why would she do that to the son she doted on? Our parents were so happy when he was born—I remember it well," she said.

There was no evidence presented in court that the defendant had any existing medical problem with his kidneys, and Mr. Tomioka looked a lean and fit man. But to him, the harm had been real, and he had nursed his grudge for 45 years. What made his complaint appear ludicrous was that, by his own admission, he drank at least three or four large glasses—roughly a liter—of Japanese sake every night. Sake is usually around 20 percent alcohol, about halfway between beer and vodka. It's a good deal stronger than the average red wine, and not something that should be consumed in such quantities if you have a kidney complaint.

The defendant also had more recent criticisms of his mother. He told the judges that she was strong-willed, and didn't really have any hobbies apart from growing vegetables in the garden. Though she was able to read *hiragana*—a simple 48-character alphabet that children usually learn from around kindergarten age—she could understand few of the roughly 2,000 kanji (Chinese characters) that are needed to read a newspaper. It was accepted by other family members that she was also difficult to live with. She annoyed them by peeping into rooms when they wanted privacy, and often talked to herself at night or in the early morning, disturbing their sleep. And she had a habit of bringing vegetables in from the garden that she tended—she was physically fit—and leaving them just inside the main door of the house.

"Was she bringing the vegetables for you and the family?" the defense lawyer asked his client.

"Yes."

"Did that annoy you?"

"They were getting in the way."

"Do you not think it was out of a sense of care for the family that that she brought in the vegetables?"

"I think she was doing what she could do as a woman in her 90s," Mr. Tomioka acknowledged.

Sometimes she would leave the vegetables on the floor of a corrugated roofed shed next to their house, which irritated the defendant because he parked his car in the shed. These all seemed trivial complaints. But if his mother annoyed him so much, why did they share the same house?

"My mother wanted us to live together. My sisters were married, so it was kind of automatic that I would look after my parents," he said.

Mr. Tomioka didn't get much by way of family assets in return for minding them. His parents gave him 5 million yen ($50,000) toward building a new house for all of them to live in. Their contribution would likely have covered about a third or a quarter of the cost of building the fashionably designed three-story wooden house, which was known locally for its bright colors and pyramid-shaped roof.

"Did you ask your parents why they lived with your brother?" the prosecutor asked the defendant's sister.

"They told me that he could look after them when they got older and weaker," she said.

It was clear from an early stage that the arrangement wasn't ideal. The three generations of the Tomioka family ate together for the first few years of life under the one roof, but then Mr. Tomioka's parents felt unwelcome at the family dinner table, so they began to have their meals separately.

"Why did your parents stop eating with you?" the defense lawyer asked the defendant.

"We wanted to have a life with our own generation," he said. "My wife continued to make food for my parents. She made the same food for them as for the rest of us, but they didn't sit down with us. They ate in their bedroom."

Even after Mr. Tomioka's father died, his mother Tefuko continued to eat in a different room, alone. "Once he passed away I thought we should eat together, but when we did that she didn't eat so much. So she went back to her room," the son said.

She must have been desperately lonely, but there was no violence at that stage. The beatings started just a few months before she was killed. The son claimed he beat his mother three times in total. He could barely remember the first time. "I punched her, I don't know if I kicked her."

"Were you drunk?" his lawyer asked.

"Yes."

"When was the second time you hit her?"

"I don't really remember."

"Why were you violent to your mother? Can you explain it?"

"I wanted her to be quiet. She was outside my bedroom making noise."

"What about the time you hit your wife?"

"That was a long time ago."

"Did you hit your kids?"

"Hardly ever."

"Did you ever injure anyone the way you injured your mother?"

"No."

Mr. Tomioka's sister met her mother one day soon after one beating. "Her face was red and I asked her what happened," the sister told the court. "She told me that her body was sore and that my brother punched and kicked her. I told her she didn't have to endure it. But she said what was done was done, and told me not to tell anyone about it."

Just as 86-year-old Kanako Mibu would tell her daughter-in-law that she didn't want to go to a hospital after her son had beaten her, 91-year-old Tefuko Tomioka wished to keep her experience of domestic violence under the family carpet.

Mr. Tomioka's sister then wrote a letter to her brother, accusing him of spending money that had been left to their mother by their father, as well as physical and verbal abuse. The prosecutor read sections of the letter into evidence, his voice cracking with emotion in parts. "You are insensitive, you don't accept your mother's senility. You are an important son to your mother. No matter how much you kick your mother, you only hurt your own heart. If you punch your mother, she will forgive you, but will it make you happy? Our mother shouldn't have to do suffer this. When will her idiot son change?"

The "idiot son," though, had much on his plate. In addition to his alcohol problem and his poor relationship with his wife, he was under financial pressure with a struggling mushroom cultivation business he had recently started. And it was, as his sister pointed out, hard to live with someone who was senile. The defendant had also started to have problems sleeping. He was prescribed sleeping pills, but didn't want to continue taking them. His mother's habit of talking to herself at night didn't help his attempts to get a good night's rest.

On one occasion he roared from his room "Hurry up and die!" When asked in court why he had said this, he explained, "I couldn't sleep, my mother was talking to herself. At first, I said it just to shut her up."

But after that incident he began to shout "Please die!" at his mother with increasing frequency. His verbal abuse seemed to distress her as much as the beatings. The defendant said that when he hit his mother, she told him, "Please kill me."

Mr. Tomioka's lawyer asked why he had gone to his mother's room on the night he did actually kill her. "I was worried about her care. I was wondering about putting her into a facility. I was thinking that my wife and I are busy with our own lives. I thought we couldn't give up work to look after her."

"So you wanted to talk to your mother?"

"I think so."

"You don't remember?"

"No."

"What did you think when your mother asked you to kill her?" the prosecutor asked.

"I don't know, I thought it's not going to happen. I thought killing her wouldn't solve the problem."

"Do you remember which part of her body you kicked in the final attack?"

"I don't remember clearly but I think it was the head. She was shouting out my wife's name. I put my hand over her mouth, I think. I don't know what else she said exactly, but they were things like, 'Help me! Stop!' She tried to stand up and she put me off balance."

"Did you fall on your mother?"

"I think I did."

"Why can't you remember so much of what happened that night?"

Mr. Tomioka didn't reply. If he wanted to shut the memories out, he wasn't the only one. His wife had heard the commotion but didn't go near it, although it must have been difficult to ignore. She said she hadn't been feeling well at the time.

The prosecutor didn't accept Mr. Tomioka's explanation that he had hit his mother a few times before losing his balance and falling on her. It was a frenzied and powerful attack, he said.

"The doctor said she was badly bruised and looked like she had been punched or kicked a lot," the prosecutor stated.

"I don't remember; I don't know," responded the defendant.

"Her bones were broken with strong force," the prosecutor said.

"It must have been when I fell on her. I don't want to think about it."

The following morning the defendant got up around 6:30 a.m. as if nothing had happened, ate breakfast, and went off to work. He claimed he had drunk so much sake the previous night that he didn't remember beating his mother. Her body was found later that morning when his wife went to check on her.

"She was lying on her side and her face had turned blue," Mrs. Tomioka said. When I touched her she was cold. "I phoned my husband and he called the police."

"Why did it happen?" his lawyer asked the defendant.

"I don't remember. The worst thing was my drinking. I didn't communicate properly with my mother. I had stress."

"How do you feel about your mother now?"

The defendant started to cry and muttered something inaudible. He then became more audible, saying he had brought a stain on the family. "The hardest thing is that I am sorry for my sister; and for my kids, if they want to get married."

"Once you get out of detention, what will you do about your drinking?" the prosecutor asked.

"I will never drink again."

Two of his daughters, both in their 20s, were in the public gallery; both crying. They had signed a statement, along with their mother and their two other sisters, saying that "as a family, we have responsibility in this incident," and that they should have done something to ease the stress the defendant had been feeling in his life. This statement included in evidence would help to mitigate the sentence, as would a similar statement by his older sister, who of the three witnesses called by the defense (along with the defendant's wife and eldest daughter) was the most hostile to Mr. Tomioka. She had previously said she would never forgive her brother. But she later had a change of heart and signed a statement saying that she forgave him. She didn't visit him during his six months of detention, however.

"Would your mother want a severe punishment?" the defense lawyer had asked the defendant's sister during her testimony.

"No."

"Would your mother want him to go to jail for a long time?"

"I don't think that she'd want that."

The prosecutor sought a six-year jail term for Mr. Tomioka. Three days after the trial and six months since the crime, judgment day arrived. Takeshi Tomioka stood in the dock. The guards took off his handcuffs. His wife and three of his daughters sat in the public gallery.

The presiding judge read the verdict and the reasons for the sentence. The crime demanded a very powerful punishment, he said. Even before killing his mother, the defendant had inflicted grave psychological and physical harm upon her. In his favor, his relatives forgave him and he had no previous convictions. He was sentenced to five years in jail, with 20 days taken off in lieu of the six months already spent in detention.

The defendant looked neither surprised nor disappointed at his penalty. The guards put his handcuffs back on. He moved as if to say something to his family, but then seemed to have second thoughts. He turned away and was led out the door.

POSTSCRIPT

After the trial had finished, I drove about an hour and a half south of Matsumoto City to the Tomioka family home in Nanakubo to ask for an interview with Takeshi Tomioka's wife. I explained who I was and what my purpose was. She declined to speak with me. "I have no interest in talking with you," she said, and closed the door.

Before setting out on the journey, I had typed the Tomiokas' address into Google maps. On Google Street View, I could see their house and the large shed where the victim, Tefuko, used to put her vegetables on the ground, to the annoyance of her son who parked his car there. Disconcertingly, the Google Street View also showed the victim, Tefuko Tomioka. In the picture she was sitting on a step in the front yard of her house, her hands clasped around her knees, wearing a loose blue top with what looked like elasticized sleeves of a type favored by female farmers. Beside her was a shopping cart. Her facial features were blurred, but she was still identifiable, and a neighbor confirmed it was her in the picture. She had been facing the Google camera truck just as it passed, in June of 2012. She would be dead within seven months.

POST-POSTSCRIPT

I also visited Setsuko Mibu, who lives just a five-minute drive from Mrs. Tomioka. The trial of her wheelchair-bound husband had just finished when I dropped by unannounced, and she came to the door with a hoarse voice, looking very ill. She said she would consider an interview when she was better. "If it helps people who are looking after the elderly," it would be worth doing, she told me. After consulting by letter with her now-imprisoned husband, she agreed to speak to me. We met at her house. In fact, we did the interview in a large room that had once been partitioned into two rooms, one of which was the bedroom that Kanako Mibu was battered in. The dead woman was there, smiling out at us through the picture on the family Buddhist shrine. She looked like a confident, intelligent, cosmopolitan woman.

What had once been a house of horror looked very ordinary now. There were two friendly pet dogs in the kitchen, and a cat roamed around the house. Mrs. Mibu was a very gracious host, eager to talk about the killing of her mother-in-law, but not in a way that absolved her husband.

She hadn't seen him for five months since his appearance at Matsumoto District Court. He was being held in the Tokyo Detention Center, a massive multi-story facility used to house remand prisoners and those on death row. Mr. Mibu had just lost an appeal against the length of his sentence, and was being held in Tokyo awaiting transfer to whichever prison he would serve his time in. His wife was planning to visit him after he moved from the remand center. "It would be too painful for us to meet each other at this point; for me and for him," she said.

She produced a letter that she had received from him. He wrote that his eyesight, a longstanding problem, had deteriorated sharply in prison. He was now blind in one eye and his eyesight in the other eye was worsening. "I think he may soon be completely blind," she said. She also said there was a "strong possibility" that her husband would die in prison. If that happened, not only would Mrs. Mibu lose the man she still loved in spite of his crime, but, she said, she would also lose their house. His disability pension of 65,000 yen (US$650) per month, which covered the mortgage, was payable only as long as he remained alive. Money had always been tight, due mainly to some bad investment and business decisions by her husband—at one point they had been forced to sell their home to pay off debt. But she remained devoted to him. "My previous husband was good with money, but bad for my heart; Mi-chan [her pet name for her husband] is bad with money, but good for my heart." Though she acknowledged that his violence toward his mother may have become a habit, she said he was not naturally a violent man. His frustration at the amputation of his leg in late 2012 and his consequent loss of independence had, she believed, sparked a change in him. A picture of the couple in happier days hung on the wall. They were both on a rare holiday to the city of Nagoya, dressed up in period European costume and smiling broadly.

After the court case had ended, she visited her five nearest neighbors to apologize for the trouble the incident had caused them. She gave each of them a small towel as a gift. "I felt so apologetic, and told them I was sorry for causing so much bother. I asked them how they felt about me remaining and living in the community. They all said, '*Ganbatte, ne*' [a commonly used expression of encouragement that in this context means something like 'hang in there']."

Looking back, she said that things might have worked out differently if respite care had been available for her mother-in-law. "If there had been an affordable facility where we could have left her once a week, or even every now and again, that would have calmed us down." She blamed herself for not seeking advice about how to deal with the worsening situation of her husband's violence. "It's my fault. There are people to help; I could have just picked up the phone. I was the only one who could have done anything. Mother couldn't have solved it, and my husband was too angry. Why didn't I look for help? When people ask why I couldn't have done that, I just say that I couldn't. I am responsible for this crime as well."

LEARNING
FROM JAPAN

THE ACCUSED

The following is an excerpt of an interview on Irish radio, RTÉ 1, in June 2014, between reporter Paddy O'Gorman and a violent criminal who had just come out of court in Dublin after appearing before a judge for violating public-order and drugs laws. The interview illuminates much of what is wrong with the system of justice in the Western world, highlighting problems that Japan has largely avoided or overcome.

Defendant: *"I was up on a stabbing there back in '07 and I got three year [sic] I did for it, and I did three year [sic] I did for a stabbing, know what I mean?"*
Reporter: *"And how was the person, how was the victim?"*
"The victim got 186 stitches across his back, know what I mean?"
"What were you in for just now?" [the man was being interviewed outside the courthouse]
"I was in for drugs and in for pupple [sic] order act, I got a strike out on that, I did."
"On the Public Order Act?"
"Yeah, but I'm back up on September the 16th on drugs, yeah."
"The incident that you did the three years for, what happened?"

"Yeah yeah. In prison, like, I had to let people know that I was no idiot, like, you know what I mean. I had to, like, show them that I was tough in prison, like, you know what I mean, and make a name for meself, like."

"And it was in prison that this happened?"

"In prison, yeah, in prison."

"And how did you have the knife in prison; how did you manage that?"

"Well I made it out of a tray, I mean, out of a tray. I snapped the tray in half, you know what I mean, I made the shiv [a knife usually made from a homemade blade such as a shard of metal or a razor blade, attached to a wooden or plastic handle—in this case, a toothbrush], you know what I mean, make a pointy shiv out of it, you get your toothbrush and file it down."

"Prison is a very frightening place, I am sure."

"Oh yeah, of course, yeah, very, very, very frightening. You have to watch your back 24–7 in prison, know what I mean."

This is an account that you would not hear from a defendant in Japan. For a start, someone on drug charges with a previous history of assault and drug convictions would simply not be walking the streets; he would have been in detention since his arrest. Also, the interviewee's savage assault on a fellow inmate with a makeshift knife to prove to his peers that he was no prison pushover would be unlikely in Japan. In Japanese prisons, speaking during mealtimes or even starting your meal before the guard has given the order to begin eating is strictly forbidden, and can lead to immediate solitary confinement. In this silent environment, where monitoring of prisoners is tight and body searches occur at least once a day, it is difficult to imagine that a prisoner would be able to break a tray and gather up a shard for later use as a weapon without attracting the attention of a guard.

Because guards have total control, there hasn't been a prison riot in Japan for decades. "In UK and US prisons, you'll hear about prisoners fighting, you'll hear about different types of dangerous incidents. You don't hear about those inside of Japanese prisons," says Matthew Wilson, a professor of law at the University of Akron, who frequently visited Fuchu prison in Tokyo as part of his academic work. Though guards have the right to carry small arms, they don't usually do so; the Justice Ministry says it has been more than 50 years since a shot was fired in a Japanese jail.

The Irish defendant in the radio interview is a stereotypical offender in Europe and the United States—he had a history of substance abuse and was poorly educated, as was clear from the multiple grammar mistakes he made when speaking and his difficulty in grappling with the name of the Public Order Act under which he had been charged. Judging by his accent, he was from one of many poorly planned housing developments in Dublin where unemployment is high, crime and drug abuse are rampant, and many children are damned by low expectation, relative poverty, and a lack of opportunity.

According to the Irish Penal Reform Trust, "Prisoners in Ireland are 25 times more likely to come from (and return to) a seriously deprived area" than one that is not deprived. Prisoners in the United States have a similar class profile, with the added dimension of race. According to the US National Academy of Sciences, 34 percent of inmates in US prisons in 2011 were African-Americans, although they made up only 13 percent of the US population.

In Japan, there is simply no parallel to the experience of Europe or the United States, where people from particular city districts or racial groups are so disproportionately imprisoned. First, Japan doesn't have any other races in significant numbers, so there isn't a large, distinct racial grouping to discriminate against. Though slavery existed in Japan, and Japanese slaves were sold abroad to China—and, in the 16th and 17th centuries, to Portugal—slaves were not brought to Japan from overseas in significant numbers. Furthermore, the country cut itself off from the wider world for around 200 years starting in the mid-17th century; it was punishable by death to leave Japan during that time. Virtually all of Japan apart from a few small trading posts was off-limits to foreigners. Japan also came to imperialism very late; its first modern colony was in 1895, when it took Taiwan as a prize for its military humiliation of China in the Sino-Japanese war. Taiwan remains the only former colony where Japan is somewhat fondly remembered, mainly for the improvements it introduced in infrastructure, medicine, and elementary education.

Japan lost all its conquered land after its own military humiliation in the second World War, and while around 0.5 percent of Japan's population today is ethnically Korean—some of them willing immigrants from the period at the beginning of the twentieth century when Japan ruled the Korean peninsula; others brought over as forced wartime laborers—it never allowed much immigration from other colonies. Today, immigration remains very tightly controlled. Over 98 percent of Japan's population is ethnically Japanese.

Japan is, of course, not without discrimination. Foreigners working alongside Japanese are usually employed on fixed-term contracts rather than as permanent employees; police are far more likely to randomly stop and question foreigners compared to Japanese; and many—probably most—landlords will not accept foreign tenants. But there is no large distinct racial grouping left on the margins of society the way African-Americans have been in the US, precisely because there is no large minority racial grouping. There is a history of discrimination against Koreans and Chinese, as well as the Ainu people, an ethnic minority who are indigenous to Japan. Bias has also historically existed against an ethnically Japanese underclass known as *burakumin*. Well into the 19th century, *burakumin* were restricted to certain "dirty" occupations such as butchering and funeral undertaking, and were stereotypically associated with poverty and criminality. Intermarriage between *burakumin* and other classes in Japan used to be rare, partly because fathers of the bride- or groom-to-be often carried out prenuptial background checks. Such checks are illegal now, and anti-*burakumin* discrimination has waned to the point where it is virtually unnoticeable today.

DRUGS AND GHETTOS

A second reason that Japan doesn't fill its jails with a particular class of people is that, unlike the West, it doesn't have large urban ghetto areas where poverty, crime, and social hopelessness all collide. This is thanks partly to a relative equality of opportunity, a culture that fosters social obedience, low unemployment, and tough laws. Some historically *burakumin* areas are still mostly populated by their descendants, but these are predominantly in rural areas, and nowadays they don't stand out as being socially or economically deprived, much less crime-ridden.

As mentioned earlier in this book, there is only one area in Japan that might loosely be termed a ghetto: the Airin district of Nishinari Ward in Osaka. Even that doesn't carry anything like the threat or menace of some ghettos in the West. Key to the relative social calm is the fact that Japan, through strict law enforcement and anti-drug advertising campaigns, has kept a lid on drug abuse, and with it the crime that drug addiction fosters. Let's again compare Japan with my native Republic of Ireland. Japan's population is 28 times that of Ireland, but the total number of drug offenses detected by the police is similar—16,471 in Ireland in 2012 compared to 19,116 in Japan. The nature of Ireland's drug problem, however, is far more serious, because much of it is caused by addiction to heroin; Japan's drug problem is mainly the abuse of methamphetamines, which are nowhere near as socially corrosive. Take a walk around inner-city Dublin and you will see poorly nourished, unemployed, drug-dependent young men and women robbed of their quality of life by their dependence on heroin or the heroin substitute methadone. In Tokyo or any other city in Japan, there is no equivalent to this phenomenon. In 2011, almost 9,000 people in Ireland were treated for heroin addiction, according to the European Monitoring Centre for Drugs and Drug addiction. In the same year in Japan, not a single person was treated for heroin or cocaine addiction, according to the Health Ministry. Just two were treated for morphine addiction, three for marijuana, one for MDMA (ecstasy) and around 4,000 for methamphetamine dependence. A ministry official stressed to me that these figures were based on reports gathered from doctors around Japan, so they give a rough but incomplete picture. Every year the bulk of drug arrests in Japan—86 percent in 2011—are for stimulants; about one quarter of all convicts are jailed for possessing or using stimulants.

By the standards of Western countries, Japan's drug problem is tiny. A World Health Organization survey from 2009 showed that 54 times more Americans had used cocaine at least once in their lives compared to Japanese (16.2 percent to Japan's 0.3 percent), and 28 times more Americans had used cannabis (42.4 percent to Japan's 1.5 percent).

It isn't that the Japanese are genetically abstemious—their alcohol consumption is broadly similar to that in the United States—it's just that the average Japanese is militantly opposed to the use of illegal drugs. Anti-drug attitudes in Japan are hardening among the young. According to research cited by government health specialist Kunihiko Kitagaki in the May/June 2011 edition of the *Japan Medical Association Journal*, the proportion of final-year high-school students (17 to 18 years old) who say that illegal drugs should "never be used" jumped from 81 percent in 1997 to 91 percent for girls in 2006, and from 69 percent to 82 percent for boys over the same period.

EDUCATION

Children in Japan may not all be born equal, but every boy and girl is guaranteed access to free high-quality education from elementary school through junior high school. High schools are also free, though they are streamed, which results in large gaps in achievement levels between the best and the worst high schools, but overall the quality of learning remains high.

OECD research suggests that the level of education in Japan is the highest in the world. In 2012, Japan topped the OECD's Program for International Student Assessment (PISA), which tests students in 65 countries and regions on math, science, and reading toward the end of their compulsory education (generally around

15 years of age). One of the keys to this success is the widespread participation of children in the teaching process. Clever pupils are used to teach slower classmates in a process of peer teaching that is educationally beneficial both to the child doing the explaining and the child being peer-taught. Slower students are not kept back in school, so classes are pulled along together.

Importantly for children whose nutrition may be neglected at home, school lunches ensure that all elementary school children and many junior high schoolers get at least one decent meal a day. At Kaichi Elementary School in Matsumoto City in February 2014, there was a different main course for each of the 19 school days that month. These included crab dumplings, chicken with lemon sauce, tomato penne, grilled fish, *oden* winter stew, pork curry, and pork stroganoff. Eighteen different soups, such as seaweed soup, tofu soup, chicken and burdock soup, and miso soup were served, as well as 19 different side dishes—mostly salads such as bean salad, potato salad, tuna salad, and cabbage salad. Three courses were served daily, except on curry day when it was just two courses. Students bring white aprons and white kitchen hats to school, and are assigned to serving and tidying up. Everyone, including the teacher, eats in the classroom. To encourage students to finish their meals, a league table of classes ranked in order of those who had the smallest quantity of leftovers is put on a board in the hall.

Healthy eating obviously helps to foster healthy minds. Fully 98 percent of Japanese students go onto high school from junior high, and 95 percent graduate from high school. Compare that to the United States, where high-school graduation reached a near record high of 80 percent in 2012. That overall US figure, however, masks a great imbalance, especially among males of different races. Research from the Schott Foundation for Public Education showed that only 41 percent of black males in Iowa who were of an age to graduate from high school did so in 2010, compared to 90 percent of whites. In the District of Columbia it was 38 percent versus 88 percent. In the United States as a whole, just over half of all black males (52 percent) who could have graduated high school did so, while 78 percent of all white males did. Again, Japan doesn't have these kinds of disparities within its society. Around Japan, rates of progression from junior high to high school for males and females are similar among the nation's 47 prefectures and regions, with a difference of just four percentage points between the top prefecture in 2012 (Iwate, where 99.4 percent of students went onto high school) and the bottom (Okinawa, at 95.5 percent).

OPPORTUNITY

Backed with a good education, young people in Japan can grow up with an expectation of getting a job—another reason behind the low crime rate. Japan is no egalitarian utopia—relative poverty is higher than the OECD average, driven by the increasing number of workers in low-paid part-time jobs; child poverty has increased; and the CEO of a large listed company in Japan made 67 times more than the average worker in 2012 (although that compares to 354 times in the United States). But unemployment is low; it has never reached 6 percent in the last fifty years. As of early 2015 it was 3.5 percent, compared to 5.5 percent in the United States and almost 10 percent in the European Union. For those who become unemployed, there is a great financial incentive to find another job, quickly. Previously employed workers may claim benefits for a limited period, but—as the OECD noted in a 2010 research paper—once that ends, "few people qualify for welfare payments, since only a person who has neither savings nor any expensive consumer goods can qualify, and assistance may be refused on grounds of insufficient job search."

For those people on welfare, there is no limit on the duration they may receive assistance. While payment rates differ somewhat depending on the region, in Matsumoto City a jobless 20-year-old would qualify for a not-ungenerous maximum of 111,480 yen (US$1,114) per month, about one-third of which is exclusively for rent. But there is a lot of pressure on recipients to find a job. Before any payment is made, parents and siblings are contacted to ask if they can help the applicant financially. Once they receive a payment, they are constantly encouraged and pressured to find work.

Each month the social welfare section in City Hall receives a monthly report of the number of visits that the unemployed person has made to the state-run job agency, Hello Work. There is also, said an official, a massive social expectation that people will look for a job, though the type of work available is increasingly likely to be part-time or contract work.

Speaking overall, a high equality of social opportunity, an absence of ghettos, a relative lack of drug problems, and a superb public first- and second-level education system all help to reduce the number of lawbreakers. A more intangible contribution comes from the historical influence in Japan of Confucianism, a set of ideas that emphasize order, integrity, and respect for seniority. Though it may be easy to overstate the influence of Confucianism—filial piety, for example, a core Confucian principle, is anecdotally stronger in China than in Japan—it is the case that Japanese are less rebellious against authority, as illustrated by the virtual absence of street riots in recent decades in Japan.

The criminal justice system in Japan, however, clearly adheres to at least one key Confucianist conviction: the belief that human beings are capable of reform.

THE COURTS

If there is one big difference between the Japanese and US justice systems, it is this: In the United States, the overriding aim is to catch the bad guy and put him in jail; in Japan, the aim is to catch the guy who committed the crime, see how bad he is, give him a second chance if his crime is low-level—sometimes a third, fourth or even fifth chance, depending on the length of time between his crimes—and if all else fails, bring him before the court, where he will generally be given a suspended prison sentence on his first appearance. If he breaks the law again, he is jailed. The most recent figures at the time of writing for Japan show that there was one prisoner for every 1,817 people in 2011, but in the United States as of the end of 2012 there was one prisoner for every 136 people. In other words, the United States had 13 times more prisoners per capita than Japan. This is partly because the United States jails more people, and partly because it jails them for longer. It is clear which system works best. Crime in the United States, as in Japan, has been falling in recent years, but it remains high compared to other industrialized countries, and very high compared to Japan. Despite—or perhaps because of—its enthusiasm for imprisonment, the United States is a much more dangerous society. As mentioned earlier, a person in the United States in 2011 was 39 times more likely to be robbed, six times more likely to be assaulted, and 16 times more likely to be a victim of murder or non-negligent manslaughter than a person in Japan.

And yet the criminal justice system in Japan is ultimately more benevolent, forgiving and softer on the wrongdoer than that of the US and most other countries. In 2011, of the 291,000 suspects accused of non-traffic penal code offenses, which include murder, theft, arson, assault, and most other serious criminal offenses, only one in 12 ended up in jail. About one in three suspects were under the age of 20 and therefore had their cases referred to courts handling juvenile cases, where detention is used as a very last resort. A further 8 percent were dealt with by a so-called summary order, which meant a fine. Another 15 percent were not prosecuted due to lack of evidence or other reasons. About one in four had their prosecutions suspended, and most of the remainder were sent to trial, but received suspended prison sentences.

There are those in Japan who complain about the leniency of the courts, and significant reforms discussed later in this chapter have been introduced to give victims of crime a greater voice in the prosecution and judgment process. But crime is not the political football that it is in, for example, a country like England, where "law and order" elements in the media hound politicians seen as "soft on crime."

So just how soft is Japan on criminals? To answer this question, it is necessary to appreciate the all-powerful nature of the prosecutor in the criminal justice system. Police may catch criminal suspects, but prosecutors, like police, can also make arrests, interrogate suspects, and investigate crimes. Prosecutors are also responsible for building up books of evidence, as well as arguing their case in court and demanding a specific penalty for the accused. But their greatest power is the ability to suspend prosecution even in cases where there is ample evidence to convict and the suspect has confessed. If a guilty party has his prosecution suspended, it means that there will be no court case and he will not face any judicial sanction at all, not even a fine. The power to suspend a prosecution is given under the catchall nature of Article 248 of Japan's Code of Criminal Procedure, which states: "Where prosecution is deemed unnecessary owing to the character, age, environment, gravity of the offense, circumstances, or situation after the offense, prosecution need not be instituted."

As mentioned above, one in four accused in 2011 was lucky enough to have their prosecution suspended. In theory, there was ample evidence to prosecute all of those cases, though anecdotal evidence suggests that sometimes prosecutors suspend prosecutions that should more correctly be withdrawn due to lack of evidence. Prosecutors generally won't suspend prosecutions in cases where a suspect against whom there is strong evidence refuses to confess. If, however, the accused confesses, pays compensation, and apologizes, and the victim doesn't push for indictment, there is a very good chance that the prosecution will be suspended, especially if the offender is new to crime and the crime is not serious or drug-related.

Though victims have no direct say in whether a prosecutor suspends a prosecution, they are an important background factor in the decision. For his book *The Japanese Way of Justice*, David Johnson carried out a survey of 235 Japanese prosecutors that included questions about the importance of the victim. The survey showed that for 76 percent of prosecutors, an important factor in deciding to suspend or continue with a prosecution was whether or not the offender had paid compensation to the victim. The victim's feeling about the punishment was important for 71 percent of prosecutors.

Aside from an interest in justice, prosecutors also need to be concerned about the victim's feelings, because victims have the right to challenge a prosecutor's decision to suspend prosecution by appealing to a Committee for Inquest of Prosecution. The great bulk of decisions by the committees, which dot the country and are made up of 11 people chosen randomly from the voting register, have historically sided with the prosecutors. But this is not always the case, and since 2009 the committees have had the power to force a compulsory prosecution in cases where the local prosecutor is unwilling to pursue a case.

Such prosecutions are very rare—around two a year in Japan as a whole. The first successful compulsory prosecution in Nagano Prefecture was in 2014, when, the *Asahi Shimbun* reported, Nagano City District Court found a judo teacher guilty of inflicting serious brain damage on a 12-year-old boy by using a risky throwing technique, and gave him a suspended sentence. The boy's parents had pushed the Committee for Inquest of Prosecution to review the case after the prosecutors in their local district had declined to indict the teacher.

Giving victims a tool to force a trial despite opposition from the all-powerful prosecutor is just one of a swath of recent pro-victim changes. As University of Hawaii law professor Mark Levin pointed out to me, "In the last 10 years, the victims' rights movement has made amazing progress in Japan: victims can be represented by counsel; they get to make statements; they get to question defendants." Since 1999, victims have also had the right to be told where the convict is imprisoned and his release date; once he is released, they are able to get biannual updates from his probation officer.

CITIZEN JUDGES

The biggest pro-victim change may turn out to be the lay judge system, which in serious cases takes much power from professional judges and transfers it to ordinary citizens. Of the cases covered in this book, five were heard before a lay-judge court, which is made up of six lay judges—though it can be four—chosen randomly from the electoral register, as well as three professional judges. A citizen can refuse to serve as a lay judge if he or she is over 70 years of age, is a student or a politician, has served previously, or can't attend a trial for an unavoidable reason. Participation rates for lay judge selection are, however, very high, suggesting a public willingness to take on what can be an onerous duty.

This system, which was introduced in Japan in 2009, is often referred to as a jury system, but lay judges are far more powerful than juries in the United States, who in most cases decide only guilt or innocence and usually have no sentencing power. Japan's lay judges can question defendants and witnesses, as well as read evidence files. They also decide on the verdict and the length of jail sentence. The three professional judges guide them on purely legal matters, but the lay judges can outvote them on the key court decisions of verdict and sentencing. The only scenario in which the professional judge carries more weight than a lay judge is when the lay judges vote to find a defendant guilty. In this scenario, at least one professional judge has to agree. But if at least five lay judges vote to acquit a defendant, then he goes free, regardless of how the career judges vote.

Lay-judge trials are also easier for members of the public to follow, since prosecutors and lawyers go out of their way to make them more understandable. In a regular trial, prosecutors and lawyers alike read their closing speeches at a rapid speed, looking only at the page they are reading. The judge and opposing counsel already have a copy of this speech, so there is no need to bother with rhythm or cadence. Judges usually aren't really listening to the closing statements; they are reading them. But prosecutors and lawyers slow down for lay judges. Defense lawyers will often move to the witness box, which is in the center of the courtroom, to give their closing statement rather than stay at the lawyers' table. Both defense lawyers and prosecutors make eye contact in the direction of the bench, and they usually talk as if they are making a speech designed to communicate rather than speed-reading a shopping list.

Lay judges are used only for serious crimes, including murder, arson, rape, and any other offenses that are punishable by death or life imprisonment, as well as certain crimes punishable by a minimum of one year in jail. Since the lay-judge system was introduced, neither the conviction rate nor sentencing has changed much. Supreme Court figures show that lay judges give slightly longer terms for sex offenses and are fractionally more likely than professional judges to give a sentence that is heavier than the penalty sought by the prosecutor.

The system has been criticized because lay judges are not allowed to discuss their reasoning for coming to a particular verdict. That criticism, however, generally emanates from those mostly influenced by the US justice system, which is unusually transparent in that jury members often speak freely after a trial, and details of criminal indictments are published before a trial. In Japan, while criminal court hearings—except cases where the defendant is under 20—are open to the public, the justice system overall remains opaque. TV cameras are never allowed into courtrooms during a court hearing, and judges rarely give interviews. Important court information, including informal briefings by prosecutors, is provided to certain journalists who are members of press clubs but freelancers and magazine writers can find themselves cold shouldered.

Japan's lay-judge system and the move toward greater victims' rights, however, are two sides of the same coin: a trend toward democratization of the court system. Greater victim participation in the process also increases the pressure on the offender to show remorse. As part of his research, David Johnson compared the responses of 57 prosecutors from Seattle, Washington to those from the 235 Japanese prosecutors questioned in his survey mentioned earlier. The biggest national difference by far related to how prosecutors viewed the importance of "invoking remorse in offenders." This ranked third out of 17 objectives among Japanese prosecutors, after "discovering the truth" and "making proper charge decisions." In contrast, invoking remorse was listed as number 16 out of the 17 by the US prosecutors.

Remorse is key for the victim in any culture; in Japan, it is presumed that the defendant will apologize. As Matsumoto-based lawyer Hirofumi Idei told me, "Everyone wants to hear the word 'Sorry'—not just the judge, but the lawyers, the prosecutor, the people in the public gallery—everyone. It is a uniquely Japanese cultural thing. When we hear an apology we feel relief. Sometimes European or American defendants, they just can't say, 'I apologize.' That makes us really uncomfortable."

Victims may be assuaged—though less so for major crimes—by a show of remorse by the perpetrator, especially if it is backed up more concretely with a payment of compensation.

In my year spent at Matsumoto City's courts, I witnessed only two cases where the perpetrator pleaded guilty but showed no remorse. Both involved a physical assault by a male defendant on a former male friend whom they felt had wronged them. Whether the remorse of other defendants was real is open to question, but it was expressed. The defendant will invariably write one, and often two, letters to the victim—a *shazaibun* (letter of apology), and a *hanseibun* (an essay of reflection). The contents are usually similar. Some are short statements; some are flowery; all are replete with words of apology and sorrow for the deed.

FORGIVENESS

Sometimes formal apologies extend beyond the perpetrator and the victim. Take Hideki Kurebayashi, who was charged with embezzling 1.7m yen (US$17,000) from a maternity clinic where he worked as a manager. His crime started small when he expensed to the company account a few dollars worth of washing powder that he had bought for his own use. Then his thieving got bigger and nastier: not only did he start taking from the company's general finances but he also began to skim off from company bonuses and ex gratia payments for workers who were getting married or retiring. Paternalistic Japanese companies usually give workers money not just for happy events but many also pay sympathy money and, separately, flower money, to workers when a close relative dies.

When the scam was discovered, Mr. Kurebayashi was fired. The high-flying manager couldn't handle the shame and the loss of status. He became depressed and suicidal.

"Did you ever think of *shindetsugunau* [atonement through death, i.e., killing oneself]?" his lawyer asked.

"Yes, for about a month or two after it was discovered, I wanted to stop the pain. I wanted to kill myself," he replied. One night he drove up a mountain road intending to slash his wrists with a box cutter. But he was saved by an image of his only child, a boy in junior high school, whom he loved. "I looked at my child's picture on the dashboard, I thought, 'If I die it will be so hard on him.'"

His wife told the court that she had delayed explaining the details of her husband's crime to her son. But when his arrest was reported in the local paper, she had no choice. "Our child said he wanted to read the paper so I gave it to him. When he read it, he cried. I cried, too," she said. That same morning, the defendant's wife went to school to apologize to some of the school staff, including the principal. She also went to the city hall, where she was employed as a part-time worker, to apologize to her boss.

"Did you think of leaving the job?" her husband's lawyer asked.

"Yes, I thought of that, but I thought if my superiors forgave me, I would continue." They did and she did.

The defendant also had offered apologies to the clinic owner, but they weren't accepted. There was no chance of a mutually acceptable financial settlement in this case. Though Mr. Kurebayashi was charged with embezzling 1.7 million yen (US$17,000) he had admitted taking around twice that amount—3 to 4 million yen (US$30,000-40,000), and had already repaid 3.5 million yen. The clinic owner, however, alleged that Mr. Kurebayashi had taken far more, and was seeking repayment of over 38 million yen (US$380,000)—money that Mr. Kurebayashi and his wife said they did not have.

Defendants, of course, express remorse not just to show they are sorry, but also to win forgiveness from the victim. The potential prize for the accused is a letter from the victim saying that all is forgiven, which is a huge help toward a lighter sentence. A request for leniency would be a further sweetener.

Few defendants are as fortunate in their victims as 22-year-old

Kohei Gozu, who was convicted of stealing unattended wallets left in a video-game arcade. (An unattended wallet in a game arcade is, I believe, a peculiarly Japanese phenomenon.) He stole the wallets to get cash to play pachinko and video games.

His doting mother gave evidence in court, partly blaming herself for his crime because she had not been strict enough with him. "When I was raising him, I was always concerned about his physical health, but that's too simple," she said, "Even when I was strict with him, my words didn't get through. I indulged him too much."

Mr. Gozu became remorseful after he was caught. He wrote a letter of apology to each of his three victims. His mother also wrote a letter of apology to each of them; so did his father, who passed away while Mr. Gozu was in detention. The Gozu family's many letters of apology to the victims, as well as the compensation they paid, had the desired effect. One of the three victims wrote to the court asking for a light sentence, even though Mr. Gozu had not only stolen his wallet, but had also thrown away his bank cards and driving license. A second victim went one better, offering Mr. Gozu a job at a small glass factory that he managed. Mr. Gozu didn't show any enthusiasm in court about the prospect of working for a man he had robbed, but he promised that he would find some sort of job whenever he was released from detention.

As it turned out, his detention lasted only until the day of the verdict. Mr. Gozu was given a suspended prison sentence—which was just as well, because his mother had testified that he was accustomed to home cooking and home comforts and didn't handle hardship so well. And if Japanese prisons are anything, they are hard. Prisons are where any indulgence in the Japanese justice system ends and uncompromising severity begins.

INCARCERATION

On its website, the US Embassy in Tokyo captures the essence of Japan's prisons very well, describing them as imposing "a strict, military-like discipline in order to maintain the security, order, and safety of the institution and its inmates. The prisoners wear prison-issue uniforms and there is a prescribed way to walk, talk, eat, sit and sleep. Doing things the wrong way or at the wrong time will be punished. Similarly, good behavior is rewarded with more privileges."

"As a result of the harsh discipline," the website states, "the guards are able to exert near complete control over the prison and so guarantee the physical safety of the prisoners. As in a military boot camp, the system seems geared towards breaking down old behavior patterns and instilling a more disciplined self-control and an ability to function in groups. Fuchu Prison [the facility in western Tokyo where foreigners who do not speak Japanese are usually held] provides continuing guidance in self-discipline and social ethics for everyday life, and there are monthly slogans and frequent personal counseling."

Unlike most countries, including the United States, Japan forces virtually all prisoners to work when in jail. According to the Justice Ministry, more than eight in 10 of the small minority not sentenced to compulsory labor (most of whom are sentenced for criminal negligence) decide to work voluntarily. For defendants who so desire, there are usually opportunities to learn a new skill and get a qualification, though some spend years doing mundane tasks. Tsuyoshi Ishii, for example, the man who burned down his brother's house as described in chapter 5, spent seven years making rice bags in a jail in Yamagata Prefecture.

Twice-convicted marijuana campaigner, Naofumi Katsuragawa, whose story is told in chapter 6, spent his first five-year jail term mainly making "paper bags and fishing lures." Mostly bags, though, he said: "A subcontractor from Osaka would cut the paper into sheets and bring them to us. It was always the same type of work. They would explain to us how to make the bags, which were made to order for shops," he said.

Depending on the prison, there may also be workshops where inmates print magazines or leaflets, make furniture, or repair cars. In Fuchu prison, "The workshop reminded me of the factory floor of a Japanese company, because it was just spotless," said University of Akron law professor Matthew Wilson. It was "very regimented, with people just going about doing their jobs."

Prisoners are paid on average about 27 yen (27 cents) per hour for a 40-hour week. The work can be extremely tedious, and many are reluctant workers. Almost 30 percent of the 53,000 solitary confinements handed out in Japanese prisons in 2012 were related to prisoners not working to the desired standard.

There are many reasons why a prisoner may end up in solitary, precisely because there are many rules. Mr. Katsuragawa told me that in the Kyoto prison where he served his five-year sentence for drug offenses, the guards had a three-point disciplinary system. A minor infraction such as saying a word during the prescribed period of silence could land an inmate with one point or more. "If you reached three points you were put in solitary confinement, where you were supposed to sit in the same position from 8 a.m. to 6 p.m."

PRISON RULES

An English-language rule book containing over 50 pages of rules, titled *Regulations for Foreign Prisoners Confined in Fuchu Prison*, is handed to all English-speaking prisoners on their arrival at the Tokyo jail. Sections of this fascinating manual posted by journalist Kevin Heldman are viewable at www.journalismworksproject.org. The preface says,

> Your sentence here in Fuchu Prison begins today. In this prison more than two thousand inmates are housed. As you know, prison is an institution where sentences are served and many convicted prisoners live together. Therefore good discipline is maintained at all times and no prisoner is allowed to act as he pleases. Accordingly, as compared to common life, there are many detailed restrictions in prison life.

Prisoners are "advised to read this book carefully until the last page so that you can avoid troubles created because of ignorance of rules. Further, it is our earnest desire that this booklet will be a useful textbook for you and aid in leading a healthy life…and help you return to society as an honest and productive citizen."

The booklet also implies that prisoners should forget any notions of rights that may exist in their home countries, that here it is wise to shut up and follow the rules.

"Like they say in the proverb, 'Do in Rome like Romans do,'" the booklet says. "Therefore, as you are in Japan, try to adapt to Japanese customs as much as possible. Try to learn at least basic Japanese language used in daily life. You should not do things in your own way, saying 'things happen to be like this in my country.'"

Activities taken for granted by prisoners in other countries, such as singing and smoking, are banned. Silence is the golden rule. On page 51, prisoners are reminded, "You are not allowed to talk loudly, make noise, or sing songs at the places where conversation is prohibited."

Such places include solitary cells, the waiting rooms for interviews, the investigation room and its waiting room, the medical examination room and its waiting room, the changing rooms, the bath/shower room, the office rooms, and the chapel. Conversation is also prohibited while eating; inmates must also work in silence apart from any softly spoken communication necessary for the job. As in wider Japanese society, the emphasis is on not causing bother to others. "You should be careful of your language and manners and always act courteously," the booklet warns. "Getting up early and cleaning [your] room, washing face or reading books will disturb others' sleep and can lead to troubles. Therefore you must avoid getting up before the rising time." Furthermore:

> At the time of leaving or returning to your cell, tidy your-self and march in a line systematically under the direction of prison officers. Avoid talking, looking around or run-ning. You should not carry clothes in your hand but must wear them properly in [the] designated way…While walking avoid folding your arms or hands, putting your

hands in your pockets, other than that avoid waving your shoulders intentionally or dragging your shoes while walking. Whenever you walk in a group of more than two persons, form a line and march in good order under the direction of the escorting officers.

On your way to and from the factory you will pass through [a] dressing room where you must take of (sic) dress completely and go through the body check quietly. Say your prison number clearly at the time of your body check. Further body check (sic) can be conducted at anytime and wherever it is thought necessary. You must not carry anything in or out of your cell or factory without permission.

You are not allowed to creep into your fellow inmate's bed...You are not allowed to do any kind of sexual play with your inmates. You should not decently (sic) expose your sex organs.

To be engaged in prison work (whatever is assigned to you) is the most important duty for the convicted prisoners sentenced to imprisonment at forced labor. It is judicially imposed so you must work hard whether you like it or not once you are assigned. If you neglect or refuse to work without justifiable reason, you will be subject to punishment. If you insist on a change of work, you will be punished as this is considered an act against your work obligations. Though work is forced upon you, you should force yourself and make an effort to find pleasure in working.

As a general rule, you work for 8 hours on weekdays. However work hour (sic) may be extended or shortened depending on circumstances.

You are not allowed to leave your work area without permission. Idle talk is strictly prohibited. Raise your hand to obtain permission from your factory guard beforehand when you have to leave your work area.

There are hundreds more regulations contained in the Fuchu Prison rule book.

ROUTINE

US citizen Christopher Lavinger, who spent 16 months imprisoned in Japan for drug possession, gave evidence in 1994 to a US House of Representatives subcommittee hearing on Japanese prison labor practices. His description of the typical prison day, summarized below, matches descriptions of prison life given to me by Japanese ex-prisoners. It is also similar in many respects to the "typical" schedules included in Japan's Department of Justice's own literature.

6:45 a.m.: Wake-up bell.

6:55 a.m.: Roll call. At this time, each prisoner must stand at military attention, completely silent and still, while he awaits a guard's command to speak his number in Japanese. If the prisoner makes a mistake or violates any of these rules, he will be taken to interrogation and then to a punishment cell for a minimum of one week. In interrogation, a prisoner is interrogated until the officials obtain a confession. When not actually being interrogated, the prisoner under investigation makes shopping bags in isolation.

7:00 a.m.: Breakfast is served. Absolute silence is mandated. Once the meal is eaten, the dishes must be washed clean, regardless of whether there is any soap to clean them.

7:15 a.m.: Breakfast is finished.

7:25 a.m.: Prisoners are let out of their cells and must stand, absolutely silent, until a guard shouts the command, "About face!" Groups of prisoners are then marched, military style, down the stairs in labor gangs, where smaller groups join a long line of prisoners. The long line of prisoners is then marched to the factories. A prisoner may not make any mistake in his marching, and may not ever look in any direction other than that of the head in front of him. Again, the rule is absolute silence.

7:40 a.m.: Arrive at work. Once in the changing room, a prisoner is not permitted to talk or even to look at another prisoner.

Talking at this time results in investigation and punishment.

7:55 a.m.: Work begins. During work time, a prisoner is not permitted to talk or look around, stand up, or use the toilet without permission. Permission is rarely granted. The guards say that they are there to watch us and not the other way around. Very serious punishments are given to those who look around or look at a guard. The logic here is that if a prisoner looks up from his work, he may accidentally injure himself, and by so doing, he will intentionally remove himself from working on the production line—something he owes to the private companies to which the Japanese government contracted out his labor.

9:45 a.m.: Tea break. Approximately seven minutes are allotted to talk to other prisoners in the factory—if the guard is in a good mood. Often the breaks can be as short as four minutes, or not be given at all.

9:55 a.m.: Back to work.

12:00 p.m.: Lunch. Absolute silence is required during all meals. Deviation from this rule will result in immediate solitary confinement for a minimum of one week.

12:20 p.m.: Lunch is finished. Back to work.

2:30 p.m.: Tea break. Same amount of time as earlier tea break.

2:40 p.m.: Back to work.

4:30 p.m.: Work ends. To changing room. Absolute silence must be maintained.

4:45 p.m.: Prisoners are marched, military style, back to the cell block where the foreigners live in isolation from other prisoners and in solitary confinement. That is, all foreigners live in solitary isolation cells for their entire sentence. The usual rules for marching apply now, more than ever, because the high-ranking prison officials come out to watch the marching.

5:00 p.m.: Roll call. The same rules apply now as for the morning roll call.

5:10 p.m.: Dinner is served. Dishes must be washed clean as for other meals, and are collected by 5:40 p.m.

6:00 p.m.: At this time, a bell chimes which means that it is permitted to unroll the prison-supplied futon, and the prisoner is then, for the first time that day, permitted to lie down on his thin mattress on the floor. At no time, even during the coldest winter nights or days, was my cell or the factory provided with any heat. At no time, even during the sweltering, humid Japanese summer, was there any air-conditioning. A prisoner may use this time to write letters (two letters per month, not exceeding seven pages, are permitted), sew a button, read a book, etc.

From 6:00 to 9:00 p.m., the radio would be played but turned off at exactly 9:00 p.m. Absolute silence must be maintained during this period.

9:00 p.m.: A bell rings which means that the prisoner must be in a prescribed position on his back, silent, and must not get up for any reason other than to use the toilet. Very severe punishments are given to those who violate room rules. A prisoner must stay in this position while sleeping—he may not roll over, turn sideways, or move the covers over his head, or he will be wakened and told to sleep on his back.

What Mr. Lavinger described has not substantially changed since his incarceration. This type of spartan regime, however, elicited virtually no objection from any of the half-dozen Japanese ex-prisoners that I spoke to while researching this book. The stern nature of companies, some schools, and even sports clubs in Japan means that Japanese people, especially men, will at some stage in their life probably endure without complaint exceptionally strict discipline (though not as strict as that found in prison).

According to lawyer Hirofumi Idei, the biggest gripe he hears from clients in detention is not about the discipline, but the food. Testimony from defendants in Matsumoto District Court certainly backs up that view. When a defendant who has experienced jail is asked in court what he disliked about prison life, the number one reply is "the food." The reason, as Mr. Idei points out, is obvious: "They complain about the food because Japanese food is usually good."

The second most common complaint is the cold. Many Japanese prisons have no heating. The Justice Ministry told me that it doesn't collate statistics on which prisons have heating, though it says that more than half do. The lack of heating leads to what the US mission to the United Nations described in 2012 as "preventable cold injuries such as frostbite" in Japanese prisons.

Matsumoto City's juvenile detention center, which houses adult prisoners awaiting trial in the local courts, as well as those sentenced before their 20th birthday, is freezing cold in winter. Temperatures in Matsumoto City are usually below zero Celsius throughout the day in January and February, and while the jail has heating, inmates say they can't feel it. "The authorities say that they turn on the heating, but it seems to have no effect," said a source familiar with the jail. "The prisoners can get up to four or five extra blankets, but it's not enough." Prisoner frostbite is a problem at the prison.

Prison heating (or air conditioning) is of course a human-rights issue not limited to Japan. A report issued by researchers at the University of Texas in 2014 found that at least 14 inmates in Texas prisons had died from heat exhaustion over a seven-year period. There is a prison refurbishment program in Japan, but progress is slow. As in any country, there is little public enthusiasm for investing resources in prisons and prisoners.

ECONOMIZING

Figures from Japan's Ministry of Justice show that taxpayers paid about 2.9 million yen (US$29,000) to keep each prisoner in jail in 2010, slightly less than the $31,000 average for the United States as calculated by the Vera Institute, and far less than the whopping €68,959 (US$77,500) it cost per prisoner in Ireland in the same year, according to Ireland's Penal Reform Trust.

In 2011, the average daily expenditure on each prisoner in Japan, excluding guard salaries, was 1,452 yen (US$14.52) per day. Spending on fuel averaged just 56 yen per day per inmate, while electricity was 349 yen, medical care 133 yen, and food 514 yen.

Skimping on heating obviously helps to keep costs down. So does skimping on medical care. An Amnesty International report from 2009 said: "Prisoners continued to have inadequate access to medical care. Due to a shortage of doctors, prisoners were often examined and given medication by nurses. Reports indicated that it was difficult for prisoners to obtain permission from wardens to visit medical specialists outside the prison due to a shortage of prison guards. Prison authorities prevented prisoners from accessing their medical records."

Not surprisingly, a system where guards demand unequivocal respect can lead to some extraordinary human rights abuses. In 2002, a scandal surfaced about the torture and fatal mistreatment of two prisoners in Nagoya Prison, one of whom suffered rectal damage during a hosing down by prison officers and died of a bacterial infection. Another prisoner died after being inappropriately held in a leather restraint, and a third was seriously injured. Seven guards at the prison received suspended prison sentences for their behavior.

This scandal prompted the first changes to the 1908 Prison Law in almost a century. One of the bigger changes was that a hitherto extremely secretive system was levered somewhat ajar with the creation of over 70 prison visiting committees under 2006 penal-reform legislation. They visit jails and can request to meet with prisoners without prison staff present. The committees represent a significant reform, but they don't have much clout. They simply make recommendations to the Minister for Justice, and he or she then summarizes and publishes them. Their suggestions and recommendations can be and sometimes are ignored by prison governors.

Since 2006, prisons also have a "suggestion box" where prisoners may put in written complaints (or, indeed, suggestions). The box may only be opened by the members of the visiting committee, though the Japanese Federation of Bar Associations points out that if a committee member makes subsequent enquiries based on a prisoner's feedback, "the nature of the proposal or comment may become apparent to the authorities to some extent." In other words, the prison officers may identify the "pot stirrer" making "suggestions."

Japan doesn't appreciate pot stirrers. The Japanese saying, "The nail that sticks up is hammered down" is often used to describe how society deals with those being awkward by seeking change. Virtually every organ of the Japanese state disdains those who make waves; probably none more so than those who run the prisons.

ISOLATION

In a 1995 Human Rights Watch report on Japan's prisons, the authors wrote of the widespread use of solitary confinement as a way to punish the pot stirrers. "In the course of our interviews in Japan, we observed a distressing pattern of punitive measures directed at prisoners who sue the prison system, hint at planning to sue, or assist someone else in a suit," the authors wrote. Human Rights Watch highlighted solitary confinement as the most common way of punishing litigious and potentially litigious prisoners. Keeping those inmates away from other prisoners also ensures that they don't infect them with their rebelliousness.

The authors of the report wrote:

> A particularly distressing case is that of Yoichi Isoe, a fifty-year-old inmate serving a life sentence in the Asahikawa prison on the island of Hokkaido. Isoe has been kept in solitary confinement since the day of his arrival in the prison, on September 3, 1982. Other than the duration itself, what distinguishes this case from other instances of prolonged solitary confinement, is the fact that Isoe was placed there immediately upon his arrival in the prison. Lawyers and prisoner rights advocates speculated that this treatment may be due to the fact that Isoe became involved in a number of conditions-related suits when in the detention center and that the suits were underway when he was brought to the prison.

Amnesty International's 2009 report into prisons found that solitary confinement is not fading away, but is, in fact, increasingly used as a punishment in Japanese prisons. "Under new prison rules introduced by the Ministry of Justice, the number of prisoners in solitary confinement increased. Those categorized as high security, exempt from time limits on solitary confinement and access to complaints mechanisms, could remain in solitary confinement indefinitely. Prisoners in solitary confinement remained in single cells, day and night, had no communication with other prisoners, and were permitted only 15 minutes' exercise a day."

Of more than 63,000 punishments handed out in Japanese jails in 2012, over 53,000 were solitary confinement. That equates to roughly one spell in solitary per prisoner every 15 months, though some prisoners will be put in solitary several times a year and others will not experience it at all.

PRISON YEARNING

Despite the tough conditions, prison life is not an unattractive option for some. Fifty-year-old Katsuhiro Matsumoto found himself before Matsumoto District Court on charges of theft and deception. He had committed his crime in a conveyor-belt sushi restaurant. Mr. Matsumoto ate 13 plates of sushi (there are usually two pieces of sushi per plate), some fried chicken, and a bowl of savory egg custard. It would have cost him 1,745 yen (US$17.45), but he never had any intention of paying.

"You told the staff straightforwardly that you had no money?" his lawyer asked.

"Yes."

"And you told them to call the police?"

"Yes."

Mr. Matsumoto, an almost penniless unemployed construction worker, had been looking for ways to go into jail. After he had lost his job he took a train to a ski resort in Nagano Prefecture without paying the fare. He told the court what happened when he got out at the Hakuba resort. "I told the station worker that I hadn't paid for the ticket. I told him I had no money, and asked him to call the police." But the station man had no interest in helping to put Mr. Matsumoto in jail. "He told me to leave the train station," the defendant said. A deflated Mr. Matsumoto then went to the *koban* police box seeking to be arrested, but the officers weren't interested in listening to his confession about traveling on the train with no ticket. He later went to apply for social welfare, but "Because I had no address, they couldn't help."

By now he was a very desperate man. "I hadn't eaten for three days. I really began just not to care any more. I had 12 yen [12 cents] in my pocket." And that was how he ended up in the sushi shop, eating food he could not pay for. At least the staff at the sushi restaurant obliged him by calling the police. Things turned out well for Mr. Matsumoto, though not in the way he planned. He ended up not going to jail; the judge gave him a suspended sentence. His state-funded lawyer negotiated on his behalf with the local government to organize an apartment for him. Once out of detention, he could move into housing and claim welfare until he got a job.

According to lawyer Hirofumi Idei, some people find the certitudes of prison life appealing. "Sometimes there are people who want to return to jail. They just like life in jail better than their ordinary life," he said.

Seventy-three-year-old Tsuyoshi Miyazawa was one such man. He had 24 previous convictions, including eight for fraud, and had been in and out of prison for decades. He had a drinking problem and low self-esteem. When he came out of prison in early 2014, he began bothering his sister for cash (it was a badge of pride for Mr. Miyazawa that he had never received social welfare in his life, though he didn't mind tapping his relations for money). But his sister tired of giving him handouts: several weeks before his capture she gave him 12,000 yen (US$120) as a final donation and told him, "Don't ever come back."

"I felt like a cockroach," Mr. Miyazawa told the court, "as if I was always getting in the way." He then left his native Niigata Prefecture to seek building work in Nagano Prefecture. And though he looked in good health, considering he was a septuagenarian alcoholic, his age presumably counted against him. He couldn't find a job. "I had worked in Matsumoto before, and asked around there, but there was no job for me. I started walking to Shiojiri (a neighboring city about eight miles away). But I had nowhere to sleep, I had no one, I was hungry, I had only 200 yen (US$2) in my pocket." He then spotted a so-called snack bar—a more homely and less expensive version of the hostess bar—where clients pay above the going rate for alcohol but can enjoy the chatty company of the (usually oldish) Mama-san and often the conversational attentions of a younger lady. Mr. Miyazawa ran up a bill of 3,900 yen (US$39) for two cups of sake, a bowl of fried noodles, and a small plate of nuts that came with each of his drinks. The Mama-san wasn't happy when she discovered that he had no money to pay her. She called the police, and Mr. Miyazawa was on the way to his ninth fraud conviction. He later wrote her a letter saying that he had nothing against her personally and that he had chosen her snack bar at random. But she remained furious and called in her statement for a strict punishment, which, of course, was what Mr. Miyazawa had wanted in the first place. The prosecutor sought a penalty of three years and six months. Mr. Miyazawa was jailed for two years and ten months.

STUBBORN JUSTICE

The Japanese justice system is a relatively good model. Investigators are thorough, and jail is used as a last resort. But those in the justice system are human: police, prosecutors, and judges can make bad decisions. And when a mistake is made and an innocent man or woman goes to jail, the system that demands so much remorse from defendants is loath to admit its error and reverse it.

Take a walk from any direction toward Tokyo District Court in the central Kasumigaseki district and you are reminded of the great power of Japan's bureaucracy. Within a stone's throw of the court building are various government ministries; a block away from the district court are the most powerful of them all, the Department of Finance and the Ministry of Economy, Trade and Industry (METI), which guided Japan to its position as the second-largest economy in the world only two decades after its defeat in the Second World War.

But outside the gates of Tokyo District Court there is evidence of the flip side of that might, the unyielding nature of a bureaucracy that is so supremely confident that it acts as if it's always correct. Middle-aged men and women (rarely younger Japanese) frequently gather outside the gates, usually lobbying for one of two things: the release of someone who they say has been imprisoned for a crime they didn't commit; or for the court to exonerate someone who has already been paroled for a crime he allegedly didn't do.

One protester I spoke to was Kazuo Ishikawa, a hardy-looking 75-year-old. He has a zest that many elderly Japanese possess and an apparent boundless optimism, which was amazing given his circumstances. Mr. Ishikawa didn't look like he was capable of killing a child. But in 1963, as a semi-literate 24-year-old, he was found guilty of murdering a 16-year-old girl, Yoshie Nakata, and sentenced to death. He was released from prison on parole after serving 32 years, and since then he has been fighting to clear his name.

Mr. Ishikawa was convicted mainly because he confessed and the victim's pen was found in his house. There are serious questions about both pieces of evidence. Regarding the pen, it took three searches of the house involving teams of policemen to discover the brightly colored pen resting on a door frame. There is a strong feeling among Mr. Ishikawa's supporters that a police officer planted it.

Secondly, Mr. Ishikawa said that the police coerced the confession out of him. He says that they threatened to jail his brother, the main breadwinner in the family, if he didn't confess, and told him that if he did admit to the murder he would only get a 10-year sentence. The police denied this. His confession, however, included details that were at odds with the crime scene. He confessed that his victim was screaming when he murdered her in a small copse, yet it turned out that there was a man just meters away working in the fields at the time Mr. Ishikawa said he killed her, and the man heard nothing.

There were other incongruous details, he told me. "I hadn't

killed her, so I didn't know how she was killed. In the interrogation, the prosecutor said, 'Didn't you strangle here with your right hand?' and I, unfortunately, said, yes. But with developments in science we know that she wasn't strangled by hand, she was strangled with an object like a rope. We have submitted that evidence to try and get them to reopen the case, so if they investigate that it will be clear."

But there is every possibility that the courts may not agree that it is clear. Judges are very unwilling to overturn a conviction, especially one where the defendant had confessed. Mr. Ishikawa believes that the police in Chiba Prefecture, where the murder took place, have exculpatory evidence that is kept tantalizingly out of reach. "The police have a two-meter pile of evidence related to this incident, but they won't hand it over. They are not interested; if they were interested they would know that I was innocent." They are under no legal obligation to hand it over. While legal changes have made it easier for defense counsel to obtain exculpatory evidence, the changes are not retrospective. Mr. Ishikawa still has a long battle ahead of him. But every now and again the courts make a ruling that vindicates the campaigners outside the gates of Tokyo District Court.

One such decision came in 2014, when Iwao Hakamada, who had spent 48 years in jail (34 of them on death row) for murdering a family of four in August 1966, was freed pending a retrial. The 78-year-old former professional boxer was released after DNA tests revealed that blood on five items of clothing that the murderer was believed to have worn was not his. Such DNA testing didn't exist at the time he was jailed, but it shouldn't have been needed, as there were other issues that should have cast reasonable doubt over Mr. Hakamada's confession. The clothing, for example, included bloodstained pants that were too small for him. Also, while he had admitted to the murder during intense interrogation, he retracted his confession in court.

One of the three judges hearing the trial believed that Mr. Hakamada was innocent, and wrote a 360-page document for the other judges arguing his case, but his colleagues overruled him. The dissenting judge finally broke his public silence on the case in 2007 and thereafter became a vocal advocate of Mr. Hakamada's innocence. Mr. Hakamada's release was reportedly the sixth time in postwar Japan that a court has approved the retrial of a death-row defendant. In four of the five other cases the defendants were subsequently found not guilty, a disturbing reminder that Japan's justice system is capable of the gravest of mistakes.

Mr. Hakamada had been in solitary confinement, like all death-row prisoners, for over three decades. In that time, his human contact—he wasn't allowed to mix with other prisoners or speak with prison guards—was largely restricted to his lawyers and his older sister, who was his staunchest supporter. One of the rules of Japanese prisons is that speaking is prohibited in solitary cells, so technically you can't even talk to yourself. As Japan doesn't tell its prisoners when they will be executed, it could always be tomorrow. "This adds psychological torture to an already cruel and inhumane punishment," according to Roseann Rife, the East Asia research director of Amnesty International.

For several years before he was released, Mr. Hakamada had started to show signs of senility. He looked utterly bewildered upon his release from prison, apparently with little ability left to communicate. He was free, but his life had been stolen from him by a system that just couldn't admit it was wrong.

"The biggest problem with the system is that once it starts running it is like a truck with no brakes," according to Matsumoto-based lawyer Susumu Ozawa. "Prosecutors only take cases where they are sure of a guilty verdict, so that leads to a situation where judges may think that because the prosecutors have taken the case, it must be correct. Judges and prosecutors are bureaucrats; they have a natural affinity with each other. If the prosecutor does his job properly—which 99 percent of them do—it works well. But mistakes happen, and in Japan, if a prosecutor is out of control, the system is like a truck with no brakes: there is nothing to stop it until it hits a wall."

UNRELIABLE CONFESSIONS

So how do these cases happen? Like some others locked up in Japan for crimes they didn't commit, Mr. Hakamada had confessed to the crime. He later alleged that his interrogators wouldn't allow him to use the toilet until he signed his confession. Confessions are a pillar of Japanese justice, and while a court can't convict based solely on a suspect's confession, having one certainly helps. Figures from Japan's Supreme Court show that every year from 2006 to 2010 between 91.0 percent and 91.3 percent of all defendants pleaded guilty, though the figure falls to as low as 69 percent for serious offenses such as murder and rape. (The rate for confessions is higher than the rate for guilty pleas, as many will confess to an offense but plead not guilty for other reasons, such as mental incapacity, illegal arrest, or that the charges breach their constitutional rights.) All justice systems would grind to a halt if people stopped confessing, especially for minor crimes, but in Japan this is especially true. Japan has neither enough lawyers nor judges that would be needed to handle cases if even a significant minority started to plead innocence. According to the Japanese Federation of Bar Associations, Japan had 3,786 citizens per lawyer in 2013, whereas the United States had 269, and the UK 430. There is a similar pattern for judges, with one judge for every 43,789 people in Japan compared to 4,010 in Germany and 9,816 in the United States.

Squeezing confessions out of suspects is made easer because, as described earlier in this book, it is legal to hold a suspect without charge for 23 days of interrogation, during which there are no legally prescribed limits on the length of interrogation sessions. The arrest and detention for 20 days of an accomplice of the gangster pimp Kenji Kakiuchi described in chapter 3, and his subsequent rearrest on another charge, shows how police can use the power to detain for such long periods to induce cooperation from suspects.

Amnesty International's 2013 report said the system of holding people in police cells and questioning them at length "continued to facilitate torture and other ill-treatment to extract confessions during interrogation." After a UN report criticized the practice of lengthy pre-charge detention and interrogation, Tokyo-based veteran journalist David McNeill wrote in the *Asia Pacific Journal* in 2008: "Critics acknowledge that the police are mostly thorough, the legal machine functions efficiently in the majority of cases and that ultimately Japan incarcerates people at a far lower rate than most developed countries. But they say the damning UN report has finally focused minds here on something known by defense lawyers for years: the system is open to horrendous abuse."

Statements made by defendants under interrogation and submitted to the court as evidence are not the words of the suspect; they are a composite or summary of what the interrogator understands the detainee to have said, though they are signed by the detainee. Again, this system is open to abuse: after days of questioning, some suspects may not be mentally strong enough to check the statement adequately.

I witnessed three defendants in separate cases object to their "confession" in court, saying that it included statements that they hadn't made. In all three cases, the defendants were admitting to their crime and pleading guilty. Alleged ill-treatment of offenders doesn't have to be physical; in fact, it very rarely is. According to lawyer Hirofumi Idei, his clients haven't complained to him about physical ill-treatment, but "we hear about suspects being shouted at or threatened."

It was that kind of nonphysical intimidation that helped to send Mr. Toshikazu Sugaya to jail for a crime he didn't commit—the murder of a four-year-old child. The former bus driver had confessed to the murder, but was exonerated in 2009 after having spent 19 years in custody. He said that he confessed because his timid character couldn't bear the constant aggressive questioning by investigators. The *New York Times* reported that he was "afraid that the police would discover he was lying and would start shouting at him again, a prospect he said paralyzed him with fear." "Confessing is the only way," according to prominent lawyer Kazuko Ito, for some suspects "to escape from prolonged detention and endless interrogations."

In the absence of irrefutable DNA or other evidence, it's very hard to overturn convictions based on confessions, no matter how dubious. Many observers believe there is enough doubt surrounding the conviction of 88-year-old Masaru Okunishi to order his release pending a retrial. But in 2013, the Supreme Court rejected a request for a retrial of Mr. Okunishi, who was jailed for poisoning his wife and mistress and three other women with wine at a village gathering in 1961.The evidence against him, including a confession that he said was coerced, was so dubious and circumstantial that he was found innocent in his initial trial in 1964.

But the prosecutor appealed to a higher court, which sentenced Mr. Okunishi to death in 1969. At the time of writing, he was Japan's longest death-row prisoner, and was still fighting for a retrial. While Mr. Okunishi has many supporters who believe he is a victim of a miscarriage of justice, Japan's judiciary remains unsympathetic. Despite the prisoner's advanced age, it took the Supreme Court fully 11 years to consider, and reject, his most recent request for a retrial. That was in 2013, and he has now used up all his avenues of appeal, according to the *Japan Times*.

Regarding the Okunishi case, his former lawyer Kazuko Ito wrote in the University of Cincinnati Law Review: "In the post-conviction litigations, his defense attorneys have proven that the scientific evidence on which the appeal court relied was falsified. Although there are large amounts of evidence and statements held by the prosecutor, presumably including exculpatory evidences, the prosecutor has not disclosed this evidence at all… In Japan, a defendant has no right to demand the disclosure of exculpatory evidence, even if his execution is imminent."

Mr. Okunishi is virtually certain to die in prison a condemned—and, as many believe, innocent—man.*

---

* Mr Okunishi died on October 4, 2015 in Hachioji Medical Prison in Tokyo aged 89 and still on death row.

COPYING JAPAN?

Cases like Mr. Okunishi's seem to be an aberration, however. Overall, Japan has a comparatively fair justice system. So how could other countries emulate it? Is it possible to transpose Japan's enviably low crime rate and low imprisonment rate onto societies in the Western world? There are some key factors that other countries may not wish to copy at all. For example, an important part of Japan's crime success is, paradoxically, its tolerance for criminals. Despite the anti-yakuza drive of recent years by the state, the mafia in Japan has a freedom to exist that is unknown in any other first-world country. They still operate in broad daylight from established offices, and openly make money from legal sources, brokering labor for the Fukushima cleanup, for example, or renting out properties. The payoff for society for such relative, albeit declining, indulgence is clear: Japan's gangs to a large extent self-police. The yakuza in general don't deal drugs that can destroy entire communities—notably heroin or crack cocaine; they don't rely very much on guns to impose their will; and in general they don't commit the type of crimes that most frighten the public, such as random assault and street robbery.

Another factor that may be too unpalatable for certain other countries to adopt is Japan's leniency toward those who commit crimes while under the age of 20, and its general softness toward adults who are first-, second-, and even third-time offenders. The power of the prosecutor to suspend a prosecution even when there is clear evidence of an offender's guilt is not unique to Japan, but it is very widely practiced in that country, and is typically cited by lawyers and prosecutors as being crucial to Japan's low crime rate. The thinking is that jailing an offender separates them so much from society that it makes reform difficult, and imprisonment should therefore only be used as a last resort. Introducing greater leniency for criminals, however, is not something that politicians in countries such as England or the United States are likely to champion in great numbers—not, that is, if they are running for reelection.

And mimicking other, more important, ingredients of Japan's crime story would be even more challenging and costly. Redesigning cities such as Los Angeles, Paris, or Manchester in a Japanese mold where ghettos do not exist and where children generally are not in any way defined by the fact that they live in a particular district would be an extraordinary feat of social engineering.

CONCLUSION

I never did get to see a not-guilty verdict in the courtrooms of Matsumoto City. The octogenarian shoplifter Kesae Shikada, who stuffed fried pork into his pocket while the equivalent of US$20,000 rested in his bank account, seemed to come closest. As his trial progressed through sporadic hearings over an 11-month period his lawyer presented an increasingly persuasive case that Mr Shikada was innocent because of senility. Ultimately, however, Judge Koji Kitamura was not persuaded to deliver that rarest of judicial decisions.

While Matsumoto City's courtrooms held few verdictive surprises, the lengthy cross examination—sandwiched between the predictable guilty plea and the inevitable guilty verdict—was always interesting and usually fascinating. There was little courtroom drama and virtually no posturing by any of the participants—judges, prosecutors, defense lawyers as well as defendants—but there was something substantial and valuable to be learned about Japan from virtually every criminal case. The cases involving the yakuza gangsters, for example, showed the mechanics of drug dealing, prostitution and protection rackets. Japan's ambivalence about the honor, or otherwise, of suicide was highlighted in the case of Satoru and Hitomi Hara whose plan to kill themselves and their unsuspecting daughter was glossed over in courtroom questioning. The stories of other defendants offered telling nuggets about things as disparate as the involvement of parents in the schools system, the big-brother approach to social welfare which scrutinizes in detail the expenditure of dole recipients, and the creaking pension system.

Aside from the yakuza criminals who generally had similar backgrounds (male, macho, working class and poorly educated) and similar motives (greed, feeding a drug habit, carrying out gang duties) most other defendants had a unique back story to their crime. They shared little in common except this: almost all showed a striking conservatism and apparent affection for traditional, old-fashioned values. They may have been outside of the establishment but, aside from the Libertarian pro-marijuana activist Naofumi Katsuragawa, they were not anti-establishment. Even the pimp Kenji Kakiuchi who, uniquely, had been openly disrespectful in the courtroom, had switched to cloying obeisance by the time of his final court hearings. Arguably his deference and that of the other defendants was motivated by a desire to ingratiate themselves with the black-robed men and women on the bench who could grant or deny their freedom. But their traditionalism shone through in other ways. Septuagenarian shoplifter Yoshimatsu Matsumoto for example, stole cassette tapes to allow him to record the old patriotic songs he loved so much. Fumiko Suzuki stole food while her savings of around $60,000 remained undisturbed because she didn't want to—irresponsibly as she saw it—become a burden on her children. The root of the misdeeds of CEO-turned-arsonist Tsuyoshi Ishii for example was his mother's failure to follow custom by passing on the family's small shipping business to him as the eldest son. He was further enraged that most of his former clients also ignored his seniority and instead gave their business to his younger brother. Those who, as he saw it, had ignored the traditional age-based hierarchy became targets for his arson.

Likewise the values of "Old Japan" loomed over the mother killers described in this book. Both Mitsutaka Mibu and Takeshi Tomioka felt trapped by the cultural expectation that the eldest boy has to care for his elderly parents. In cases that carried more than a scent of Shakespearean tragedy the men felt forced to live with a mother whom they hated. And both "solved" their problem in the most terrible of ways. Similarly, the story of 24-year old

Natsuki Takenouchi could have formed the plot of a 19th century novel. He put a knife to the throat of a colleague to extort him because he wanted to clear his debts and win back the heart of his loved one. He may have been unorthodox in his methods but his goal was boringly conventional—marry young, settle down.

Conventional too was Satoru Hara, who, before he and his wife came up with a plan to burn their house and kill their daughter, was a clean-living accountant; shy but ever ready to help with the local resident's association. He was, however, so obsessed with family honor that he believed he couldn't live if his neighbors knew him as a man who couldn't pay his housing loan. Murder-suicide was better than the shame of leaving an unpaid debt to a bank. Death rather than dishonor.

Even Kenji Kakiuchi who made a living brokering the bodies of girls as young as 14 was anxious to portray himself as someone who helped the weak—an allegedly traditional samurai virtue commonly espoused as a core principle of yakuza gangs. For Mr. Kakiuchi, the weak were not the teenage girls whose bodies he exploited but fellow gangsters who had fallen on hard times. He repeatedly emphasized in court how much he valued loyalty and honor. He did not receive any of either from the former employees who testified against him but for each hearing up to a dozen supporters turned up to show their loyalty to him. At the end of every appearance as he was being handcuffed, Mr. Kakiuchi would briefly address the band of well-wishers. He would bow and tell them politely to not to worry about him, while thanking them for their presence. He would then leave through one courtroom door with his guards, and his supporters would leave through the public door, rush down four flights of stairs and regroup at the back of the court building. There, they waited for Mr. Kakiuchi to reappear as he was led into a prison van. They shouted words of encouragement and he would give a smile and join his handcuffed hands together in a prayerful show of gratitude.

After his final hearing, when he was sentenced to eight years, they gathered again—mostly men in their late 30s and women who were far younger, as well as Mr. Kakiuchi's ex-wife and young child. This time he briefly mounted the door ledge of the Honda people carrier that would ferry him to detention. It was just minutes since he received his sentence but he was all smiles, bravado presumably. As the prison car pulled away his supporters bowed him all the way out the gate. There was no attempt to block the vehicle or interfere with the guards or shout abuse at them. Most of those who gathered looked like thugs but like the defendants of Matsumoto's courts they understood the unspoken rules of order and observed them. Even as their friend, one of the region's most hardened criminals, was being taken away to begin a sentence that was long by Japanese standards, decorum was maintained. Like all of the other days on which I attended the courts of Matsumoto City there would be no disturbance that day.